# MAKING THE DEC RECOMMENDED PRACTICES "COME TO LIFE"

## ABOUT THE AUTHORS

**Aaron R. Deris, PhD,** is a Professor and Program Coordinator of the Early Childhood Special Education Program in the school of education at MN State University, Mankato (MSU, Mankato). Prior to joining MSU, Mankato in 2011, he worked as an infant/toddler, public preschool and elementary teacher, charter school teacher, Early Steps Provider, special education coordinator, consultant, and trainer. He has worked in the field of early childhood since 1998 and holds teaching licensure in early childhood special education, developmental disabilities, emotional behavioral disorders, and specific learning disabilities. He has visited the infant/toddler and preschool programs in Reggio Emilia, Italy and surrounding regions, incorporating this knowledge into the Early Childhood Special Education Academic Programs at MSU, Mankato.

**Cynthia Fontcuberta DiCarlo, PhD,** serves as the Executive Director of the Early Childhood Education Laboratory Preschool and is a Professor and Program Coordinator of the Early Childhood Education Teacher Education Program in the LSU School of Education. Prior to joining LSU in 2004, she worked as an infant/toddler teacher, public preschool teacher, Early Steps Provider, consultant, trainer, state assessor, and NAEYC validator. She has worked in the field of early childhood since 1993 and holds a teaching certificate in early intervention and Birth to Kindergarten. She has visited the infant/toddler and preschool programs in Reggio Emilia, Italy and surrounding regions, incorporating this knowledge into both the ECELP and the Early Childhood Academic Programs at LSU.

# MAKING THE DEC RECOMMENDED PRACTICES "COME TO LIFE"

## Using Case Method of Instruction in Early Childhood Special Education

*By*

**AARON R. DERIS, PhD**

*Minnesota State University, Mankato*

*and*

**CYNTHIA F. DICARLO, PhD**

*Louisiana State University*

CHARLES C THOMAS · PUBLISHER · LTD.
*Springfield · Illinois · U.S.A*

*Published and Distributed Throughout the World by*

CHARLES C THOMAS • PUBLISHER, LTD.
2600 South First Street
Springfield, Illinois 62704

© 2021 by CHARLES C THOMAS • PUBLISHER, LTD.

ISBN 978-0-398-09346-4 (paper)
ISBN 978-0-398-09347-1 (ebook)

Library of Congress Catalog Card Number: 2020037405 (print)
2020037406 (ebook)

*With* THOMAS BOOKS *careful attention is given to all details of manufacturing
and design. It is the Publisher's desire to present books that are satisfactory as to their
physical qualities and artistic possibilities and appropriate for their particular use.*
THOMAS BOOKS *will be true to those laws of quality that assure a good name
and good will.*

*Printed in the United States of America*
*MM-C-1*

**Library of Congress Cataloging-in-Publication Data**

Names: Deris, Aaron R., author. | Dicarlo, Cynthia, author.
Title: Making the DEC recommended practices "come to life" | using
   case method of instruction in early childhood special education /
   by Aaron R. Deris and Cynthia F. Dicarlo.
Description: Springfield, Illinois : Charles C Thomas, Publisher, Ltd.,
   2021. | Includes bibliographical references.
Identifiers: LCCN 2020037405 (print) | LCCN 2020037406 (ebook) |
   ISBN 9780398093464 (paperback) | ISBN 9780398093471 (ebook)
Subjects: LCSH: Early childhood special education. | Children with
   disabilities—Education (Early childhood). | Early childhood special
   education—Case studies. | Children with disabilities—Education
   (Early childhood)—Case studies.
Classification: LCC LC4019.3 .D47 2021 (print) | LCC LC4019.3
   (ebook) | DDC 371.9/0472—dc23
LC record available at https://lccn.loc.gov/2020037405
LC ebook record available at https://lccn.loc.gov/2020037406

*This book is dedicated to the next generation of early childhood special education teachers. Our hope is that this text will provide you with foundational knowledge of the DEC Recommended Practices and insight into the lives of the children and families you serve.*

# PREFACE

The focus of this book is to assist new early childhood special education (ECSE) professionals in entering the field. While ECSE candidates receive formal training to advance their knowledge and skills, this book supplements the ECSE candidate's education by providing realistic situations that may be encountered as a new practitioner. The book responds to a critical need for highly qualified personnel who have an understanding of how to navigate professional situations in consideration of the DEC RPs in their work with young children and their families.

Fifty-five case studies are provided, including seventeen solved case studies and thirty-eight unsolved case studies. The case studies are aligned with the current recommended practices (RPs) from the Division for Early Childhood (DEC) of the Council for Exceptional Children (2014). These cases mirror situations practitioners are likely to encounter in their practice. These cases are provided for ECSE candidates to consider, with support from faculty, in the context of their educational preparation. This book can also be used in professional learning communities, to generate conversation among working professionals on how to handle tough situations in consideration of the RPs.

Each of the case studies include questions for further thought and discussion, making these ideal for starting conversations around recommended practices. The unsolved cases allow the reader to consider strategies that could bring the proposed situation to a mutually beneficial resolution. The solved cases invite the reader to critique the resolution of a situation and consider alternative strategies that may have been applied.

Included in the front matter of the book are the DEC RPs and a chart of cases presented in the text, organized by the RPs. The end of the text includes supporting research citations and resources for further understanding on Case Method of Instruction. We hope that the cases provided aid in your understanding of the application of the DEC Recommended Practices in your work with young children and families.

A.R.D.
C.F.D.

# ACKNOWLEDGMENTS

We would like to recognize the graduate students in the ECSE program at Minnesota State University, Mankato, for sharing their stories in their work with young children and families. We are particularly grateful to our colleagues, who provided feedback on an earlier draft of this book, including Elizabeth Beavers, Karen Eastman, Kiersten Hensley, Bernadeia Johnson, Meghan Purcell, Steven Reuter, and Dana Wagner.

# CONTENTS

# MAKING THE DEC RECOMMENDED PRACTICES "COME TO LIFE"

# OVERVIEW OF DEC
# RECOMMENDED PRACTICES

The Division for Early Childhood Recommended Practices (RPs) (2014) provide guidance to practitioners and families on practices in delivering services to young children who have or are at-risk for developmental delays or disabilities. These RPs were used as the basis for the cases in this text to help preservice and inservice teachers in the implementation of these practices.

## ASSESSMENT

- **A1**. Practitioners work with the family to identify family preferences for assessment processes.
- **A2**. Practitioners work as a team with the family and other professionals to gather assessment information.
- **A3**. Practitioners use assessment materials and strategies that are appropriate for the child's age and level of development and accommodate the child's sensory, physical, communication, cultural, linguistic, social, and emotional characteristics.
- **A4**. Practitioners conduct assessments that include all areas of development and behavior to learn about the child's strengths, needs, preferences, and interests.
- **A5**. Practitioners conduct assessments in the child's dominant language and in additional languages if the child is learning more than one language.
- **A6**. Practitioners use a variety of methods, including observation and interviews, to gather assessment information from multiple sources, including the child's family and other significant individuals in the child's life.
- **A7**. Practitioners obtain information about the child's skills in daily activities, routines, and environments such as home, center, and community.

- **A8**. Practitioners use clinical reasoning in addition to assessment results to identify the child's current levels of functioning and to determine the child's eligibility and plan for instruction.
- **A9**. Practitioners implement systematic ongoing assessment to identify learning targets, plan activities, and monitor the child's progress to revise instruction as needed.
- **A10**. Practitioners use assessment tools with sufficient sensitivity to detect child progress, especially for the child with significant support needs.
- **A11**. Practitioners report assessment results so that they are understandable and useful to families.
(DEC, 2014, p.8)

## ENVIRONMENT

- **E1**. Practitioners provide services and supports in natural and inclusive environments during daily routines and activities to promote the child's access to and participation in learning experiences.
- **E2**. Practitioners consider Universal Design for Learning principles to create accessible environments.
- **E3**. Practitioners work with the family and other adults to modify and adapt the physical, social, and temporal environments to promote each child's access to and participation in learning experiences.
- **E4**. Practitioners work with families and other adults to identify each child's needs for assistive technology to promote access to and participation in learning experiences.
- **E5**. Practitioners work with families and other adults to acquire or create appropriate assistive technology to promote each child's access to and participation in learning experiences.
- **E7**. Practitioners create environments that provide opportunities for movement and regular physical activity to maintain or improve fitness, wellness, and development across domains.
(DEC, 2014, p.9)

## FAMILY

- **F1**. Practitioners build trusting and respectful partnerships with the family through interactions that are sensitive and responsive to cultural, linguistic, and socioeconomic diversity.

- **F2.** Practitioners provide the family with up-to-date, comprehensive and unbiased information in a way that the family can understand and use to make informed choices and decisions.
- **F3.** Practitioners are responsive to the family's concerns, priorities, and changing life circumstances.
- **F4.** Practitioners and the family work together to create outcomes or goals, develop individualized plans, and implement practices that address the family's priorities and concerns and the child's strengths and needs.
- **F5.** Practitioners support family functioning, promote family confidence and competence, and strengthen family-child relationships by acting in ways that recognize and build on family strengths and capacities.
- **F6.** Practitioners engage the family in opportunities that support and strengthen parenting knowledge and skills and parenting competence and confidence in ways that are flexible, individualized, and tailored to the family's preferences.
- **F7.** Practitioners work with the family to identify, access, and use formal and informal resources and supports to achieve family-identified outcomes or goals.
- **F8.** Practitioners provide the family of a young child who has or is at risk for developmental delay/disability, and who is a dual language learner, with information about the benefits of learning in multiple languages for the child's growth and development.
- **F9.** Practitioners help families know and understand their rights.
- **F10.** Practitioners inform families about leadership and advocacy skill-building opportunities and encourage those who are interested to participate.
(DEC, 2014, p. 10-11)

## INSTRUCTION

- **INS1.** Practitioners, with the family, identify each child's strengths, preferences, and interests to engage the child in active learning.
- **INS2.** Practitioners, with the family, identify skills to target for instruction that help a child become adaptive, competent, socially connected, and engaged and that promote learning in natural and inclusive environments.
- **INS3.** Practitioners gather and use data to inform decisions about individualized instruction.

- **INS4**. Practitioners plan for and provide the level of support, accommodations, and adaptations needed for the child to access, participate, and learn within and across activities and routines.
- **INS5**. Practitioners embed instruction within and across routines, activities, and environments to provide contextually relevant learning opportunities.
- **INS6**. Practitioners use systematic instructional strategies with fidelity to teach skills and to promote child engagement and learning.
- **INS7**. Practitioners use explicit feedback and consequences to increase child engagement, play, and skills.
- **INS8**. Practitioners use peer-mediated intervention to teach skills and to promote child engagement and learning.
- **INS9**. Practitioners use functional assessment and related prevention, promotion, and intervention strategies across environments to prevent and address challenging behavior.
- **INS10**. Practitioners implement the frequency, intensity, and duration of instruction needed to address the child's phase and pace of learning or the level of support needed by the family to achieve the child's outcomes or goals.
- **INS11**. Practitioners provide instructional support for young children with disabilities who are dual language learners to assist them in learning English and in continuing to develop skills through the use of their home language.
- **INS12**. Practitioners use and adapt specific instructional strategies that are effective for dual language learners when teaching English to children with disabilities.
- **INS13**. Practitioners use coaching or consultation strategies with primary caregivers or other adults to facilitate positive adult-child interactions and instruction intentionally designed to promote child learning and development.

(DEC, 2014, pgs. 12-13)

## INTERACTION

- **INT1**. Practitioners promote the child's social-emotional development by observing, interpreting, and responding contingently to the range of the child's emotional expressions.
- **INT2**. Practitioners promote the child's social development by encouraging the child to initiate or sustain positive interactions with other children and adults during routines and activities through modeling, teaching, feedback, or other types of guided support.

- **INT3**. Practitioners promote the child's communication development by observing, interpreting, responding contingently, and providing natural consequences for the child's verbal and non-verbal communication and by using language to label and expand on the child's requests, needs, preferences, or interests.
- **INT4**. Practitioners promote the child's cognitive development by observing, interpreting, and responding intentionally to the child's exploration, play, and social activity by joining in and expanding on the child's focus, actions, and intent.
- **INT5**. Practitioners promote the child's problem-solving behavior by observing, interpreting, and scaffolding in response to the child's growing level of autonomy and self-regulation.
(DEC, 2014, p. 14)

## TEAMING AND COLLABORATION

- **TC1**. Practitioners representing multiple disciplines and families work together as a team to plan and implement supports and services to meet the unique needs of each child and family.
- **TC2**. Practitioners and families work together as a team to systematically and regularly exchange expertise, knowledge, and information to build team capacity and jointly solve problems, plan, and implement interventions.
- **TC3**. Practitioners use communication and group facilitation strategies to enhance team functioning and interpersonal relationships with and among team members.
- **TC4**. Team members assist each other to discover and access community-based services and other informal and formal resources to meet family-identified child or family needs.
- **TC5**. Practitioners and families may collaborate with each other to identify one practitioner from the team who serves as the primary liaison between the family and other team members based on child and family priorities and needs.
(DEC, 2014, p. 15)

## TRANSITION

- **TR1**. Practitioners in sending and receiving programs exchange information before, during, and after transition about practices most likely to support the child's successful adjustment and positive outcomes.

- **TR2**. Practitioners use a variety of planned and timely strategies with the child and family before, during, and after the transition to support successful adjustment and positive outcomes for both the child and family.
(DEC, 2014, p. 16)

# CHART OF CASES

| Chapter 2: Assessment | | | |
|---|---|---|---|
| **Title of Case** | **Solved/ Unsolved** | **Age level B-3, 3-5** | **Page #** |
| Revolutionary Referral | Unsolved | B-3 | 30 |
| Split Decisions | Unsolved | B-3 | 35 |
| Time for a New Diagnosis? | Solved | 3-5 | 38 |
| Nature vs Nurture | Unsolved | 3-5 | 40 |
| Special Education Graduate | Solved | 3-5 | 44 |
| Do Something | Unsolved | 3-5 | 47 |
| **Chapter 3: Environment** | | | |
| **Title of Case** | **Solved/ Unsolved** | **Age level B-3, 3-5** | **Page #** |
| Baby Blues | Solved | B-3 | 53 |
| Too Much | Unsolved | B-3 | 57 |
| The Comfort Zone | Solved | B-3 | 60 |

*continued*

*continued*

| Chapter 5: Instruction | | | |
|---|---|---|---|
| **Title of Case** | **Solved/ Unsolved** | **Age level B-3, 3-5** | **Page #** |
| Culture Shock | Solved | B-3 | 118 |
| The Next Step | Unsolved | B-3 | 124 |
| Giving in is so Much Easier | Unsolved | B-3 | 126 |
| Alex's Tornado | Solved | 3-5 | 132 |
| Let's Count | Solved | 3-5 | 136 |
| I Want | Unsolved | 3-5 | 139 |
| **Chapter 6: Interaction** | | | |
| **Title of Case** | **Solved/ Unsolved** | **Age level B-3, 3-5** | **Page #** |
| Patience Running Thin | Unsolved | B-3 | 144 |
| New Babies | Unsolved | B-3 | 148 |
| Parenting a child with special needs while having special needs | Unsolved | B-3 | 151 |
| The Distant Child | Solved | 3-5 | 155 |
| Daily Dilemmas of a New Teacher | Unsolved | 3-5 | 157 |
| Concerning Social Interactions in a Small Town | Unsolved | 3-5 | 159 |

*continued*

*continued*

| Chapter 8: Transition | | | |
|---|---|---|---|
| **Title of Case** | **Solved/ Unsolved** | **Age level B-3, 3-5** | **Page #** |
| Daycare to Preschool | Unsolved | B-3 | 207 |
| A Long Way from Home | Unsolved | B-3 | 209 |
| Transitioning to Preschool | Solved | B-3 | 212 |
| Time for Kindergarten | Solved | 3-5 | 215 |
| Sam and Sue | Unsolved | 3-5 | 218 |
| Will It Work Out | Unsolved | 3-5 | 220 |
| Your Opinion is Important | Unsolved | 3-5 | 225 |

# Chapter 1

## OVERVIEW OF CASE METHOD
## OF INSTRUCTION

I (Cyndi) was first introduced to Case Method of Instruction (CMI) as a graduate student in an alternative certification program for early intervention. As a non-education undergraduate major, I had not experienced student teaching and had no prior experience working with families of children who had disabilities. I was not yet a parent and did not even have that perspective. I had begun teaching the previous semester on a temporary teaching certificate while concurrently taking coursework toward early intervention certification. Having a few teacher education courses under my belt, I enrolled in a course on "families" for the summer. One of the textbooks for the course was *Working Together with Children and Families: Case Studies in Early Intervention* (McWilliam & Bailey, 1995).

In this summer course, we used cases from the McWilliam and Bailey (1995) text as a basis for class discussion. The use of cases allowed us, novice teachers and young professionals, to gain valuable information and insight into the perspective of the family, while also introducing us to key issues in the field. We learned how to advocate, listen to, and understand the issues that families with young children with special needs encounter and how to work together with families to formulate plans of action. If I was unsure about my love for working with young children, that summer course solidified my resolve in this path. I eagerly read the entire book over a weekend. Years later when *Lives in Progress: Case Stories in Early Intervention* (McWilliam & Kersgard, 2002) was published, I bought it immediately and read it cover to cover. The stories in this book provided me with an excellent introduction to the field and a deeper understanding and perspective into the lives of families who had children with disabilities.

I (Aaron) was motivated to use CMI in my graduate early childhood special education (ECSE) courses after receiving an Office of Special Education Personnel Preparation grant, entitled Project PREP. The focus of the grant was to increase the number of teachers certified to work in ECSE. This grant shifted the composition of my courses, as I now had an increasing number of students in a master's degree program with no prior experience in special education. With an additional focus Project PREP was to develop students' knowledge and skills regarding evidence-based practices, including the Division for Early Childhood's Recommended Practices (DEC, 2014). Students enrolled in the grant were from a variety of geographical areas of the state of Minnesota and with a wide range of skills (i.e., some were new to the field of education, some were licensed in general education, and some were already licensed in another area of special education).

I needed to find an effective teaching tool to be used to translate the DEC Recommended Practices (RPs) into something that would be practical for the practitioners to both learn about and be motivated to use. I knew of the CMI from my own educational training, but was not consistently using it as a teaching method. I knew that CMI would be an effective method in meeting my goal of having practitioners both learn about the DEC RPs and as a method for them to demonstrate understanding of the RPs.

Both of us as the authors of this text teach a *Methods in Early Intervention* course and began having students read cases to help them gain perspective. Over time, we recognized the need to have context-specific cases for our students. This book is the outgrowth of several years of instruction on both the use of CMI and the process of writing cases.

## WHAT IS CMI?

Case method of instruction (CMI) is an instructional strategy demonstrated to support application of teaching practices as well as enhance problem-solving, decision-making, and reflective thinking skills (Snyder & McWilliam, 2003). Analysis of real-life case situations allow learners to reflect on their own beliefs and ideas while applying content knowledge in order to make decisions about complex problems. Case studies provide teachers and students with a "bridge between theory and practice" (Pindiprolu, Peterson, Rule, & Kraft, 2003, p. 1). It is inevitable that practitioners will face innumerable challenges in their professional practice, making CMI an especially useful instructional strategy.

CMI has been used in a variety of disciplines including education (Silverman, Welty, & Lyon, 1992; Svinicki & McKeachie, 2013), management (Watson & Sutton, 2013), medicine (Sutyak, Lebeau, Spotnitz, O'Donnell, & Mehne, 1996) and higher education (Johnson & Marietta, 2009) for both professional development and college teaching. Early work in early childhood special education has demonstrated the effectiveness of CMI within special education preservice training (Bailey, McWilliam, & Winton, 1992; McWilliam, 1992; Snyder & McWilliam; 1999). The book *Lives in Progress: Case Studies in Early Intervention* (McWilliam & Kersgard, 2002) is a text and accompanying instructor's manual featuring both solved and unsolved early intervention case studies that incorporate real-world dilemmas preservice teachers were likely to encounter in their professional practice. This text, and other cases, have been used in personnel preparation to spark discussion and get students thinking about how to use the Division for Early Childhood's (DEC) recommended practices (DEC, 2014) when interacting with families, guardians, practitioners, and other professionals.

## BENEFITS OF CMI

Case method of instruction has been demonstrated to promote critical thinking and decision-making skills (Boeher & Linsky, 1990; Carter, 1999) for those partaking in either training or coursework. Learners are challenged to analyze problems, make inferences based on limited information, make decisions on uncertain, ambiguous and conflicting issues that simulate real-world problems (Banbury, Janz, & McDermott, 2003; Boeher & Linksy, 1990; Carter, 1999; Svinicki & McKeachie, 2013). Cases provide students with real-world practice in the synthesizing of information and use of professional judgement in order to make an informed decision. Well-written cases prepare students or pre-service teachers for situations they have not yet encountered in the context of the classroom environment, where they can discuss the implications of decisions they consider making within the case study. In-service teachers can use cases as a way to work through challenges they may be having or have had in the past and reflect on possible differences in ways to work through these challenges. As with practice, there can sometimes be information that is important in decision making and other times information that is not relevant. The use of cases gives students practice in making these discernments. Cases can be crafted to make content more salient to help students think through the most challenging situations that are illustrative of both ethical issues in early childhood intervention and adherence to specific recommended practices.

Some proponents of CMI favor long and complex cases (Naumes & Naumes, 2000), as they consider the complexity of redundant information plus the incorporation of gaps as making the case more "real world." Other CMI proponents (Erskine et al., 2003) prefer the inclusion of relevant information with few or no gaps. Both sets of researchers agree that cases should be real rather than fictional, should include narrative and contain characters with which students are able to identify in order for the case to be engaging to students (Whitehouse, 2012).

## CMI DEBATE

One dilemma or debate regarding CMI is which is more important the need for a *skilled facilitator to lead discussion* (Shulman, 1992; Snyder & McWilliam, 2003) or having a *well-constructed cases* (Barnett, 1991; Dolmans, Snellen-Balendong, Wolfhagen, & van der Vleuten, 1997; Erskine, Leenders, & Maufette-Leenders,, 1998; Schmidt, Norman, & Boshuizen, 1990). With more and more teacher preparation programs offering content and/or course work online (Hendricks & Bailey, 2016), it becomes increasingly important to have well-constructed cases (Kim et al., 2006).

Those who advocate for a skilled facilitator recommend that instructors are comfortable working together with students to co-construct knowledge from both the course content and case dilemmas (Sudzina, 1999; Kerns & Watkins, 2007). The use of cases requires several things from the instructor: to be familiar with the case and to be open to alternative interpretations; to know their students well; and to provide feedback and redirection without being authoritarian (Sudzina, 1999; Kerns & Watkins, 2007), as this will have the effect of silencing students from sharing their own understanding.

In one of the early articles on CMI in ECSE, Snyder and McWilliam (2003) discuss the CMI Decision-Making Process, first outlined in McWilliam & Snyder (1993). This model provides guidance to instructors in preparing questions that will help facilitate the discussion on the case. The authors explained that this model is used to help the facilitator develop questions that prompt the student to:

> (a) open the case discussion, (b) identify and analyze dilemmas/issues and contributing factors, (c)consider differing perspectives, (d) project actions that might be taken, (e) consider likely consequences of a particular action, and (f) summarize major insights or highlight learning that has occurred as a result of the case discussion. (p. 289)

This model relies on the facilitator to guide the students through their discussion of the case. In addition to the facilitator's preparation of guiding questions, supplemental strategies include allowing enough time for the students to spend on the discussion, strategies for including everyone in the discussion and summarizing strategies to keep the conversation moving, using boards or flip charts to capture case discussion and address affect (e.g., "You seem to feel strongly about that; do you know why?").

## HOW CMI IS USED

CMI can be a useful tool in introducing a new concept, helping facilitate a shift in students' attitude or dispositions, in introducing students to different cultural, ethnic, and/or linguistic diversity and different perspectives, or to summarize and discuss the students' learning gained from the lecture and discussion of a new concept. Cases can also open discussions about controversial issues, such as families living in poverty, single parenting, or LGBTQ parents. ECSE faculty can use CMI in a variety of ways; below are a few examples.

**Independent Work.** Students can be assigned case studies as an extension of their course readings. Cases should address concepts covered in the course and should highlight perspectives that bring the content to life for the student. This strategy can be used to enhance learning by itself or can prepare the student for class discussion.

**Pair and Share.** Students can be assigned to read cases at home and come to class prepared to discuss with a partner. Within this activity, students can be asked to respond to questions on their own first, then discuss with their partner. When there are differing responses, students should be directed to ask probing questions, using details from the case and their course content knowledge to substantiate their points.

**Small/Whole Group Discussion.** Students can read and discuss cases in class within small groups, highlighting details from the case to respond to questions. After each group has completed their discussion, the instructor can serve as a facilitator in guiding the students through discussion (Shulman, 1992; Snyder & McWilliam, 2003).

**Ongoing Case Discussion.** A case can be presented in the beginning of the semester, slowly providing students with pieces of information to facilitate content across an entire course (Kerns & Watkins, 2007). Researchers suggested that this method can help students understand the impact of a disability across time.

**Role Play.** Students can assume the role of parent or team member for a specific child within a case (Kerns & Watkins, 2007). Students can read the content of the case and conduct a mock team meeting from the case, where different students assume the identity of team members from the information gained from the case. This twist on the use of CMI can help students to engage with the content of the cases and maximize the impact of case content.

## BARRIERS TO USING CMI

While there are multiple benefits for students when using the CMI, there are also barriers. One often cited difficulty expressed by higher education faculty is the time it takes to create cases that are a perfect fit the instructional situation (K. Hensley, personal communication, June 11, 2020). Another issue is having enough cases to use that are appropriate for the content being taught and the age ranges covered is problematic (M. Purcell, personal communication, June 8, 2020). Many ECSE faculty have previous experience using one or both of the McWilliam texts; however, as laws have been reauthorized and recommended practices have evolved, ECSE faculty are in need of more current cases.

Each country, state or community has characteristics that make it unique and oftentimes, these characteristics may also make a case less relatable for students. This problem can be remedied by having more senior students create cases, based on their personal experiences, that are specific to a locale.

CMI requires preparatory work on the part of the instructor. Instructors must be well versed in the case; must be comfortable in facilitating case discussions (skill in improvisation can help here); must be able to provide extensive feedback to students; and have adequate resources of time to work with students (Gideonse, 1999; Kerns & Watkins, 2007).

## FRAMEWORK FOR A WELL-DEVELOPED CASE

In developing the rubric, we looked across previous research to guide the development of our rubric. Of particular interest were works by Banbury et al. (2003), Ertmer & Russell (1995), Kim et al. (2006), and Kim et al. (2005). Below, we share the essential elements from each article that contributed to our final rubric.

Banbury et al. (2003) developed rubrics for a variety of teaching methods to be used for personnel preparation programs. The format followed by Banbury et al. was to provide an overview of the teaching method and the benefits and concerns and then the rubric. The rubric was organized by *preparation* (i.e., development of the case), *implementation* (i.e., how to use the case in a live/in person class), and *questions to be used for debriefing*. For our purposes, we were most concerned with the *preparation* of the case which Banbury et al. had included 13 items that we organized into four categories to assist in our goal of determining how to develop a case. The four categories containing the 13 standards are (1) course standards (*related to course content and objectives; links theory to practice; encourages application for course content is appropriate length* (paragraph 29), (2) characters (presents various perspectives; *portrays both observable event(s) and internal thoughts/feelings of charac-ters; uses dialogue* (paragraph 29), (3) authenticity (*focuses on a provocative dilem-ma or issue; allows for alternative actions/solutions; captures participants' interest; authentic* (paragraph 29), and (4) format (*conveys sufficient detail; clear, well orga-nized, and minimizes extraneous details;* and *decides on techniques to facilitate dis-cussion* (paragraph 29).

**Course Standards.** The standards of the course need to be used as the basis for the case as the case must be related back to learning goals. It is rec-ommended to determine which course standards will be aligned with the case, and ensuring that the learner is able to determine the link between the-ory informing practice and practice informing theory, as well as allowing the learner to apply information already known. For example, if a case is being developed for a professional development of in-service teachers then the facilitator needs to determine what is the main area that should be focused on and what are the goals and objectives that I have for this training.

**Characters.** When developing the characters and setting of the case there should be information to provide depth to the characters. To add depth to the characters, there should be sharing of actual dialogue between the characters and the perspectives of the characters. For example, provid-ing names of characters and giving background information known about the character, having dialogue between characters, and allowing for the char-acter to have an internal monologue of their own perspective on what is occurring that may not be shared in the dialogue between the characters.

**Authenticity.** The authenticity of the case can be achieved if based on act-ual or authentic event(s), allows the reader to focus on a particular dilemma, and has more than one way to solve the case. For example, when examin-ing the goals and objectives for the training there may be a past experience that either the facilitator has had or has heard about from another profes-sional. This past experience could be the basis for a case that will be developed.

**Format.** It is important to be mindful of the format of the case. While developing the case, one should be mindful of including enough detail for the reader to have an understanding of what is occurring, organizing the information for the reader in a logical manner, and how the case will be facil-itated for discussion. For example, prior to sharing the case, the facilitator should ensure that the reader will have enough information to understand the case and that the case is presented in a manner for general understand-ing of the details. Also, the facilitator should determine how the case will be presented and the follow-up discussion will occur.

Ertmer and Russell (1995) provided guidelines for developing a case. These researchers suggest the following questions be considered: *what's the big idea?, what's the story?, who are the characters?,* and *what's the dilemma?* (pp. 27–28).

**What's the Big Idea?** The big idea would be the central concept of the case or what is the main concept area that will be in the case. For example, the main idea might be evidence-based instruction. The case will have an overall focus area of evidence-based instruction (p. 27).

**What's the Story?** The story would be what is going to be discussed that will keep the attention of the readers. There has to be a story that will engage the reader. For example, if the focus area is evidence-based instruction, the story may include a challenge between a parent and a teacher. The challenge would include details to intrigue and engage the reader. Also, if basing the case on a real-story, this will add to the realism and believability of the story (p. 27–28).

**Who Are the Characters?** The characters need to be carefully chosen and should be multifaceted. The characters need to display both strengths and areas of growth. If continuing the case study example of evidence-based instruction, perhaps the father has some knowledge of the need for this type of instruction but is in denial of behavioral issues his child might be displaying. The father's weaknesses of understanding and admission of this issue will add to the depth of this character (p. 28).

**What's the Dilemma?** The dilemma should be complex and more engaging if the issue is not able to be resolved as this will mimic real-life when most issues are not completely resolved. The unresolved case will also be more engaging for the reader. Again, with our example of the evidence-based instruction and the dad not understanding the impact of his son's behavior, perhaps the school team members suggest a more restrictive setting, this setting might allow for more intense instruction, it might impact the child's ability to interact and be around his typically developing peers. While the issue of the child's ability to thrive academically is increased, his social skills might be negatively impacted and the parents may not be completely happy with this decision.

Kim et al. (2006) suggest that to have a well-developed case, four key components are necessary. The case must be relevant, realistic, engaging, challenging, and instructional.

**Relevant.** The case should *reflect the backgrounds, needs, and diversity of learners.* For example, when writing a case for a college course, it would be important to differentiate the level of knowledge the reader has. An undergraduate student would likely not have as much background knowledge on the content as a graduate student; therefore, more descriptions and details may be needed to aid with understanding. The case should include instructional goals and objectives of both learners and teachers. For example, if the case is being used for professional development with practitioners the goal for the learners could be to demonstrate understanding of a practice. The case should contain *realistic and relevant settings . . .* and *should be provided at the* *beginning of the scenario.* For example, one would state the setting of the case in the first few sentences of the case, and would ensure that the setting is relevant to the audience as you would not provide a case set in a manufacturing plant for teachers as this would not be relevant (Kim et al., 2006, p. 870).

**Realistic.** The case should have a basis in *real-world settings.* The real world setting will assist the learner to generalize the information gained to their actual work. When writing a case, one should add *authentic materials, distractors or non-pertinent features, and gradual discourse of information. Authentic materials* for a case may be incorporated with having a dilemma or complex situation as part of the case, just as in real-life most situations are not black and white and solved with one solution. It is important to have *distractors* because in real-life, we don't always have all of the information needed when working with others and we also sometimes have additional information that is not needed. For example, in a case regarding a child transitioning between settings, one might add information regarding how the child is close with his uncle, even though this has no bearing on the case and then you might omit specific information on all of the pros and/or cons of the proposed setting. The *gradual discourse of information* is important as this is how one generally finds out information, all of the information needed is not provided to a person and then one is able to solve the issue. For writing a case, you will want to provide the information needed throughout the case and not all provided to the reader in the first paragraph (Kim et al., 2006, p. 870).

**Engaging.** The case should contain *rich and sufficient content that allows multiple levels of interpretation.* For example, providing a case with more than one way to solve the problem would be one way to ensure multiple levels of interpretation. The case should have *multiple voices and perspectives.* This can be achieved by providing the thoughts of the characters in the case and ensuring that there is more than one character in the case. Ensure that the *course* and *outcome of cases* [are] *dependent on learner's actions.* For example, a case may include the needs and values of both parents, and while both parents may have worthy goals, solving the case in favor of one parent over the other will impact the relationships between the characters in the case (Kim et al., 2006, p. 870-871).

**Challenging.** The case should have a *degree of content difficulty.* For example, not providing enough information, providing multiple perspectives of the characters, and allowing for multiple solutions will all add to the difficulty of the case. The case could vary the structure of information shared. For example, providing key details out of sequence would add to the complexity of the case and challenge the reader in obtaining the information to develop a solution for the case (Kim et al., 2006, p. 871).

**Instructional.** The case should *build upon prior knowledge.* For example, you will want to ensure that you are utilizing information that the reader has to apply to the case. If you know that a reader understands the need for evidence-based instructional strategies, then a case regarding teaching and learning would be appropriate as this will assist with generalizing and building on one's knowledge. The case should allow for assessment. This assessment could be through evaluation of the cases by the instructor or the learner in the usefulness of the content of the case and application of the information (Kim et al., 2006, p. 872).

Kim, Utke, and Hupp (2005) conducted a study on the use of case studies and also the use of *application questions.* Application questions prompt students to consider previously-learned concepts to solve problems in new situations. These types of questions require students to apply what they have learned, rather than recite information verbatim. Researchers found that the use application questions helped in facilitating small group discussion, which could contribute to student understanding. We need not only well-written cases, but also well-written questions.

Case studies can be written describing a problem or situation that has just arisen, and remains unsolved, or a situation that has already occurred or solved. As practitioners, we are likely to encounter situations that are in process, as well as situations that have already occurred, making both solved and unsolved cases beneficial for preservice teachers. McWilliam (1992) considers unsolved cases ripe for discussion, as there can be several possible alternative solutions. Unsolved cases can generate discussion and potential solutions to the dilemma; the focus is on decision making, not on a right answer (Boavida, Aguiar, & McWilliam, 2014). Ertmer and Russell (1995) also note that cases that are unresolved can be the most engaging to students. However, solved cases give us the opportunity to examine how a process has unfolded and make retrospective decisions, in light of outcomes. Having solved cases that are models of adherence to recommended practices, as well as those that are not, can both be valuable for learning.

## DEC RECOMMENDED PRACTICES

The Division for Early Childhood (DEC) is one of 18 subdivisions for the Council of Exceptional Children. The primary focus of DEC is to work on behalf of young children with a disability or at risk for a disability and their families. The DEC has provided recommended practices (RPs) to guide families and practitioners in their work with young children and are recognized as high leverage practices in special education (Council for Exceptional Children & CEEDAR, 2017). The RPs are based on current evidence from the literature, and have been found to be practices that allow for the best outcomes for children with disabilities or at risk for a disability. The RPs have been updated twice (2009 & 2014) since first being introduced in 1993 (DEC, 2018).

The Division for Early Childhood's Recommended Practices (2014) served as the framework for developing the cases in this text. As an initial assignment, students were asked to read and respond to case studies posted online. The next step was to use the case study rubric to assess cases for components that represented standards for writing well-constructed cases. The culminating activity was for students to use the *DEC Recommended Practices Case Study Rubric* to develop their own case studies. In the graduate program there is a range of experience from seasoned practitioners to newly working teachers. These students were tasked with writing cases for 7 of the 8 practices, based on their personal experiences (the RP of leadership was not included, as students did not yet have leadership experience in ECSE). They were given license to combine different elements from their own personal experience or experiences of their colleagues in order to create cases that were illustrative of each practice. This scaffolded process helped students to have a better understanding of the structure and power of the case method of instruction.

While all cases may include elements with multiple RPs, they were asked to primarily focus on one recommended practice topic area, noting individual practices within the topic area. The final step was to provide a framework for the development of cases using previous literature as a guide.

## CASE STUDY RUBRIC

When developing the cases for this book, we created a rubric that incorporated information regarding CMI from a variety of authors (Banbury, Janz, & McDermott, 2003; Ertmer & Russell, 1995; Kim et al., 2006; Kim, Utke, & Hupp, 2005). Students enrolled in a graduate early childhood methods course were instructed on how to create cases and also taught about the Division for Early Childhood's Recommended Practices (DEC, 2014) as a framework to be used to base the case and ensure alignment with evidence-based practices.

| DEC Recommended Practices Case Study Rubric | | |
|---|---|---|
| **Criteria** | **Points** | **Feedback** |
| **Introduction:** Relevant—Provides a title for the case study that ties to the RP addressed, and if the case is "unsolved" or "solved" (e.g., *Introduction*—"This is a (solved or unsolved) case study which references the DEC Recommended (insert the topic area)." | /5 | |
| **Content:** Engaging—Starts with a 'hook' to draw in the interest of the reader | | |
| 1. *Background*—sets context of case—child age, child characteristics, setting. Introduces all characters by name and role. Explain relationship among characters. Realistic—can include extraneous (or missing) details and/or gradual introduction of content. | /5 | |
| 2. *Dilemma*—problem of the case is clear, uses language from DEC RPs; includes positive aspects of the situation (i.e., resources); analyzes contributing factors (i.e., existing constraints, time limitations). Authentic—problem that SPED teachers would encounter, even if it is unusual. | /5 | |
| 3. *Perspectives*—family, teachers, therapists (at least 2); this can be dialogue [in quotations] or internal conversation/thoughts [in italics]; provide enough detail for the reader to evaluate the pros and cons of the situation. | /5 | |
| 4. *Questions.* Instructional—Provides at least 5 questions that can be used to help guide a discussion and/or to probe students' thoughts and refer the reader back to the RP. | /5 | |
| **Format:** Length is no more than 4 pages; Follow APA to include a title page and headers; Spell out all acronyms first time used; Provide objective #s for the Recommended Practices used. | /5 | |

## How to Use the Book

This book is intended to provide practitioners with an understanding of the DEC Recommended Practices (DEC RPs) through the use of case studies written in alignment with standards on the development of case studies. These cases are written to illustrate the DEC RPs and can be used in a variety of ways, with or without the aid of a facilitator. We hope these cases can assist future ECSE practitioners in a greater understanding of both the DEC RPs and a better perspective of the needs of children and families.

# Chapter 2

# ASSESSMENT

## OVERVIEW OF RECOMMENDED PRACTICE

The Division for Early Childhood has defined Assessment as "the process of gathering information to make decisions" (DEC, 2014, p. 8). Assessment is used as an encompassing term that is used for multiple purposes, such as screening and evaluation, planning instruction, and measuring and monitoring of child and family outcomes as performed by the team members on the child's IEP or IFSP.

The major tenets of the assessment process include a team approach that includes the family, consideration of the child's development, and is culturally sensitive. Assessment information should draw from a variety of sources across time and settings. Assessment should be sensitive enough to measure incremental child progress and results should be easily understood by families.

DEC recommends the following assessment practices for practitioners:

- **A1**. Practitioners work with the family to identify family preferences for assessment processes.
- **A2**. Practitioners work as a team with the family and other professionals to gather assessment information.
- **A3**. Practitioners use assessment materials and strategies that are appropriate for the child's age and level of development and accommodate the child's sensory, physical, communication, cultural, linguistic, social, and emotional characteristics.
- **A4**. Practitioners conduct assessments that include all areas of development and behavior to learn about the child's strengths, needs, preferences, and interests.

- **A5**. Practitioners conduct assessments in the child's dominant language and in additional languages if the child is learning more than one language.
- **A6**. Practitioners use a variety of methods, including observation and interviews, to gather assessment information from multiple sources, including the child's family and other significant individuals in the child's life.
- **A7**. Practitioners obtain information about the child's skills in daily activities, routines, and environments such as home, center, and community.
- **A8**. Practitioners use clinical reasoning in addition to assessment results to identify the child's current levels of functioning and to determine the child's eligibility and plan for instruction.
- **A9**. Practitioners implement systematic ongoing assessment to identify learning targets, plan activities, and monitor the child's progress to revise instruction as needed.
- **A10**. Practitioners use assessment tools with sufficient sensitivity to detect child progress, especially for the child with significant support needs.
- **A11**. Practitioners report assessment results so that they are understandable and useful to families.
(DEC, 2014, p. 8)

The following six cases were designed to represent the recommended practices (RPs) for assessment as a whole. Each case is illustrative of a combination of the 11 RPs for assessment and each case does not demonstrate each of the practices. When reviewing the case studies for the RPs for assessment, it is advised to use this chapter in the following ways. One, have individuals read each case and answer independently as a way to determine the individual's understanding of assessment and the corresponding practices. Two, have individuals independently read a case study and, in small groups, discuss what they learned regarding assessment and the corresponding cases. Three, have small groups read case studies and contribute to a whole group discussion. You can use any and all of these suggestions as it fits with your purposes for the teaching or review of the RPs.

## SECTION 1: CASES FOR BIRTH TO AGE 3

## Revolutionary Referral

*Unsolved*

### Background

Caroline looked at the referral paperwork in front of her. To say she was overwhelmed would be an understatement. *Where do I even begin?* Caroline thought. The referral came from a local pediatrician for a nine-month-old girl, Htay Kbru Say. The pediatrician had indicated overall developmental concerns for Htay Kbru Say that included lack of head control, unable to roll from stomach to back, underweight, no reported babbling or sound imitation, no hand to hand transfer, does not turn head to sound, and no social recognition of caregivers. Caroline continued to read the referral. Htay Kbru Say's family are recent refugees from the Karen State in southern Myanmar. The family included Yu Zaw Htay (Mother 23 years old), Eh Baw Say (Dad 31 years old), brothers Reh Yu Say (5 years old), Htet Min Htay (4 years old), and Ko Ye Htay (2 years old). The family has only been in the country for 90 days. They have been fleeing their home country for the last two years, having lived in various refugee camps in Thailand and Malaysia. When they finally arrived in America, they originally settled near Detroit, Michigan. Less than 30 days later, they moved to a small rural community in Minnesota. As they settled, the family was connected with many local social services that assisted them. The family was referred to a local clinic for health care services. The referral came after the initial pediatrician visit for Htay Kbru Say.

Caroline, as the intake coordinator for all early childhood referrals for the local school district that served four communities, had never encountered a Burmese referral. Of course, she has had referrals for other cultures and languages. However, typically this has been limited to the Hispanic population. Caroline wondered how to begin to proceed with this referral. Caroline thought, *I know one thing for sure, I need to reach out for help and find resources in working with families of the Karen culture.* Caroline set out to make contacts and begin planning for the assessment. In her local school district agency, there were no Karenni interpreters available. Caroline contacted a local larger district that she knew would have the resources that she needed. Caroline was referred to the Karen Organization of Minnesota (KOM) and requested an interpreter through their website. After several phone and email exchanges, Caroline's district was able to contract with a Karenni interpreter, Htoo Paw Hte.

"Whew!" Caroline said when she called Htoo Paw Hte. "I am so relieved to have found you!" With Htoo Paw Hte as resource, Caroline set up a meeting with the Early Childhood Special Education (ECSE) intake team, including Terrie (ECSE birth-3 teacher), Emily (District Physical Therapist, PT), Ryan (District Occupational Therapist, OT), Michael (District Licensed School Social Worker, LSW), Moses (ECSE Speech and Language Pathologist, SLP) and Staci (School Psychologist).

## Dilemma

The ECSE intake team had many questions and concerns about this referral. At the forefront of their intentions was to conduct a meaningful assessment while being sensitive to the family's culture and experiences. The team knew the assessment needed to be completed in the child's native language and that Htoo Paw Hte would be able to assist in that regard. However, their bigger concern was with the cultural differences and how the assessments would be able to truly measure development for a child with such a diverse background. "Where do we even begin?" Terri asked Caroline. "I am worried about how to assess this child appropriately." Caroline reassured Terrie, "The team will have Htoo Paw Hte's expertise at every step. We will do this together."

During the initial staffing, Htoo Paw Hte shared rich information about the background of the Karenni culture and experiences. "The Karenni people are resilient, gracious people with a great sense of humor. They have a very strong work ethic, and don't complain. They live out of a basic belief that life is difficult, so you do what you have to do in order to survive." Although he did not know this family yet, he was also able to relate what the refugee experience was like for the Karenni population that had relocated to America. "Due to the ongoing civil war in Karenni State, many people were forced to leave their home and move to government-controlled relocation sites. These refugee camps were located along the border of Thailand. Life in the camps is tightly controlled and refugees are kept isolated from the outside world." Htoo Paw Hte continued, "Some residents have lived in camps for almost 18 years. Children who were born in the camps don't know any other life." Htoo Paw Hte shared information about the relocation process, "Before being accepted for resettlement in the United States, the Karenni refugees had to first pass the United Nations High Commissioner for Refugees (UNHCR) screening. After this initial screening, the successful candidate for resettlement had to pass additional screenings, such as medical checks, and to attend cultural orientation training for 3 to 4 days. When someone successfully passed through all the necessary stages, the individual could then prepare for moving to the host country, such as the United

States." Htoo Paw Hte thought about his own refugee experience and couldn't help thinking about how difficult the journey for this family must have been.

The team listened carefully and began to seek additional feedback. Terri asked, "How are developmental milestones defined in the Karenni Culture?" Htoo Paw Hte shared, "Monitoring of developmental milestones is not a familiar concept. They often use instinct and comparison with siblings or community peers to identify developmental differences." Caroline asked, "How do the Karreni people recognize or define disabilities?" Htoo Paw Hte stated, "Physical disabilities are common and are generally more accepted within communities. Children with physical disabilities are typically integrated into family life and traditional school settings without resources or supports. If disabilities are severe, children are isolated at home."

At the end of the meeting, team members were more familiar with some of the cultural background. "How can we conduct a meaningful assessment?" Caroline questioned the team. Team members shared their thoughts about moving forward. Htoo Paw Hte suggested "Let the family share and become comfortable with you." Terri and Moses agreed that the team should keep the cultural context in mind, while they take an honest look at Htay Kbru Say's needs. They decided the next best step was to meet with the family and solicit their feedback about the evaluation. Htoo Paw Hte made contact with the family and set a meeting at their home for the following week.

**Perspectives**

The team arrived on time at the home of Yu Zaw Htay and Eh Baw Say. After initial greeting and introductions, the team sat on the floor of the two-bedroom home. Many team members already knew of this home location as it was one of a few Housing of Urban Development (HUD) homes in their small rural community. The home was dilapidated and needed many repairs. There were sparse furnishings in the home that consisted mostly of blankets, pillows and various cushions. The floor was bare wood. The children were roaming the home aimlessly and had few items to play with. Yu Zaw Htay was holding Htoo Paw Hte in her arms, but there was little interaction or response between mother and baby. Immediately, Michael started to make mental notes of resources this family was in desperate need of. Michael thought of resources in the community that would be able to provide some furniture, clothes, dishes, and toys.

Caroline began the conversation with the parents. She asked, "How have you been doing since settling into your new home?" Through Htoo Paw Hte, the family shared, "We are grateful to be here, and many people are helpful. We are worried about our children and how they will do in American school." Caroline assured the family "Your children will be welcomed and cared for at school. I can make the school aware of any concerns you have." Caroline gave the family a warm smile and reassurance. However, Caroline was worried about how the refugee and relocated experience may have affected all members of this family. Caroline thought "I wonder if members of this family are experiencing Post Traumatic Stress Disorder (PTSD) and how will this play out the evaluation process?" Terrie took note of the other children in the home but began with asking simple developmental questions about Htay Kbru Say. Terrie asked, "What are your concerns for Htay Kbru Say?" The parents indicated "We understand the doctor's concerns about Htay Kbru Say." They elaborated with comparisons of her development to that of her brothers. However, they didn't seem knowledgeable about specific developmental milestones. Htoo Paw Hte indicated mom and dad reported that they had not considered Htay Kbru Say to be "behind" in her development. Moses asked. "How is Htay Kbru Say's eating routine and how do you feel her growing is?" Both parents indicated that their daughter was not as big as their boys had been, but they felt that was due to her being a girl. During the time they were fleeing to America, Htay Kbru Say was born in a refugee camp. Yu Zaw Htay had breastfed her during this time, but Yu Zaw Htay did not have access to proper nutrition or food on a regular basis. Yu Zaw Htay stated, "Since arriving in America, Htay Kbru Say has been drinking formula and eating some baby food, but often will have problems keeping it down." Moses asked the parents to give examples of sounds or vocalizations that they observe of Htay Kbru Say. Both parents were unable to describe any communication attempts. Moses noted that Htay Kbru Say did have limited cooing and brought that to their attention. Both parents agreed with Moses' observations. Emily and Ryan followed with some questions about fine and gross motor development. Specifically, Ryan asked "Does Htay Kbru Say demonstrate grasp and what she might grab on to?" The parents were able to share that their daughter will grab at her bottle. Emily asked. Can you please lay Htay Kbru Say on a blanket?" As Htay Kbru Say lay on her back, Emily observed there was no attempt to roll or lift her head. Caroline and Staci began to wrap up the visit with information about the evaluation and assessment process. Staci asked, "We would like to know, what are your concerns for Htay Kbru Say?" Yu Zaw Htay and Eh Baw Say said "We are thankful for any help and we know that Htay Kbru Say needs help. We are not sure what is the best way we can help our daughter." Staci stated, "We are going to work together as a team, with you, to help Htay Kbru Say. The evaluation will give us the information to work together to address her needs."

**Final Results**

It was determined to move forward with a formal evaluation for Htay Kbru Say. The team gathered all of their information collected on Karenni culture, the pediatrician report, and information gathered from previous interviews with the family including the child's strengths and areas of concern. Caroline scheduled another meeting with the family and Htoo Paw Hte to go over the evaluation plan and assessments. Caroline wanted to make sure the family and their feedback were included. Observations were set to be done at home and in the community at the grocery store, park, and other places that they take Htay Kbru Say. The team retained Htoo Paw Hte during the entire evaluation process, to ensure assessments were conducted in her native language, and looked for his feedback on each component. Several questions remained for the team to determine. How to find the best assessment tool? How to find the best way to communicate the needs for the assessment? How will the team adapt the assessment materials to be culturally sensitive? Caroline also thought about how, in their culture, children with severe disabilities remained isolated at home, and wondered what the family's opinions on this are and how this could impact implementing services in the future. The district and ECSE evaluation team were embarking on new territory. They embraced the experiences as a learning opportunity and looked forward to how this will benefit them personally and professionally.

## QUESTIONS

1. Which DEC practices for the topic area of Assessment did you see supported in this case study?
2. Which of the DEC practices for the topic area of Assessment were not supported in this case study? How might these have been addressed?
3. How could the refugee and relocation experience have had an effect on the early development of Htay Kbru Say?
4. Besides involving Htoo Paw Hte for interpretive purposes, in what other ways could he be a resource to the team?
5. The team must consider language and cultural barriers when planning evaluations, how was this demonstrated?
6. Oftentimes, in very young children and infants, developmental delays are a result of chromosomal, genetic or medical abnormalities. How could the team explore this possibility?
7. What are some alternative informal assessments that could provide a clearer picture of Htay Kbru Say's overall development?

# SPLIT DECISIONS

*Unsolved*

## Background

It was a busy fall for Michael and his mother, Jackie. They moved from Illinois to Minnesota and everything here was new. Jackie's family all lived in Illinois and she only knew one person in Minnesota, Michael's dad, James. With Jackie's new part time job and Michael to be turning 3 in a few months, Jackie decided to enroll in early childhood family education classes that included both her and Michael. Jackie was excited for Michael to be around kids his own age and hopefully they could both make some friends. They went to the classes three days per week and Michael also started seeing his dad for a few hours on the weekend so they could get to know each other better. Jackie and Michael were settling into their new routines and getting used to having James in their lives. However, all of this sudden change was difficult for Michael, and the previous concerns Jackie had about some of his behaviors were now worrying her again. Michael liked things to be predictable and the same each day. At first, Jackie thought *all kids like consistency. Michael just likes it a little more than others.* But now, Jackie was noticing that Michael's tantrums were becoming worse when things varied even slightly from the usual routine and when she'd pick up Michael from school he was almost always playing alone with the trains.

Overwhelmed, she set up a meeting with Michael's teacher, Kate, to see if she also noticed these behaviors at school. At the meeting, Kate agreed with Jackie's observations. "Besides Michael's need for a strict routine, I also notice that he seems to avoid loud noises," said Kate. She also agreed with Jackie that Michael didn't really play with other children. He either played alone or next to other children. At the end of the meeting, Kate mentioned that they were going to be doing their early childhood screening next week and that she could connect Jackie with the early childhood special education (ECSE) teacher, Marie, as a resource.

## Dilemma

A few days later, Michael completed his early childhood screening. With the screening results and Jackie's input, the ECSE program referred Michael for further evaluation. With this support and feeling like something could happen to benefit Michael, Jackie was relieved and felt positive. When it came to James, however, it was a different story.

On Saturday, Jackie dropped Michael off with his dad. As they exchanged greetings, Jackie mentioned the struggles she was having and her concerns about Michael's behavior. She also mentioned that she was relieved that he was going to be evaluated by the ECSE team. James shook his head and said, "I don't think anything's going on with Michael. He's a four-year-old kid. Of course, he's going to be hard to deal with sometimes. If you're going to go through with this, I want to be part of it. After all, I have legal rights as his father." After Jackie left, James couldn't stop wondering how in the world Jackie could actually feel relieved thinking that there was something wrong with their son.

## Perspectives

The evaluation team, Michael's teacher Kate, Jackie, and James met to discuss the evaluation results and propose a plan for Michael. "Let's first go around and introduce ourselves and our role on this team, OK? I'll go first. I am Marie and I'm the early childhood special education teacher." The rest of the team, including Jackie and James took their turns.

"We each did some assessments and observations with Michael over the past week and we want to discuss those results and propose some ways that we might be able to use that information to help Michael be successful at school and at home. We also want to hear from you, Jackie and James, since you are an important part of this team. Kate, since you know what he's like in your classroom, feel free to add anything you've observed as well," Marie explained.

Before anyone had a chance to share anything, James spoke up. "Excuse me, but is this really necessary? I mean, he's a two-year-old almost three-year-old kid. He's going to have tantrums. Maybe if his mom didn't give in to him or use her iPad to babysit him, he would be fine." Although Marie could feel herself tense up, she didn't show her surprise and said, "I hear what you're saying, but I want to back up a little and talk about what we have observed. You two will be able to give us lots of insight into what Michael is like at home. I am guessing we will find some areas that we are in agreement about. Any areas that we don't see eye to eye on we can discuss further." With that, James nodded and the specialists began to talk about their assessments and results.

First, the speech-language clinician, Karen, talked about Michael's language development. "Michael's receptive language skills are on track. He understands what is being said and follows simple verbal directions without any problem. One thing I did notice, and I know Kate and Jackie mentioned, was that he sometimes struggles with expressing his feelings, which results in him screaming or having a tantrum instead of using his words," she said.

It seemed like everyone was seeing the same things and that the proposed IFSP would be approved and implemented to support Michael. Jackie was feeling optimistic. That is, until it was James' turn to share. James said, "I don't want my son labeled. I don't want people to think there's something wrong with him because he might be a little different. Aren't all kids different in one way or another? I do NOT want my son to have some kind of a label so kids can make fun of him or teachers can treat him differently."

Jackie started to cry. "You don't know what it's like. You only have him a few hours at a time. Maintaining the structure that he needs and dealing with his behavior is really hard. I need help. He needs help. That is all that these people are trying to offer us," she sobbed.

Kate, who had mostly only chimed in to support others' ideas and observations so far, spoke up, "James, I get where you're coming from. I want to let you know we are all on the same team. We are all trying to advocate for what's best for Michael, just like you. One of the things I see is that Michael is alone and upset every day. I want this whole team of people to help us help him so he doesn't feel that way every day."

James simply replied, "You're wrong!"

## QUESTIONS

1. Which DEC practices for the topic area of Assessment did you see supported in this case study?
2. Which of the DEC practices for the topic area of Assessment were not supported in this case study? How might these have been addressed?
3. James was worried about Michael being "labeled." What are some strategies that the team could have used to respond to James' concerns?
4. The team focused on Michael's needs. How could they have better focused on Michael as a whole person?
5. What could the team have done differently to address James' concerns?
6. How could assessment data be used in this discussion?

## SECTION 2: CASES FOR 3-TO-5-YEAR-OLDS

## Time for a New Diagnosis?

*Solved*

### Background

Logan is a five-year-old kindergarten student who currently has an individualized education plan (IEP) for a diagnosis of emotional/behavior disorder (EBD). Logan has a history of aggression, which includes incidents in child care settings that result in injury to other children. He shows aggression and has tried to hurt his two-year-old sister and mother on various occasions.

Logan injured one of his kindergarten classmates, which resulted in him being suspended. He demonstrates attention seeking behaviors in the kindergarten classroom that interfere with the safety and learning of his peers. He strives to get a "rise" out of his peers and adults, and will sometimes resort to physical contact in order to gain that attention.

Logan's mother, Tanya, does not know what to do regarding Logan's behavior or how to help him. He has been kicked out of child care twice, most recently for biting other children. At home, Tanya does not feel she has any control and it seems like everything she tries is ineffective.

Logan's kindergarten teacher, Ms. Thomas, and the school counselor, Mrs. Nelson, have been working with Logan on how to appropriately gain others' attention and build peer relationships. Mrs. Nelson sees Logan once a week and describes him as "pleasant," but also indicates that his inability to take turns during a conversation is a large obstacle to him building peer relationships. "Even in a small group, he always has to be noticed."

### Dilemma

Ms. Thomas has expressed her concerns about the amount and variation of techniques and consequences used so far. Nothing has produced consistent change in Logan's behavior. She has tried extrinsic motivational techniques, consequences, and has done her best to remain consistent but has not found a strategy that works to control his emotional outbursts and aggression. In Logan's classroom environment, he has his own space at the carpet and while doing desk work in order to minimize aggression towards his peers. He is given breaks throughout the day during which he is able to move his body to release excess energy.

Currently, the majority of Logan's special education services are provided within his general education classroom in order to embed his social skills instruction into routines, activities, and environments to provide relevant learning opportunities. There is evidence that Logan is utilizing his social skills strategies, however, he is still exhibiting aggression towards his peers at school and his mother and sister at home.

## Perspectives

During his most recent IEP meeting, the team learned a few new things about Logan. Logan has quite a bit of anxiety when he is at home. His mother stated that Logan is "afraid of the dark and does not sleep in his own bed." She also shared that he is often worried about the unknown, and is afraid of storms, fire, and car accidents. He is constantly asking his mom about natural disasters and seems fixated on things that can hurt him and others, along with being sensitive to loud sounds. When Logan's IEP team asked about how long Logan has exhibited these behaviors, his mom said, "Logan has always seemed hyper-aware of distressing situations, and when I tell him that it is something adults are supposed to worry about and that it is my job to keep him safe, he still seems uneasy."

Logan's mom also shared that she is often concerned about his nutrition and his ability to gain weight. Since he started eating solid foods just after turning one-year-old, he has been very picky about what he eats and has been on the low end of body weight percentages. She explained that he likes to eat a lot of plain foods: bread with nothing on it and noodles. He rarely eats any meat or fruits. He likes to smell food before he will consider eating it. His teacher said she noticed Logan close to his school lunch tray to smell the food.

Logan's IEP case manager, Ms. Thomas has tried several different strategies throughout the school year. "There have been a few strategies that have seemed to decrease Logan's attention seeking behaviors, but most last only a few weeks." Some of the strategies that have been used include social stories, video self-monitoring, sticker charts, time outside of the classroom with a peer, friendship groups, and a check in/check out system. "It is difficult because some of his peers also show some aggressive and attention seeking behaviors in the classroom and together, they seem to escalate. Logan has the skills to "be a leader" if he can channel his behavior in a positive way rather than through anger and outbursts.

Logan has not yet shown the ability to connect on a personal level with a "best friend," and often struggles to make connections and maintain meaningful relationships with adults and his peers. As a result of this disconnect, Logan's parents and teachers struggle with finding the "currency" that will get him to continually make choices that are not a danger to himself, or others.

## Possible Solution

Upon learning about Logan's anxiety and nutrition concerns from his mother, the school team felt that an evaluation for Autism Spectrum Disorder (ASD) was appropriate. Logan has an evaluation that will be due next year. The team knew that changing the label on his IEP would not alter the type of services he receives. The team discussed the possibility of moving up his assessment, but determined that waiting until the evaluation was due would not affect the quality of his services. The team decided to make some changes to his goals and objectives, and to provide some accommodations and modifications to his educational setting that would be similar to those of a student with autism. At the end of the IEP meeting, Logan's mom suggested that it may be time for him to be evaluated by a professional psychologist, and that she would like for him to begin some outside play therapy in hopes of relieving some of his anxiety and aggression.

## QUESTIONS

1. Which DEC practices for the topic area of Assessment did you see supported in this case study?
2. Which of the DEC practices for the topic area of Assessment were not supported in this case study? How might these have been addressed?
3. What are Logan's strengths, needs, preferences, and interests? Have these been recognized and used in planning for intervention?
4. Who else can provide information about Logan's challenges and strengths?
5. Do you think the proposed changes to Logan's IEP will be enough support for him to make progress?

## NATURE VS. NURTURE

*Unsolved*

## Background

Sonya is a three year, four-month old girl who has been attending three-year-old preschool for approximately six months. She lives at home with her mom, Nancy, and three older brothers, Danny (twelve), Alex (nine) and Peter (seven). Sonya's mom and dad are not living together. She sees her dad occasionally but does not have regularly scheduled visits. Nancy has shared that Sonya's dad is diagnosed with Emotional Behavioral Disorder (EBD) and has self-regulation issues. Nancy works in the school district as a paraprofessional with elementary-aged students. Danny and Alex were both diagnosed with Autism Spectrum Disorder (ASD) at early ages. Danny exhibits more extreme physical behaviors than his brother Alex although Alex does exhibit physical behaviors as well. Mom describes the youngest boy, Peter as "quirky" but he is developing as expected as compared to same-aged peers.

Sonya has been exhibiting some odd behaviors in class since the beginning of the year. The behaviors have increased in frequency and are causing a disruption to Sonya's ability to learn. Sonya will say things like, "I eat it?" when referring to non-food items in the classroom. When the teacher responds with, "No, we do not eat that," Sonya smiles, repeats her phrase over and over until the teacher ignores her. Sometimes she will then put the item in her mouth and sometimes she doesn't. She smiles at everything, even at very inappropriate times, such as when she's angry or frustrated. She will often disrupt another children's play and watch how they react, smiling through it all. Sonya also has very excessive drool; her mouth is often open in a smile and she does not seem to notice or care that her chin and shirt are covered with drool. During circle time, Sonya will often leave her spot on the carpet and drape herself across the teacher's lap. Her body goes limp and the teacher has to physically lift Sonya off her lap. She does this with other teachers during free choice, as well.

Sonya's behaviors have increased with becoming extremely non-compliant during times of transition. She will hit and push her peers, lay across the teacher's feet and refuse to transition to the next task. When it is time to put winter clothes on to play outside, she has started running away in the hall, laying/rolling around on the floor, and refusing to put her winter clothes on. If staff assist her with these tasks, she often takes everything off once it's on. Staff will then bring her items into the classroom, close the door, and wait for her to do it independently on her own terms. This can sometimes last up to 15 minutes. At dismissal, Sonya exhibits these same behaviors with the staff. Every day the staff have to ask Nancy to come into the classroom and help Sonya get ready to leave. Again, this sometimes takes between 10-15 minutes. More often than not, Nancy is usually carrying Sonya out to the car as she is half dressed in winter clothes, kicking and screaming.

Cognitively, Sonya has demonstrated a lot of inconsistencies. During large and small group, teacher-lead activities, Sonya will sometimes engage appropriately by following directions, raising her hand, and trying to answer questions. She has an age-appropriate vocabulary and talks in full sentences, sometimes omitting words. Sonya does have difficulty with articulation, and it is sometimes difficult to understand what she is saying. She will often say things out of context, which makes communication with staff and peers difficult at times. Sonya is very inconsistent when answering questions, oftentimes answering questions off topic.

## Dilemma

The dilemma in this case study is to determine the best assessments for determining Sonya's eligibility for services. The teaching staff will have to provide accurate informal assessments to be able to provide supporting evidence regarding Sonya's behaviors and achievement in the different developmental areas (social emotional, physical, cognitive, language, literacy and math. Because Sonya has been exposed to significant behaviors from her brother, who is on the Autism Spectrum, a big question that has been posed by the assessment team is whether Sonya is exhibiting behaviors that she would have exhibited naturally or if she is exhibiting behaviors that are only learned from her environment.

## Perspectives

The general education teacher, Sarah, talked to Nancy during parent teacher conferences in November regarding Sonya's progress and some concerns she had with Sonya's behavior. During the conference meeting Sarah and Nancy collaborate by determining ways to support Sonya's development in preschool. Sarah said they would continue to monitor Sonya's progress and keep Nancy updated, as needed. Sarah and her staff started collecting Behavior Incident Reports (BIR) in December when they started to see the increase of behaviors. It has been difficult for Sarah to accurately assess Sonya in many of the developmental areas due to her inconsistencies. Using Teaching Strategies (TS) GOLD, which is a valid and reliable observation based assessment system used by the Early Learning Department in the school district, Sonya demonstrates lower than typical scores for social/emotional, language, and cognitive developmental areas. Sarah was concerned with Sonya's behavior in November and, now seeing the progression of significant behaviors in February, would like to discuss this further with Nancy to see if she would be open to the teacher submitting a referral for a special education assessment.

During conferences, Nancy said that she was seeing some of the same behaviors at home but was not concerned. Nancy felt that Sonya was developing at a much higher rate than Danny or Alex were at that age and that she did not feel a referral was necessary at that point. Nancy did share some scenarios that may affect Sonya's development. Oftentimes, at home, Danny will become physically aggressive with his siblings and Mom. Sonya has observed Danny hitting, punching, kicking and breaking household items. Nancy also shared that there have been occasions when Sonya's Dad has been verbally abusive towards Nancy. When this happens, Nancy will put her hands over Sonya's ears and sing loudly hoping to drown out the verbal abuse.

Sarah consulted with the Early Childhood Special Education (ECSE) teacher, Jane. Jane serves students in Sarah's classroom and she shared her observations of Sonya. They had discussed early on in the year that Sonya definitely had some quirky behaviors and, as the year continued, Jane shared similar concerns as Sarah. Some of the observed behaviors were smiling when angry and/or causing harm to a peer, laying across a teacher's lap and feet when seeking attention, difficulty sitting in a chair during table activities (could only perform tasks when standing), non-compliance, throwing tantrums, and inability to answer questions on task.

Sarah also consulted with the Speech/Language Pathologist (SLP), Lisa, to discuss a possible speech referral. Lisa had the opportunity to pair Sonya up with a couple other children who also receive speech services to do an informal assessment in a quiet, more controlled setting. After this informal assessment, combined with her observations in the classroom, Lisa felt that it would be beneficial to move forward with a formal speech and language assessment.

About two weeks ago, Sarah requested a meeting with the school psychologist, Anna, and Jane to discuss the BIR's she has collected. Unbeknownst to Sarah and Jane, Anna was somewhat familiar with the family, as she had worked on the teams for Danny and Alex. Anna understood the severity of the behaviors Sonya was probably exposed to daily with her siblings. Sarah, Anna and Jane all agreed that the behaviors Sonya has been exhibiting were very atypical and very similar to behaviors observed in children with Autism Spectrum Disorder. However, the resounding opinion was that Sonya was looking for reactions to her behaviors and they almost all tended to be attention-seeking. Jane posed the question, could the behaviors be learned from Sonya's environment and siblings, but not necessarily reflecting that Sonya may be on the Autism Spectrum?

The Early Childhood Special Education Teacher, Jane, would like to assist Sarah in providing additional information to Sonya's family to assist in making the best decision. If the family decided to move forward with an assessment, she would also utilize several of the assessment checklists provided on the Early Childhood Technical Assistance (ECTA) Center website.

## QUESTIONS

1. Which DEC practices for the topic area of Assessment did you see supported in this case study?
2. Which of the DEC practices for the topic area of Assessment were not supported in this case study? How might these have been addressed?
3. What impact does having two siblings with autism have on Sonya?
4. If Sonya's mother decides not to move forward with the early childhood special education assessment, what would the next steps be for Sarah?
5. What challenges do you foresee with this case study?
6. What assessments would you recommend to the team, if Nancy gave approval to move forward?

## SPECIAL EDUCATION GRADUATE

*Solved*

### Background

Is Ian ready to graduate? Ian is a 5-year-old child receiving special education services at a community based preschool program 3 mornings a week for 2 and one half hours each day. Ian was referred to special education services by his pediatrician due to concerns about his cognitive, social-emotional, and speech development. Ian qualified for special education under the category of Developmental Delay at the age of 2 and began attending preschool in March of 2014, when he turned 3. While in preschool, Ian has worked with Wendy, his speech pathologist, and Anna, his special education teacher/case manager. Ian received a new preschool teacher this year but remained in the same program and setting. Being Ian's third year of preschool, he is very familiar with the routine and environment. Outside of school Ian lives in an apartment with his older brother Caleb and mother Tami.

### Dilemma

Children in early childhood special education services must be re-evaluated every 3 years to determine if they continue to show a need for special education services and support. Ian is currently due for his 3-year re-evaluation, to determine if he continues to show a need for special education services. Ian has shown great success in preschool as evidenced by ongoing assessments used to monitor his progress. Leading up to the re-evaluation, the special education team has communicated with Ian's mother about the possibility that he may no longer need special education services as he transitions into kindergarten. Ian's mother is worried about the transition to kindergarten and feels uneasy about Ian making the transition without any special education support.

## Perspectives

At conferences Ian's mother, Tami, expressed her concern about the transition into kindergarten. She feels it is a big transition in itself without also taking away special education services. Tami agrees with the special education staff that Ian is having success in preschool, but feels that the new environment and routine of kindergarten combined with Ian's shy personality could result in Ian "slipping through the cracks."

Ian has made enormous gains in preschool and requires little to no prompting from the special education staff to move throughout his preschool day. The special education team feels that Ian may be behind his peers when it comes to naming letters and numbers, but otherwise shows the great skills in following directions, completing multi-step art activities, and participating within the large group. The special education team consisting of the speech pathologist and case manager will be testing Ian in the areas of cognition and communication to see if he continues to show a need for special education services. The team has sent home a Prior Written Notice to Ian's mother so that she is aware of the testing. Included in the testing are the Preschool and Kindergarten Behavior Skills (PKBS) and Adaptive Behavior Assessment System (ABAS) questionnaires to be filled out by Ian's preschool classroom teacher. Also, Anna the case manager will complete the Mullen Scales of Early Learning, classroom observation, and file review of Ian's previous testing. Lastly, the Preschool Language Scales (Fifth Edition), language sample and file review of previous testing will be completed by Wendy. The special education team split up their testing and varied their days so that Ian did not become overwhelmed or miss too many classroom activities. The testing was completed over the course of 2 weeks. Upon completion of the testing, the special education team found that Ian no longer met criteria to receive special education services. Ian's test results showed him at or above age level in all areas.

**Final Results**

Once Ian's test results were compiled, the special education team and Ian's mother Tami got together to discuss the outcome. The special education team thoroughly explained the observations, the testing they completed along with the scoring of the instruments, and how the scores compare to Ian's typically developing peers. After seeing the scores and hearing about what a great job Ian did while testing, Tami's anxiety of kindergarten was lightened. Tami did not ask many questions but did seem to understand the results and what was being described. The special education team agreed to let Ian finish out the preschool year receiving his current special education services and organize a transition meeting with kindergarten staff. A transition meeting will allow Tami to meet the kindergarten staff, describe Ian, and ensure that they are aware of him and keep him on their radar. The following day Ian's evaluation report was sent home. Tami signed and returned the report indicating that she agreed with the report and the proposal of discontinuing services.

## QUESTIONS

1. Which DEC practices for the topic area of Assessment did you see supported in this case study?
2. Which of the DEC practices for the topic area of Assessment were not supported in this case study? How might these have been addressed?
3. What else could the special education team have done to ease Tami's fears of kindergarten?
4. While the focus of this case is assessment, there will likely be concerns regarding instruction when Ian is in Kindergarten. Which instruction recommended practices should the team be mindful of as he transitions to Kindergarten?
5. Was the outcome the best solution for all parties involved? Why or why not?

# DO SOMETHING

*Unsolved*

## Background

Sherri (Paraprofessional) walks into the resource room exasperated and tells the special education teacher, Ms. Stokes, "You have to do something, this is ridiculous that no one is doing anything for Rachel."

Mrs. Stokes (Special Education Teacher) looks at Sherri and says, "Calm down and tell me what is going on."

Rachel is a four-year-old child in Ms. Stokes Pre-K classroom. She has been performing well academically, though the classroom teacher has noticed some odd behaviors, but has stated she is not concerned about Rachel, due to her strong academic skills. Rachel's parents have not previously brought forward concerns to the school. However, the classroom paraprofessional has noticed some behaviors she finds concerning and is finding that Rachel is taking a considerable amount of her support to perform daily classroom routines with success. Concerns being raised by staff around the school include Rachel's inability to independently complete bathroom tasks, such as wiping and hand washing. Additionally, it has been observed that she often sits with her back to the group during instruction, moving her hands in unexpected ways. School staff are concerned that Rachel may be displaying behaviors indicative of Pica, the ingestion of non-food objects including pencils and rocks. The team includes Sherri (classroom paraprofessional), Ms. Dean (classroom teacher), Ms. G (recess supervisor), members of the Teachers Assisting Teachers (TAT) team and the OWL Squad (school behavior team).

## Dilemma

The team does not yet have all the data and several members of the educational team are not seeing eye-to-eye on the difficulties Rachel is displaying. The team needs to collect data to discover what concerns exist, to come up with a plan to support the learner.

## Perspectives

**Sherri** (paraprofessional). Sherri is fed up with having to be the one to deal with all these items when she has other children that need her help too. She feels the classroom teacher is oblivious to what is going on. She has observed that Rachel will sit with her back to the group and her hands look like puppets talking, she isn't talking out loud, but her hands are constantly moving. She will not go to the bathroom by herself and while in the bathroom she will not wipe herself. The teacher can be sitting five feet from the classroom sink and Rachel will not wash her hands unless the teacher goes with her to the sink.

**Ms. Dean** (classroom teacher). Ms. Dean has seen some of the behaviors described by other team members, but feels that they are not interfering with Rachel's academics. She doesn't see them as areas of concern.

**Ms. Stokes** (special education teacher). Ms. Stokes is concerned that some of the behaviors being described to her might be an indication of Autism. When the classroom teacher says she isn't concerned, she responds by saying, "We understand that Rachel is very bright and that you have no concerns right now with her academics, however, early intervention may be needed to be considered to decrease the chance that these behaviors will negatively impact Rachel in the future."

During the TAT (Teachers Assisting Teachers) meeting, Ms. Dean states that she is not sure why she is there. Ms. Stokes asks Ms. Dean to talk about what Rachel has been doing in class. The other teachers seem concerned, and give ideas on how to deal with the different behaviors. The team agrees to develop an intervention plan to address the major areas of concern. Ms. Dean agrees to support these interventions and help with progress monitoring, to determine if the interventions are successful. The plan is documented below:

### Bathroom (not wanting to go in by herself):

1. Leave the door open enough to stick your hand or foot in, so Rachel does not feel alone.
2. Give her a flashlight attached to a doll. This can help in case she is scared of the lights going out and also gives her "company."
3. Provide a story-based intervention on going to the bathroom.

### Sink (needing an adult standing beside her at all times):

1. Gradually make the space between teacher and adult larger, 1/2 foot to 1 foot at a time.
2. Provide a story-based intervention on going to the bathroom and washing your hands independently.

Ms. Dean agreed to work on these things and to come back in six to eight weeks to discuss how things were going with Rachel.

During afternoon recess, Ms. Stokes was called to the playground for assistance. Rachel was laying on the ground eating rocks. She continued despite redirects from recess supervisors to stop.

"Rachel, are you ok? Did you fall down?" *No reply from Rachel.* "Rachel, this is Ms. Stokes, I just want to make sure you are ok. Can you sit up and talk with me?" *Ms. Stokes sits down next to her and Rachel rolls over with a big smile.* "What is going on Rachel? You have people worried about you."

Rachel smiles and simply says "I'm hungry." This stunned Ms. Stokes a bit, as Rachel sounded sincere.

"Well, I can understand being hungry. Do you think eating rocks is the best solution?"

Still smiling, Rachel says "No, but they taste so good and I am really hungry."

Ms. Stokes and Rachel talked about how rocks can be harmful to Rachel's belly. They discuss other choices Rachel could make when she is feeling hungry. Afterward, Ms. Stokes went to visit with Ms. Dean about how the intervention plan has been working. *Ms. Dean felt that the interventions were showing promising results.* Ms. Stokes informed her of the situation on the playground. Ms. Dean shared that Rachel has been eating her pencil in the classroom. Confused, Ms. Stokes says, "You mean chewing on them?" "No, she eats the whole pencil, the metal, the eraser and the wood. I have other students that chew on their pencils, they are just nervous."

Ms. Stokes is shocked. "Ms. Dean, this is not a common thing. It is very concerning that Rachel is eating these items, this can be detrimental both physically as well as socially. I feel as though we need to call her mom and let her know what is happening, talk to Rachel and put a plan in place."

The next day the OWL Squad is called to Ms. Dean's classroom. The OWL Squad is a team of teachers, paraprofessionals, and administration who've received training in dealing with severe behaviors. Once in the room, the team sees Rachel crawling on the floor, acting like a dog. She is growling at her classmates and at anyone that comes near her. Ms. Dean says that she saw Rachel chewing on a pencil, told her no, and tried to take it away. Rachel started growling at everyone, crawling around and tried to leave the room. Ms. Dean is asked to take the other children out of the room. The team decides that there is no need for everyone to be there and that it might calm Rachel down if there are fewer people. Ms. Stokes and Ms. G. stayed with her. Anytime one of the adults tries to talk to her, Rachel either growls or tries to run from the room saying, "It's a game now!" Ms. Stokes asks Ms. G. to stand by the door, so Rachel cannot leave the room. Ms. Stokes starts a conversation with Ms. G. about being hungry.

MS. STOKES.   "Ms. G. I am pretty hungry; I wonder what is for lunch."
MS. G.         "I think we are having Chicken Alfredo today."
MS. STOKES.   "That sounds good. Do you know what time it is?"
MS. G.         "It is a little after eleven, do you think you can wait an hour to eat?"
MS. STOKES.   "I'm not sure, I am really hungry."
MS. G.         "I am sorry to hear that. What do you think you could do?

*Rachel stops moving around the room and is watching the teachers.*

MS. STOKES.   "Ms. G. do you think I could have a snack?"
MS. G.         "I think that is a great idea! I see that there are some cereal or graham crackers here, which would you like?"
MS. STOKES.   "May I have a graham cracker, please?"

*Ms. G. gives Ms. Stokes a graham cracker.*

After a few minutes, Rachel moves closer and asks, "Can I have some too?" Ms. G. smiles and says "Sure, here you go. It is hard to do your work when you are hungry isn't it?" Rachel finishes her graham cracker and Ms. Stokes asks her what happened today. Rachel says, "I was hungry, and I had to wait for lunch; I couldn't wait and the pencil tastes really, really good." "Well," Ms. Stokes replied, "do you think you can use your words to tell Ms. Dean how you are feeling, and to get a snack instead of eating a pencil?

Ms. Stokes tells Ms. Dean that she is going to call a meeting together with the principal, school psychologist, school occupational therapist and the two of them. She also tells Ms. Dean that they need to talk to Rachel's mom and that she would like to sit in on it.

## QUESTIONS

1. Which DEC practices for the topic area of Assessment did you see supported in this case study?
2. Which of the DEC practices for the topic area of Assessment were not supported in this case study? How might these have been addressed?
3. How could the paraprofessional, classroom teacher and special education teacher address this situation differently?
4. There were several meetings to discuss Rachel's behavior needs. Which team member was left out of those discussions and how could that information be obtained?

5. What did you think of the proactive actions the team proposed? What additional actions would you propose?
6. What next steps would you suggest for the team?

# Chapter 3

# ENVIRONMENT

## OVERVIEW OF RECOMMENDED PRACTICE

D EC (p. 9) states that environments include, ". . . the space, materials (toys, books, etc.), equipment, routines, and activities that practitioners and families can intentionally alter to support each child's learning across developmental domains. The environmental practices we address in this section encompass the physical environment (e.g., space, equipment, and materials), the social environment (e.g., interactions with peers, siblings, family members), and the temporal environment (e.g., sequence and length of routines and activities)."

The major tenets of the environmental practices are to ensure access and participation while maintaining the safety of children in either natural or inclusive environments. Practitioners and families will work together to ensure that any needed modifications, adaptations, or assistive technology are provided for access and participation. The principles of universal design for learning are to be considered when determining an appropriate environmental setting.

DEC recommends the following environment practices for practitioners:

- **E1**. Practitioners provide services and supports in natural and inclusive environments during daily routines and activities to promote the child's access to and participation in learning experiences.
- **E2**. Practitioners consider Universal Design for Learning principles to create accessible environments.
- **E3**. Practitioners work with the family and other adults to modify and adapt the physical, social, and temporal environments to promote each child's access to and participation in learning experiences.

- **E4**. Practitioners work with families and other adults to identify each child's needs for assistive technology to promote access to and participation in learning experiences.
- **E5**. Practitioners work with families and other adults to acquire or create appropriate assistive technology to promote each child's access to and participation in learning experiences.
- **E6**. Practitioners create environments that provide opportunities for movement and regular physical activity to maintain or improve fitness, wellness, and development across domains.
(DEC, 2014, p. 9)

The following nine cases were designed to represent the recommended practices (RPs) for the environment as a whole. Each case is illustrative of a combination of the six RPs for environment and each case does not demonstrate each of the practices. When reviewing the case studies for the RPs regarding the environment it is advised to use this chapter in the following ways. One, have individuals read each case and answer independently as a way to determine the individual's understanding of assessment and the corresponding practices. Two, have individuals independently read a case study and in small groups discuss what they learned regarding assessment and the corresponding cases. Three, have small groups read case studies and contribute to a whole group discussion as a whole. You can use any and all of these suggestions as it fits with your purposes for the teaching or review of the RPs.

## SECTION 1: CASES FOR BIRTH TO AGE 3

### Baby Blues

*Solved*

## Background

Jamie and her son Charlie, live with her dad and brother. Her father and brother worked long hours, so Jamie was alone most of the day with Charlie. They encouraged Jamie to find some friends, but she spent most of her day lying on the couch. It took many months to understand she had postpartum depression. She started therapy when Charlie was 9 months old. Charlie was not reaching his developmental milestones. He was not cooing or babbling, and he could not sit up on his own. After Charlie's 9-month checkup, and with Jamie's permission, Charlie's pediatrician referred Charlie to the local birth-to-three program. This is where Liz came in. Liz is an early childhood special education (ECSE) teacher. Charlie was assessed for all areas of development and it was determined that he qualified for ECSE services. Liz, the ECSE teacher and Joe, the physical therapist provides Charlie and his mom, Jamie with ECSE services.

## Dilemma

When the ECSE teacher, Liz, arrived Jamie answered the door. Liz smiled, and said, "You must be Jamie." Jamie looked towards the floor, and then towards Charlie and said, "There he is. There's my boy." Charlie was near the couch rolling around in a Pack 'n Play. Jamie told Liz she could sit on the couch. She sat on the floor. Jamie played with her hands. Liz smiled at Charlie, and asked questions. Jamie responded with mostly yes and no answers.

Jamie explained to Liz that she would not make it without her father and brother. Liz asked if Charlie could play on the floor. Jamie laid Charlie on the floor on his back. She mentioned the pediatrician telling her Charlie needed lots of tummy time when he was a baby, but he didn't really enjoy it much.

Liz asked Jamie what she hoped for from the visits. Jamie's response was, "I want you to teach him to do stuff. I want him to be like other babies. His doctor said he was behind other kids. I want him to smile at me. All he does is lay in the pack n play and stare at his hands all day." Liz told Jamie she could teach him stuff too, and that they could work together. Jamie said she'd try, but she was tired and sad most of the time. Then she said, "My therapist said I should always at least try." Liz said, "Trying is all we ask. Being a mom is hard work." They decided on 3 goals together. One would be for Charlie to sit independently. Another goal was for Charlie to learn to walk. The final goal would be for Charlie to say mama. Liz explained the program to Jamie. Liz would visit Jamie every other week. Once a month she would bring the physical therapist, and once a month she would bring the speech and language pathologist. Jamie could also attend a parent/child group she held one Friday a month. She could meet other moms and Jamie and Charlie could play in the large motor room.

After the visit Liz reflected on the needs of the family. Charlie needed his natural environment to provide more opportunity for movement. She knew both Charlie and Jamie would benefit from the inclusive setting of the parent/child group. Jamie needed more confidence in her parenting. She needed coaching on how to interact positively with Charlie.

## The Next Visit

When Liz arrived for the next visit she brought along Joe, the physical therapist, and introduced him to Jamie and Charlie. Liz smiled, happy to see Charlie in her hands this time and she asked Jamie how things were going. Joe asked Jamie's permission to get Charlie, and his blanket from the pack n play. He laid the blanket out on the floor. Liz said, "Jamie, does Charlie have a favorite toy? Can you bring something over from the basket?" Jamie grabbed a green ball that Charlie liked to suck on. Joe showed Jamie how to support Charlie in sitting on his own. Liz coached Jamie on how to promote Charlie's language. Before they left Jamie was back on the couch. She said she was tired. Liz said, "You tried. And you succeeded today." Jamie almost smiled. Jamie looked forward to the visits from Liz. Liz encouraged Jamie to spend 15 minutes in the morning and 15 minutes in the afternoon on the floor with Charlie. They found a big blanket to put down, and placed toys near the edges. She told Jamie to talk to Charlie about the toys and encourage him to go get them. Jamie started to feel proud of Charlie, and she was proud of herself. Soon when Liz knocked on the door Jamie would answer with a smile. She was excited to show Liz, and Joe, or the Speech Language pathologist what Charlie had learned. Liz watched as Jamie showed her how Charlie could sit on his own. She coached Jamie to praise Charlie. Liz watched Jamie repeat mama, while pointing to her mouth, just like Liz had shown her. After two months of visits, Jamie told Liz she was ready to try the parent/child group.

Jamie found herself spending more than just 15 minutes on the floor with Charlie two times a day. She wasn't as tired anymore. She would giggle with Charlie and he would giggle back. Charlie learned to crawl. He began pulling himself up on the floor. Jamie cried when she heard him say, "Mama." At 16 months she captured his first steps on video. Jamie liked being a mom. When Charlie was 18 months, as planned, Liz met him and Jamie at the door, and they walked down the street to the park. Charlie moved around waving at people passing by saying, "Bye-bye," over and over again. He pointed to the swing. Charlie loved to swing. Joe arrived at the park. They laid a blanket out for lunch. This would be their last time together. Charlie was back on track developmentally, and Jamie had enrolled in the local community college. She wanted to be like Liz. She wanted to work with babies and help other mothers. Jamie told Liz she felt like her old self again. It was a hard 9 months, but she made it. She was nervous to start school. Jamie's school had a child care center where Charlie would stay while she was in class. Jamie was also nervous that Charlie would stop learning once Liz no longer came for home visits. Liz told Jamie, "Keep doing what you're doing. You're his best teacher." Jamie said, "I'll try." They both smiled. Liz felt proud of Jamie. She worked with Charlie for those 15 minutes twice a day. She was the one who taught Charlie to sit on his own, to crawl, and learn to walk. She was the one who spoke carefully and purposefully to Charlie. Liz was confident Charlie would continue to grow. As part of the program Liz would follow up with Jamie and Charlie on his birthday each year until he turned 5. As Liz was leaving, she told Jamie to keep up the good work with Charlie. Jamie said, "I'll try." They both smiled.

## Perspectives

Jamie was experiencing postpartum depression and was not engaging with her child as she should have. Once she received the treatment that she needed she was able to help Charlie get caught up and is feeling so happy and proud to be a mom. Jamie is even wanting to go to school to be able to help other families in need. Liz was very supportive and gave her the encouragement and provided Jamie the services that she and Charlie needed. Joe provided the last piece of support that was needed for Charlie to improve his gross motor development.

## QUESTIONS

1. Which DEC practices for the topic area of Environment did you see supported in this case study?
2. Which of the DEC practices for the topic area of Environment were not supported in this case study? How might these have been addressed?
3. What other ways could the PT and ECSE teacher adapt the environment to help Charlie develop his gross motor skills?
4. What are the opportunities for the use of assistive technologies in this case study?
5. What are additional ways to promote learning during daily routine in this case?
6. What other options are there for this family to be in an inclusive environment that would help Charlie reach his goals?
7. How might Charlie's uncle or grandfather have been involved in Charlie's learning?

# TOO MUCH?

*Unsolved*

## Background

Sadie is a 17-month-old who experiences signs of Sensory Processing Disorder (SPD), also referred to as Sensory Integration Dysfunction. She is currently enrolled in daycare at The Learning Center where the ratio is 7:1 and she has 17 other kids in her class with three teachers. Her teachers' names are Rachel, Jonie, and Mora. Sadie is seen twice a month by an Early Childhood Special Education (ECSE) teacher Harriet, who works in the district, as well as Jasmine, who is a Speech and Language Pathologist (SLP).

## Dilemma

Harriet has reached out to Rachel, the classroom lead. "Rachel, how do you feel Sadie has adjusted since she started in your room a little over a month ago? I know when she first began in your room she seemed overwhelmed by the drop-off and took a long time to regulate into the routine of the day. How does that seem to be going?" Rachel responded with some less than promising news. "Well, Sadie still cries at drop-off, she cries through hand-washing and breakfast, and then cries through diaper changes up until we go outside. This is a little over an hour span of time where she seems very distraught and is seemingly inconsolable. The three of us (Sadie's teachers) are still trying to figure out what her triggers are beyond drop-off and what engages her enough to distract her from being so upset. She is slowly getting more comfortable with each of us and we are really trying to build up our relationships with her. We are hoping that with more time, Sadie will become more comfortable with us and this will help with her behaviors."

## Perspectives

This information does not seem to be discouraging or surprising to Harriet. "What sort of strategies have you used to attempt to help Sadie with transitioning into the classroom more successfully? Has her transition time seemed to lessen in length since she first started in your room? Harriet took notes as she intently listened to Rachel's response "We have spent a lot of time considering the aspects of the morning that could be affecting Sadie's transition time. Some of these things include turning the lights off in case they are painful to Sadie's eyes or potentially making noises we do not hear.

We have lowered our voices to more of a loud whisper in hopes that it is more calming, and we have sat with her holding her tightly for compression. Sadie also uses a teething necklace, as she is oral. This calms her for a few seconds at a time but is not a long-term solution for her being upset. Often, we put it in her mouth for her to use it. She is slowly learning to use it as a tool."

Harriet asked Rachel what moms experiences were regarding how sensitive Sadie was to lights and sounds. Mom mentioned when she took Sadie to the grocery store she seemed agitated by the lights. It was hard for Sadie to be in a store for much more than ten minutes at a time. She also stated that Sadie struggled with parades, she equates to loud noise.

In her last classroom, Sadie was very aggressive toward other children. She bit many times a week and seemed to seek out two to three specific children. It appeared to her last teachers that Sadie was attempting to be social, not violent. The teething necklace appeared to be lessening the number of times this happened but was not a cure all. Through the use of the teething necklace, Rachel is using assistive technology to promote participation in learning, or in this case to lessen the biting incidents in order for Sadie to participate more socially with other children. Since moving into her current classroom, Sadie has not shown aggression towards any of the children or experienced any other behaviors they had been witnessing in her last classroom. Her teachers are wondering if this will change as she becomes more acclimated and comfortable in the classroom with her peers and teachers. This will become apparent over time.

Rachel spent some time talking to Sadie's previous teacher, Miranda, about what she experienced and strategies they tried. Rachel asked, "What triggers did you see that seemed to escalate Sadie's biting other children?" Miranda replied, "It was so hard to determine. It appeared, outwardly, that Sadie was just waiting for something to do. It happened so randomly and at seemingly odd times. Sadie would be playing by herself or with other friends and suddenly, without any obvious disagreement from peers, she would walk up and bite. Unfortunately, it often happened to children's faces. We concluded, after many times, that Sadie wanted so badly to be social with her peers and didn't know how to do so."

Rachel, Jonie, and Mora want to help provide Sadie with the tools and skills for self-regulation as well as limit the level of stimulation in the room at one time as much as possible. Other things Sadie's three teachers and both Jasmine and Harriet have talked about is trying to find a safe place for Sadie to be in the classroom. They are unable to change the ratio of student to teacher, but they can attempt to find Sadie her own space in the classroom. There is a separation in the classroom from the hard floor where they eat, to the carpet area where the kids spend most of their day. Sadie was given a seat on the hard floor. This is where they offer for her to go, anticipating the other children will not bother her. When she goes there, her teachers provide her with a few options of toys, puzzles, and a couple books. This has yet to visually make a difference for Sadie, but her teachers are going to continue this option for a few weeks and see if this lessens decreases Sadie's stress during the transition time after drop-off.

"Rachel, I'm not sure this is working. We've been giving Sadie this area by herself for over a week now and she doesn't seem to be calming down any faster. We tell her this is a safe place she can be by herself and she just cries when we put her there. Why are we still putting her in this spot at the table by herself?" Mora asked. Rachel understood Mora 's frustration however, as teachers, we know that it takes many days of repetition and consistency to know if a change will have positive effects. "I know it seems like it's not doing any good but we've all discussed how overwhelmed Sadie seems in the classroom with all these new faces and she's still not used to having so many people in one room at the same time. It gets loud and I think she could really benefit from having some space to herself. We can't force her to sit there and be calm, but we can make it a space available to her if she chooses. We will keep trying it for a few more weeks and reassess at the end of the month. "As a team, they are hoping this provides Sadie with some space where she feels comfortable and safe in an environment that is potentially really overwhelming for her.

Two months after Sadie's initial transition into toddlers, she is still taking more than 45 minutes to calm down enough to join the class in daily routines. Her teachers are feeling defeated after trying so many different strategies; changing the environment the best they can, working on distractions, finding things Sadie enjoys, giving her a space by herself away from the other kids, and working on building relationships with peers as well as her teachers.

## QUESTIONS

1. Which DEC practices for the topic area of Environment did you see supported in this case study?
2. Which of the DEC practices for the topic area of Environment were not supported in this case study? How might these have been addressed?
3. How can Sadie's teachers support her when she joins the class in daily routines?
4. What are some strategies Sadie's teacher could use when it gets too loud for her in the classroom?

5. What type of sensory items has her teacher tried and which does Sadie prefer? Which sensory items did not work? What are some other sensory items Sadie's teacher can use?
6. How might the number of peers in Sadie's class be affecting her behavior?

## THE COMFORT ZONE

### *Solved*

### Background

The early intervention team got a call from a mother with concerns about her 20-month-old son, Sam. The mother, Sally, indicated in her initial phone call that her son did not talk very much and was very active. One of her neighbors said that Sam might be able to get some help if she called this number. Upon calling the intake number and hearing further information about the Early Intervention Program, including that a global evaluation would be done and that it was a home-based service, Sally started questioning her decision, she just agreed with the woman to get out of the conversation. An intake packet was mailed to Sally. The Early Childhood Special Education (ECSE) teacher, Jenny, followed-up the next day with a phone call to schedule an initial evaluation meeting and walk her through the evaluation process. Although Jenny left three messages, Sally did not call her back. The paperwork was never returned. *Jenny felt as though she was wasting her time. If the parents didn't care enough about Sam's speech to return a phone call, how far did she have to go to contact them?*

### Dilemma

The next week, Jenny had some extra time between visits and decided to call Sally one more time using a district cell phone. Sally answered and seemed startled when Jenny introduced herself. She replied that she was expecting a different call and that the caller ID did not indicate it was the school calling. Jenny explained that she was between home visits and asked if Sally was still concerned about Sam's language skills. Sally said that she may have overreacted when she had called, and Sam was grunting a bit more now and sometimes even looks up at her when she talks to him. Jenny said, "It sounds like there are still some concerns for his age. I have my calendar with me, so let's get something scheduled. If Friday works for you, the speech therapist and I could come over in the morning to meet with you and

Sam." Immediately, Jenny could sense Sally's hesitation. Sally seemed to be making excuses—the kids didn't have a consistent nap schedule, her house was a mess, and her husband had to sleep due to shift work.

## Perspectives

Although Jenny realized that the team would gather a lot of information about Sam by seeing him in his home environment, she was afraid that Sally was going to back out. That meant that Sam wouldn't get the help he need-ed. She asked if it might be easier for Sally to bring Sam into the school. She suggested that Sam may enjoy playing with some of the toys in the class-room, and they could talk while he explored. Sally replied, "Yeah, I think that might be easier for Sam. If I can bring my baby girl with me too, I could come in on Thursday or Friday—as long as it's after 9:00." Sally was relieved. The idea of having someone in her home made her very anxious.

During the initial meeting and two follow-up evaluation sessions in the school environment, Sally slowly opened up about her current home situa-tion. The therapist and teacher seemed to genuinely want to help Sam and surprisingly weren't judging her. It felt like she was talking to a friend, though Sally couldn't help being a little guarded after her previous experi-ence with social services. Sally shared that they couldn't afford a plumber to fix the kitchen sink, so she often had piles of dishes, both of which were embarrassing to her. In addition, a neighbor had called social services a few months ago when Sam got out of the house and was found on the sidewalk a block away. Sally would rather decline the help for Sam than run the risk of him getting taken away. The paperwork was not completed because Sally had trouble reading and understanding it.

The evaluation sessions, as well as the first month of visits, were done at the school to help Sally feel comfortable and develop greater trust and rap-port. Since Sam moved quickly between activities and dumped things, Jenny quickly learned that she needed to have fewer items out at a time. She had Sally help pick out bins of toys that she thought Sam would enjoy, and they used a picture schedule to transition from one item to the next. After Sally observed Jenny using this process, Jenny asked Sally if she could prompt Sam with the visuals. This gave Jenny the opportunity to coach Sally through prompts and pauses in order to facilitate requests from Sam. Sally shared that she had put a lot of extra toys in shoe boxes at home. She had noticed that Sam played longer with toys when she got only a few new things out of the box at a time. He also had started to tap her and point at the cupboard where the toys were kept on occasion. Jenny noticed how relaxed Sally seemed to be at visits lately. She seemed to be enjoying them.

As the relationship grew, Sally expressed many concerns. She thought her attempts to keep Sam quiet while her husband slept may be at fault for his lack of talking; plus, she didn't read him many books because she felt she was a bad reader. Also, she described how stressful it was for them to take Sam anywhere in public (because he would run), that she felt "stuck" at home because they had no family in the area, and a desire to meet other moms. This gave Jenny the opportunity to move the focus to natural family settings.

Visits were scheduled at the grocery store, parks, the library, and an Early Childhood Family Education (ECFE) classroom. Jenny noticed how quickly Sam showed interest in the water fountains and pushing and pulling things. There were tools within each environment that Sally slowly learned to use to engage Sam. They made use of the small grocery carts, large plastic book bins, and a variety of playground equipment as they saw his verbal and non-verbal communication improve. They also discovered that Sam responded well to visual parameters, such as a sidewalk or doormat to keep him in a desired location-or at least away from the doors. Sally slowly became more confident in her skills to help Sam be successful, and she signed up for a weekly ECFE class. After five months of community visits, Sally told Jenny, "Sam is becoming more frustrated at meals. He has started throwing his plate and climbs in and out of his chair. Could you do a visit during breakfast or lunch? I'm just not sure what to do!"

The majority of home visits from that point forward were done in the home environment. Sally's husband joined a few of them, too. Jenny quickly saw how busy Sam looked in the small two-bedroom home. As she learned Sally's expectations and parenting style, they brainstormed movement and sensory activities that Sam could participate in to "help." He enjoys his jobs of pushing the full laundry basket and moving the bottled water from the packaging onto the cupboard shelf. Both Sally and Sam also liked dancing to music, so re-arranging the furniture allowed for more floor space. Jenny could see Sally's own confidence continue to grow.

## QUESTIONS

1. Which DEC practices for the topic area of Environment did you see supported in this case study?
2. Which of the DEC practices for the topic area of Environment were not supported in this case study? How might these have been addressed?
3. Would it have been more beneficial for Jenny to do the initial visit at Sally's home? Why or why not?

4. Do you think starting visits in the community right away might have been a better choice than in the school environment? Why or why not?
5. What other community environments might be beneficial for eliciting language?
6. As Sally seemed fully invested in the community visits, should Jenny have asked about home routines sooner rather than waiting for Sally to ask? Why or why not?
7. What was the most important outcome of this home visiting relationship?

## SECTION 2: CASES FOR 3-TO-5-YEAR-OLDS

## Gentlemen Start Your Engines

*Unsolved*

### Background

All Tony could think as he walked into school was Gentlemen Start Your Engines! He had graduated full of energy, hope, and believed he was well prepared with knowledge of current evidence-based practices. Now he was only four months into his first job as an Early Childhood Special Education (ECSE) teacher, and he was already feeling like he was out of ideas. The school had given Tony his own center-based classroom, and he felt like he had done his best in setting up the classroom based on what he learned in his teacher education program.

While all his students had Individual Education Programs (IEP) and a primary disability category of developmental delay, they still showed a wide variety of different skills and needs. Tony had made sure to thoroughly read the paperwork describing his students and done his best to take that into account when he decided on his classroom layout. Signs with words and pictures told his students what each area of the room was for, and he had been careful to teach all of his students the expectations for every area. Tony had felt that he created a classroom where all of his students have access to a variety of learning experiences and had opportunities for movement.

### Dilemma

Despite all of this, Tony did not feel like his classroom was under control. He dreaded center time every day, as his carefully designed classroom turned into what he described as "every child running everywhere at the same time." He spent his time reminding students to walk and stopping them from hitting each other at full speed and never had time to address the individual goals of his students. Tony continued to think about the recommended practices he had learned about in school. He wanted to ensure that he was addressing all of the aspects of the environment (physical, social, and temporal). He didn't know what was wrong and had no thoughts on where to start.

## Perspectives

"How's it going?" asked Jane, the team lead for ECSE. "Anne said that you wanted to talk with me this morning." Anne was the teacher in the room next to Tony's. He had confided in her that he was feeling frustrated with center time in his classroom, and she had suggested talking with the team lead and recommended he contact Jane.

Tony was quiet at first. He had worked so hard to become a teacher, and now he felt like a failure. Tony reminded himself that Jane was the team lead for his team, and part of her job was to help him when he had a problem. So, he took a deep breath and began explaining.

His first design for his classroom had been too closed off. He found that students would go to a center but seemed to get stuck staying in the same area instead of exploring other areas of the classroom and would rarely interact with their peers. In response, he opened up his classroom more, so that his students could see peers in other areas and look at other things to do in the classroom.

"That makes a lot of sense," said Jane. "While it is important for each center to be distinct, we also need to let the students learn by moving and exploring. How did that plan work?"

Tony got a sheepish look on his face. "All of my students are now playing together during center time- "

"Love to hear that!' interjected Jane.

"-but the only game they will play in a group is Run and Scream in the classroom," Tony finished.

"Oh."

Jane and Tony went to look at his classroom. She found that everything was much as he had described it. When dismissed from the circle, they would group up, and then would start screaming with excitement as they ran from one center to another as fast as they could. He explained how he had added a new part to his dismissal where he went over the expectations again, and how he had tried to make the entrance to each center more closed and distinct while still making the classroom an open and inviting environment, in an attempt to help the children stop at each area and become engaged there.

"I really like how hard you are working on solving this problem." Jane started. "I think the biggest problem with your arrangement is that your open area is too big! When you cleared out the middle of the classroom, and then closed off the centers, you made one gigantic open area. No wonder your students are running so much, they have the space to do it in!"

Tony was a little confused. He had thought that he was supposed to encourage his students to move and be active in the classroom, so the open area seemed like a perfect solution! Jane commiserates with his dilemma. "This is a phrase I was told every day in school: 'Behavior is functionally related to the learning environment'" Jane said. "It means that if you are seeing a behavior, look towards a change in the environment to see if you can help the student meet the function of their behavior in a more appropriate way. What can you do with the physical and temporal environment to help students be successful during center time?"

Jane and Tony continued talking. They decided as a pair that it seemed like his students saw a big open space as a place to run, maybe like how they view the playground. Tony decided to rearrange his room again so there was a toy center in the middle of the running space and see if his students will change their behavior.

Two weeks later, Tony found himself back in Jane's office. Moving the toys to the center of the open space had stopped his students from crisscrossing the classroom, but now he had a new problem: they were racing around the toy center instead! Now he was really out of ideas: he had tried open spaces, closed spaces, gotten help from his team lead and re-taught his expectations for every center. In response, his students had changed from chaotic running to... running in circles. How could he keep his students interacting with each other but still have some control over his classroom?

## QUESTIONS

1. Which DEC practices for the topic area of Environment did you see supported in this case study?
2. Which of the DEC practices for the topic area of Environment were not supported in this case study? How might these have been addressed?
3. How is Tony following RPs at this time even though he feels that his classroom is out of control?

4. As Tony rearranged his classroom, what choices did he make that followed RPs, and what choices did not? If you think his choice did not follow RP,s why do you think he made that choice anyways?

5. Tony spent time working on the physical environment of his classroom. How might he change the social environment or the temporal environment to solve his dilemma of running students?

6. What other factors in the classroom could have an effect on the behaviors being observed by Tony that were not mentioned in the case study? Why do you think those factors are having an effect?

7. How could you balance the need for students to move with the need for safety and development in domains other than physical in the classroom?

## ROCKY

*Unsolved*

### Background

Megan stood by the door of her 3's and 4's preschool classroom, eagerly awaiting the arrival of her morning preschool students. Her students had shown high interest in a book she read about Emperor Penguins, that she decided to create the Arctic in her classroom. Overnight, Megan's classroom was completely transformed. She hung snowflakes and white material from the ceiling and down the walls. Her individual center areas were set up with ice painting, igloo building, and fishing in a play-pool complete with magnetic fish and poles. In the block center, Megan added Arctic animals and plastic blocks that looked like ice for building. The sensory table was filled with snow, scoopers and shovels. The reading center was stocked with books about the Arctic and the animals that live there. She even planned an activity where the students would pair up and pretend they were Emperor Penguins and try to pass eggs to each other using only their feet. Her classroom definitely looked like the Arctic and she couldn't wait for her students to arrive.

### Perspectives

Anna arrived a few minutes later. She has worked as an assistant teacher with Megan for two years and she loves her job. Anna thought Megan was an amazing teacher and the two of them worked well together. Anna's mouth dropped open as she surveyed the room and stated, "Wow! This looks amazing!" Megan had a great ability to create learning activities that reflected the children's interest and aligned with learning goals. In the past, she transformed the classroom into China, a forest, and even an ocean. Megan's classroom was always busy and engaging, but it was also cramped. Anna felt there were too many things that would lead to distraction in some of her students who found it difficult to focus. In some parts of the room, the centers were so close to each other in proximity, it was difficult for the students to transition from one center to another. The children were constantly bumping into each other as they moved around the room. The set-up did not allow the teacher a clear view of her students. Anna couldn't see the children when they were playing in the block center, unless she was standing right next to that area. Although Anna felt that she could help Megan improve the classroom set-up in a more Universal Design, she did not feel comfortable voicing her concerns.

Meanwhile, Nolan's mother Terri sipped her morning coffee at the stoplight, her mind busy with the usual worries. *Will Nolan do well in school today? Will she receive a call from Miss Megan about his behavior again?* Terri couldn't understand why Nolan chose to hit, push, or scratch his classmates. Consequently, Nolan didn't have many friends and the invitations for play dates were dwindling. Nolan is a child who had trouble articulating his words and was receiving speech services for expressive language. He was working with Mr. Ray, a speech and language pathologist twice a week. Mr. Ray pulled Nolan out of class to work with him one on one. Mr. Ray indicated that Nolan was making progress, but Terri wasn't sure. Nolan had been in speech for six months, but still wasn't talking as much as other children his age. At home, Nolan was a sweet and kind three-year-old little boy who loved to play with sharks and dinosaurs. Yes, he was quiet, but he always had a smile on his face and gave hugs to everyone. At school, that wasn't the case. Nolan would often play by himself and if another child wanted to join him, Nolan would push the child and yell, "No!" He would also observe a classmate playing and then run over and take a toy out of their hand. If the child protested, he would often hit him/her. Terri didn't remember this type of behavior with Nolan's older brother, Chase, who also had Miss Megan for a teacher. In fact, these days Chase was the only one Nolan would play with nicely. Terri felt like this was a point of contention with her husband Tom. He completely disagreed with his wife's concerns and gave Nolan the nickname of Rocky. "He has a great left hook," he would say jokingly. "Boys will be boys. He will learn. One day he is going to hit the wrong kid and that kid is going to hit him right back. Then he will learn his lesson."

As Terri pulled into the preschool parking lot, she reminded Nolan to use kind hands and ask a teacher if he needed help. Nolan quickly exited the car and grabbed his mother's hand as they walked into the school. He looked down as he passed other teachers and the office staff, not making eye contact. "Are you feeling shy today?" Terri asked him lovingly and patted him on the back. "Be kind to your friends and have a super day," she told him as she entered the hallway to his classroom. She gave him a big hug. The doorway to the classroom was congested with parents and their children entering the room. Terri chose to let Nolan enter the room by himself. She always said goodbye to him in the hallway. "Please have a good day, baby," she whispered under her breath as he walked inside the classroom.

## Dilemma

Megan greeted Nolan as he entered the room and watched his eyes light up as he looked around with awe at their Arctic classroom. Nolan smiled at Miss Megan and pretended to be a polar bear as he gave her a big hug, complete with a friendly growl. Nolan then asked, "Where Miss Anna?" Nolan simply adored Miss Anna. He loved to play with her and he especially liked when Miss Anna read stories to the class. He giggled when she made up funny animal noises and talked like a baby. Miss Megan pointed to the other side of the room to where Miss Anna was standing. As soon as she saw Nolan she called out, "Good morning Nolan!" Nolan gave Miss Anna the biggest bear hug he could muster. *Megan was glad to see that Nolan was in a good mood that morning. She had grown concerned because Nolan was displaying some aggressive behavior lately, and she felt that those behaviors were escalating.* While she tried daily, she couldn't find a pattern for his behavior. She tracked what he was doing when the hitting, pushing, or scratching occurred and there didn't appear to be a consistent cause. Megan often sat with Nolan and discussed what words he could use to talk to his friends, in place of grabbing items or hitting them. She even instituted a classroom timer as turn taking technique and showed Nolan along with the children how to use it. Nothing seemed to work. She was starting to get phone calls from other parents concerned about Nolan's behavior. Anna approached her, "My little buddy Nolan is in a great mood today. Hopefully, he will keep his hands to himself." Megan responded, "I hope so, maybe he will be content exploring the classroom. Let's keep an eye on him just in case."

A happy chatter arose in the classroom as the children explored the centers and new materials. The block center and dramatic play area looked a little congested as Megan circulated around the room. The plastic ice blocks were a popular manipulative and she watched as the students' built homes for the family of arctic foxes. Nolan was enthralled with the sensory table, which was filled with snow. He was using a little scooper to create a snowman. Anna attentively watched as Patrick walked over to the snow table and picked up a scooper. Nolan looked at Patrick and kept working on his snowman. Two other boys soon joined them. Mason reached in front of Nolan to grab a scoop and accidentally knocked down his snowman. Nolan lifted his scooper as though he was going to hit Mason with it. Anna rushed over and blocked Mason's head with her arm. The scooper landed with a thud on Anna's arm. Meagan hearing the commotion, rushed over to the table. She didn't see the incident from where she was sitting on the floor with the children.

Nolan stood silently as tears welled up in his eyes. He didn't mean to hit Miss Anna, he was just so mad that Mason broke his snowman. He didn't like all his classmates around him when he was playing. They always broke his stuff and they wouldn't share. Nolan hugged Miss Anna and said through the tears, "Sorry, I'm sorry." Anna patted his back and said, "It's ok Nolan. Thank you for apologizing," and gave him a hug. Anna quietly told Megan what happened as Nolan clung to her leg. Megan asked Nolan to come talk to her out in the hallway. There wasn't really a place in the classroom that was away from the other children, and due to his disposition as a result of the incident she needed to talk to him privately. She knew he felt terrible about what happened and didn't mean to hit Anna, but if she hadn't been there, Nolan would have hit Mason in the head. "Nolan sweetie, I know you didn't mean to hit Miss Anna, but you need to use your words or get an adult when you are upset. Mason knocked over your snowman by accident. You cannot hit."

Mr. Ray was walking in the hallway when he noticed Megan talking to Nolan. He overheard their conversation and asked Nolan if he would like to take a walk with him. Megan appreciated the offer. Nolan needed to calm down and the class needed to start cleaning up to get ready for circle time and snack. Thank goodness Nolan didn't hit Mason. She recently had a conversation in which Mason's mother referred to Nolan as a bully. Megan knew this incident would just fuel her fire. Megan felt just terrible, she felt as though she was failing Nolan.

## QUESTIONS

1. Which DEC practices for the topic area of Environment did you see supported in this case study?
2. Which of the practices for the topic area of Environment were not supported in this case study? How might these have been addressed?
3. What factors in the classroom environment do you feel are contributing to Nolan's behavior? Why?
4. Creating an open, honest, and supportive relationship with parents is crucial for educators. How would you address Nolan's behavior with

his parents, specifically with his father who doesn't seem to feel there is a problem?

5. What support can Megan provide to increase Nolan's appropriate interaction with peers in the classroom?

6. What improvements and/or supports within the classroom do you think Miss Anna would suggest in consideration of the RPs?

7. How would you modify and adapt the physical, social, and temporal environments to promote Nolan's positive participation in learning experiences?

## VISUAL SCHEDULE

*Unsolved*

### Background

Eli, a four-year-old in Miss Laura's Pre-K class, has been extremely tired for the past three weeks during class time. Kara, the Early Childhood Special Education (ECSE) teacher assigned to Lisa's classroom, walks into Lisa's Pre-K classroom at the end of the day to check in on how Eli has been doing recently. "Eli has been having a difficult time following our normal routines and being kind to friends due to being overly tired." Lisa said, looking exhausted. "I asked Eli why he has been so tired, and he did not know why. I was able to touch base with his mom, Tina, at pick up today and she stated he has not been sleeping." Lisa and Kara both agreed that they should schedule a meeting with Eli's mother to discuss assistive technology that would help support a consistent bedtime routine for Eli.

Kara also began thinking about ways she could help with this situation, including any assistive technology she could implement in the classroom to make Eli's day go a little smoother. Kara wonders if a visual schedule would provide the support Eli needs to be successful in the classroom.

### Dilemma

On Wednesday morning, Tina, Kara, and Lisa met to discuss a few possible tools to help Eli and his mom maintain a consistent sleeping schedule at home. Kara began the meeting by asking Tina how things have been going at home recently. Tina responded, "Eli is really struggling with maintaining a regular sleep schedule. He is sleeping more during the day and then stays up until around 3 am. This is part of the reason he has a hard time getting up for school." Lisa states, "that must be a difficult schedule for you at home. Do you have any ideas on why this is occurring?" Tina explains that she recently switched shifts at work and is getting home from work much later. Eli wants to stay up so that he can see her when she gets home.

Kara and Lisa explain that they have been noticing a change in Eli's behavior for the past few weeks. Lisa states, "Eli, he has been struggling in class as well. He does not want to follow our daily routine, including participating in large and small groups, something he used to love." Kara added, "he is also struggling to get along with his peers. I am wondering if the changes in his sleep schedule are affecting his behaviors here at school."

Kara begins talking about the possibility of implementing assistive technology into Eli's daily routines. "The first possibility we could try is a visual schedule at school and at home to help him get back into a normal routine," says Kara. "How will I know how to use it?" Tina asks. Kara produces an example of a visual schedule that they use at school to provide Tina with some knowledge on how to use it. Lisa describes the visual schedule, "this is an example of a schedule that we might use at school. It is placed on the board so everyone can see what is going to be happening throughout the day. Once we have finished an activity, a teacher goes to the schedule and turns the card around. This shows the children that activity is done for the day."

Tina asks a few more questions about the visual schedule and agrees that this could be beneficial for her and Eli to use at home as well. Kara tells Tina, "I will need you to write down what a typical day is like in your household. Every routine that you have will have its own card. I will also have a picture of Eli that he can clip onto the routine that he is supposed to be doing."

Lisa explains that the schedule will give Eli a concrete visual to see what he should be doing at any time of the day. Tina suggests, "I should also try to get to bed sooner so that Eli will know that it is time to go to sleep." Lisa nods in agreement and states, "modeling for him is an excellent way to teach him a routine." Everyone left the meeting feeling hopeful that the visual schedule would help Eli start to have a more consistent sleep schedule at home.

**Perspectives**

Kara has completed Eli's visual schedule for school and home. She takes schedules to Lisa and asks Lisa to send home the schedule in Eli's backpack. Kara then calls Eli's mother, Tina. "Hi Tina, it's Kara. I just wanted to let you know that the schedule we made and reviewed for Eli is done and will be coming home in his backpack." Tina said "great, he is still struggling with sleeping and in turn struggles with everything else." Kara and Tina review ways to use the schedule and then hangs it up. Kara thinks *I hope this works for Eli.*

It has been two weeks of using Eli's his schedule at school and at home. After class one day, Lisa briefly met with Kara and told her that she is seeing some improvements but tells Kara "Eli still seems tired and emotional. She explains, "although the schedule is helping, especially with transitions, he just is still not himself." At the end of their conversation, Kara says that she will call mom and check in to see how things are going at home.

Kara begins her phone conversation, "Hi Tina, it's Kara. I was just calling to touch base with you and see how the visual schedule is going at home." Tina begins, "it's not going very well. Eli refuses to use the schedule and it is just easier to let him sleep when he wants." Kara lets Tina know that she understands that this is going to be a big change for both her and Eli. She also emphasizes that it is important to continue to try using the schedule and to be as consistent as she can with it. Tina states, "I don't know what to do, it just isn't working. I am currently trying to get my work schedule changed, or I will have to look for a new job." Kara empathizes with Tina, "I'm sorry that the visual schedule isn't working as well as we had hoped. I will brainstorm some other solutions that we could have you try at home. Please continue to let me know how everything goes in your end."

Kara realizes that using a visual schedule may not work for Tina and Eli if it is not used consistently. She is going to talk with her colleagues and brainstorm other ways for the family to use assistive technology to improve Eli's sleep schedule.

## QUESTIONS

1. Which DEC practices for the topic area of Environment did you see supported in this case study?
2. Which of the DEC practices for the topic area of Environment were not supported in this case study? How might these have been addressed?
3. What other ways can Kara help mom incorporate a schedule into their nightly routine?
4. What are some other forms of assistance technology that Kara could use to help Eli at school and at home?
5. What are other environmental factors that may be impacting Eli's sleeping?
6. Eli's mother stopped using the visual schedule after 2 weeks. What additional information could the team have shared when presenting the use of the visual schedule?

# FINDING THE PERFECT FIT

*Unsolved*

## Background

Johnny East is a three-year-old boy who recently transitioned out of Birth to Three services and is now receiving services within his new classroom setting at Smart Academy Preschool under Part B services. He is enrolled in an inclusive classroom that is made up of ten typically developing peers and five students that receive services. The needs of these five students range in level of severity and need. Of the five students, Johnny is the individual that requires the most support from the staff as he has a diagnosis of cerebral palsy, which greatly affects his motor development. He is currently non-verbal and responds through rough sign language or by pointing to what he would like, want or need. When provided with visual choices, Johnny makes a choice by pointing. For example, if shown the choice of yogurt or cereal, he can choose the item he would like. This also allows him to participate with peers during large group time. He utilizes a walker to move about his setting, which is a recent transition from the Rifton gait trainer that he used up until three months ago.

Natalie Gains is Johnny's current case manager. She works with him and the other children enrolled within Smart Academy preschool. She is in her second year of teaching early childhood special education at Smart Academy. Natalie does not act as the lead preschool teacher in Johnny's classroom but rather works alongside the teacher and classroom assistants to adapt/modify the classroom and curriculum to meet the students' needs.

Angie Lower is the lead preschool teacher in Johnny's classroom. She has been teaching for nearly 20 years, most of which were at a private school, ranging in grades preschool to second. She recently switched jobs and began working at Smart Academy Preschool three years ago. In the past, Angie has had limited experience working with students who have special needs and often is unsure of how to further help them from beyond what she already has planned for the class. She wants to provide a positive, inviting classroom to all her students but struggles to remember all the different needs for the five students she works with on Individual Education Programs (IEP) in addition to teaching the other ten students in her class.

Classroom Assistants-Laurie Johnson and Megan Rivers are the two classroom assistants (Paraprofessionals) within Johnny's classroom. Their first role is to support the five students within the classroom on IEPs. This will be Megan's second year working with Natalie and Angie. It will be Laurie's first year working at Smart Academy. Laurie has worked as an assistant in a preschool setting in the past, some of which were with children that had special needs. Megan has two children of her own who currently receive special education services at the elementary level. Both started in preschool with Part B services.

## Perspectives

As Natalie drove home from work, she thought back on the meeting she just finished with her co-workers. "I am really just struggling to remember all of the different modifications that he needs," Angie stated after Natalie began the meeting by asking how the team felt the week had gone. Natalie recalled that she had heard this from Angie last week when she had asked why Johnny's cutting assignment had not been printed on cardstock. "Is there something that I can do along with the printed list of modifications to help you to remember what activities need to be modified?" Natalie asked, hoping for a positive response. "The list is wonderful, but I often forget to check it when I am creating my lesson plans or having the para's prep for me," Angie responded. Natalie turned to Laurie and Megan, who were busy getting items ready that Angie had asked them to complete for the lessons on Monday. "What ideas do you ladies have that could help to have the modifications made? You are a part of the team and I would like your input as well." Laurie and Megan looked at one another and Megan responded, "If we could have a copy of the list of what needs to be modified that would be helpful." Natalie had asked Angie to share this list with the paras when it was initially made three weeks ago. "Oh, I must have forgotten to give them their copy," Angie stated quickly. "I will get it to them first thing on Monday morning. I actually have to get to an appointment though," she stated as she began to gather her coat and purse to leave the room. "I guess we can finish on Monday then once you have given Laurie and Megan the list," Natalie somberly replied. Angie always appeared to have a reason to leave when Natalie was trying to work with her on meeting Johnny's needs.

This was the third time the group had to meet to discuss Johnny's needs, modification and adaptations that should be utilized within the classroom to make him as successful in the inclusive classroom as possible. With three adults in the classroom setting, she still struggled to find the reason that specific adaptations were not happening, such as having all of Johnny's cutting work printed on cardstock or letting him utilize the thicker writing utensils. She could not tell if members were intentionally not following through or if it was just an honest mistake. What other supports could she provide to the team to help them with their follow through?

## Dilemma

Natalie reflected on the various times that she had entered the classroom to find that adaptations were not being completed for Johnny. The first week of school Natalie had asked Angie to discuss the current layout of the room. While it provided appropriate boundaries to designate the various areas of the classroom for the students, it simply did not allow enough space for Johnny to independently navigate the room on his own with his walker. For example, a quiet space/library had been created in the corner of the classroom using two bookshelves to create a small entry into the space. The bookshelves were turned in toward the space and then beanbags had been set out for students to read in. The students really enjoyed this space and utilized it often, but the entrance to the space simply was not large enough for Johnny to enter with his walker. Natalie had asked Angie to either widen the space or at least turn one of the bookshelves outward so that Johnny had access to the books from the outside and could find a different spot to read. "I don't want to take away from the design of the quiet corner by changing the bookshelves, because this will then affect the building area," Angie had defensively replied when Natalie asked her to move the shelves to allow Johnny a chance to get into the library with his walker. She did agree to turn one of the shelves around. However, when Natalie was in the classroom the other day, now two weeks into the school year, this still had not been done. When she approached Angie about this, Angie reported that it had simply slipped her mind.

Natalie had noticed that whenever the class moved about the school to the cafeteria, gross motor gym or to go to the outdoor playground, Johnny was always last in line. After observing the class a couple of times, Natalie realized that when it was time to get in line, Johnny was always dismissed last. This resulted in him always being the last person in line. When Natalie brought this up to Angie, Angie conveyed that her intent had been for Johnny to have an easier time to navigate the room to the lineup area since his peers would already be lined up and out of the way. Angie also stated that it takes Johnny a lot of time to transition to the other areas of the school, in part because he was distracted by what was going on in the hallways and it often holds up the rest of the class if he was not at the end. Natalie and Angie had come to an agreement that on three out of five days a week Johnny would be dismissed at random times like the rest of his peers so that he could be in different places in the line. This would help Johnny to learn that he needed to keep up with his peers and it also would not isolate Johnny from his peers by always being last in line. This appeared to work right away but then after a week or so, Natalie noticed that Johnny was always being dismissed last again. When she approached Angie about this, Angie again stated that she simply had forgotten.

Natalie often observed assignments and would then provide feedback to Angie on how this could be appropriately modified for any student. For example, the class often had cutting practice. For students that struggled with these skills, Natalie had brought in and suggested the use of spring-loaded loop scissors to help strengthen the students' fine motor muscles. Not only was this something that could be done for Johnny but could be beneficial to others as well. Natalie had also asked that Johnny's cutting assignments be printed on cardstock to allow him to more easily manage the paper. This again was something that other students could benefit from as well. Angie said that she could certainly try these ideas but was concerned that she may not remember all the different things to do.

One of Johnny's IEP goals was to promote and gain independence within the classroom setting. Without these specific adaptations and modifications, Johnny is now having to rely more on adults to help him. Natalie was still working to find a way to convey to all staff the importance for Johnny to be more independent and in order to be independent, these adaptations and modifications must happen. So far, Natalie has expressed to Angie that she could be responsible in making modifications to the assignments and curriculum if she had ample time to do so. This way it is one less thing that Angie must remember to get ready.

What often took place was that Natalie was told the morning of the assignment what would be happening. This then allowed little time for it to be modified. Natalie's next plan is to meet with the classroom team every Friday to discuss the upcoming week's lesson plans. This way she could discuss assignments that needed to be modified and show the classroom assistants how to modify the lessons as well. Her hope is that by working as a team to work on and create these modifications, the follow through will be more consistent. However, Natalie is concerned that she will be met with another report from Angie that this is just one more item for her to remember.

## QUESTIONS

1. Which DEC practices for the topic area of Environment did you see supported in this case study?
2. Which of the DEC practices for the topic area of Environment were not supported in this case study? How might these have been addressed?
3. What supports could Natalie provide to Angie when working with Johnny?

4. How could the classroom assistants be utilized to incorporate the adaptations?

5. At what point does Natalie need to bring her concerns to a higher administrator?

6. Should Natalie speak with Johnny's parents about the adaptations that they are already using at home that could be transferred to the classroom? Why or why not?

# PREPARING FOR KINDERGARTEN

*Unsolved*

## Background

Emma's mother reports that she is easily distracted, has difficulty taking turns, is very talkative, and is excessively loud at times. Also, she usually does not follow directions or listen to what she has been told. At the age of three and a half, Emma went to preschool screening. Based on the screening, it was suggested that she may have attention deficit hyperactivity disorder (ADHD). The screening prompted her parents to visit her to see her primary care doctor, who diagnosed her with ADHD. She does not have any other health issues.

Emma attended a daycare center between the ages of eight weeks to two years. Then, from the ages of two to four, her mother stayed at home to take care of her. Emma recently resumed attending the same child care center she did when she was younger. She is at the daycare center for five days a week while her parents work full-time jobs. There are 17 four-year-old children in Emma's class. Accommodations for children with special needs are lacking in this program. The majority of the activities are done in small or large groups, with very little one-on-one time between children and staff.

Emma qualifies for special education services under the category of emotional behavioral disorder. Prior to Emma returning to the child care center, Becky, the Early Childhood Special Education (ECSE) Teacher, visited with Emma and her mother, Julie, in the home. Becky followed Emma to the child care center to provide the weekly one-hour ECSE services, instead of continuing the home visits.

## Dilemma and Perspectives

A conference was held in November to discuss Emma's progress. In attendance at the meeting were Emma's parents Steve and Julie, Kimberly who is one of Emma's preschool teachers, and Becky, the ECSE provider. Emma will be starting kindergarten the following year and the members at the meeting have some concern. Julie stated, "We are afraid to take Emma out in public because of her tendency to wander away from us." Kimberly expressed similar concerns, she said "We have had two situations where Emma has left her preschool class and has walked into another preschool class." The three preschool classrooms are connected by doors. Kimberly assured the team that "The staff took quick notice when these wandering episodes occurred, and the issue was handled appropriately." Since these occurrences, Kimberly confirmed, "Higher-quality safety door knob covers have been placed on the doors between the preschool classrooms and this seems to be a sufficient solution to the problem." Emma's safety is still a matter that requires attention, Kimberly expressed. An example was a recent field trip the daycare went on. Kimberly stated, "Emma consistently wanted to go in a different direction from her group. The leader of Emma's group held onto Emma's hand the entire time; however, Emma was extremely resistant and did not want to comply."

Kimberly also stated that Emma has been displaying some negative behaviors. "During nap time the children are expected to rest quietly. Emma has had some outbursts in which she talks in a very loud tone of voice and is disrespectful to the teachers. These outbursts disrupt the other children in the room and keep them from resting." Steve agreed and added "Emma has thrown fits when we go shopping which draws attention and concern from other people in the store."

When Becky has observed children in the preschool, she has noticed Emma is not willing to share toys with the other children. "If she wants a toy another child has, she will grab it from the child without asking." Kimberly further commented, "Emma seems to have difficulty in forming and maintaining friendships. Some of the children have told Emma they do not want to play with her."

Environment plays a key role in a child's education process. The parents feel that Emma might do better in a home-based child care setting that has a smaller number of kids. A smaller child-to-adult ratio would offer more individual assistance than the child care center Emma currently attends. However, Becky feels the setting of the child care Emma is currently at closely resembles the setting she will be in for kindergarten and would provide Emma with more opportunities to practice social skills. Kimberly, the preschool teacher feels that additional behavior support is necessary. All team members agree that interaction and engagement with peers is needed for Emma's social skills to improve.

## QUESTIONS

1. Which DEC practices for the topic area of Environment did you see supported in this case study?
2. Which of the DEC practices for the topic area of Environment were not supported in this case study? How might these have been addressed?
3. Based on the information in the case, which setting do you believe would be most beneficial for Emma—a home child care or a child care center—and why?
4. Emma has been presenting negative behaviors such as speaking in an excessive tone and inability to cooperate with peers. What adaptations to the environment might be used in shifting Emma's behavior?
5. Safety door knob coverings were installed to prevent Emma from wandering into another classroom. What adaptations could be made in the classroom to improve Emma's safety?
6. What proactive strategies could be implemented to make for a more supportive environment?

## SPEECH IN SPEECH

*Unsolved*

### Background

Danielle is helping students gather their things to go home with the help of her teaching aid. Little Amy's mom, Jennifer comes into the classroom to pick Amy up and asks to speak with her about a problem they are having at home with Amy.

"Miss Amanda (Amy's speech teacher) has requested that we practice her speech sounds at home and Amy refuses, says Jennifer. "I have tried everything I can think of to get her interested in working on her speech with me and her father, but she always says "NO, I do speech with Miss Amanda!" and goes into a fit if we push the subject. I really want to help Amy with her speech, but I'm starting to feel frustrated and overwhelmed. I don't know what to do at this point."

"Have you spoken with Miss Amanda about this problem?" Danielle asked. Thinking that this would be a problem for her to solve. Or one they could work on together.

"I haven't had the chance. I only see her at IEP meetings. I was hoping that you and she would work with me on the problem" Jennifer explained.

"I think Amy would benefit from using her speech sounds in the classroom too, then maybe she would see that she isn't only supposed to work on them with Miss Amanda."

"I agree. I think Amy needs to be working on her speech sounds with me in the classroom as well as with you and her father at home." Replied Danielle "I will be sure to get a hold of Amanda and we will talk about ways to help Amy and I will be sure to get back to you!"

"Thank you so much! That would take a lot of pressure off of us at home." Jennifer replies happily.

Danielle has been Amy's early childhood teacher for 2 months now. Amy is a 3 year and 4-month-old girl with normal academic and intellectual functioning. When Amy was 2, her parents were concerned about her speech, as she was unintelligible to many listeners and she had many ear infections previously. A hearing test was conducted, showing no hearing loss, so she was referred to a Speech Language Pathologist, Amanda. Amanda, diagnosed Amy with an articulation delay and has been working with her for 45 minutes, once a week since the June before Amy started early childhood classes.

In the classroom, classmates and educators struggle to understand her speech due to her articulation errors and this sometimes causes communication breakdowns. Amy tends to get frustrated with her peers when they do not understand her and often needs the help of her teachers to fix the situation.

## Dilemma

Danielle calls Amanda, "Hi, so we have a problem with Amy. Her mom came to me today and said that she refuses to work on her speech sounds at home with her or her dad. Jennifer has expressed concern that Amy only wants to work on her speech sounds with you and will throw a fit when she is asked to try. This is causing quite a few headaches for Jennifer and her husband at home; She would love for us to try and find a solution to this problem." Danielle says.

"Oh dear! I had no idea that this was going on; I was under the impression that Amy was practicing her speech and sounded well with her parents." Amanda replies.

"Apparently Amy isn't giving us all of the information then. I have noticed that she doesn't use her correct speech sounds in the classroom either. I do agree that her articulation errors are causing problems in the classroom, as her classmates struggle to understand her at times. I am often the only time the only adult in the room that can decipher what she is trying to say."

"Well we definitely need to do something to help Amy and Jennifer then!" Amanda exclaims.

## Perspectives

"Can you tell me more about how she talks and acts in your classroom?" asks Amanda.

"Amy is pretty shy; she tends to keep to herself and watch other kids play. I do see that she gets frustrated when people don't understand what she is trying to say. It's not often that I struggle, but her classmates do and that creates problems. Amy gets upset when her classmate doesn't understand her and acts out; she either raises her voice or takes the object she wants away from her classmate." Danielle replied. "I have tried to work on a few of the sounds when I hear that she is producing them incorrectly, but Amy always gets mad. She always tells me, "NO, with Miss Amanda." Jennifer says that's how she responds at home as well. She requested our help in showing Amy that working on her speech in different environments will help her. Any ideas?"

Danielle had a few ideas of how to interest Amy in practicing her speech sounds in the classroom daily, and she couldn't wait to run them by Amanda.

"I have had the conversation with Amy about how important it is to work on her speech with all of the adults in her life." Amanda replied. "It is hard for children this age to understand that concept. Would you like to meet and brainstorm some ideas on how we can help Amanda and her mom?"

"I think that is a great idea!" Said Danielle.

The two educators set a time the next day to discuss the problem and brainstorm solutions for Amy to practice her speech sounds in different environments that would create more interest. Some of the ideas that they came up with were changing the content, by finding topics and games Amy loved and incorporating her speech sounds into those in all environments. They decided that manipulating the environment of her speech sessions would help; They decided to do this in two ways, having Amy's parents sit in and participate in some of the speech sessions to create continuity between the therapy environment and the home environment.

Danielle will work Amy's speech sounds into the classroom's daily routine, so that Amy was working on her speech sounds often. Danielle could choose large group reading books geared towards the speech sounds Amy was working on and have the entire class work on the sounds within the reading.

Danielle feels confident that the changes she, Amanda and Amy's parents are going to incorporate into Amy's daily routines will really help her to see that her speech is a big part of all aspects of her life, not just in speech class. Everyone is excited that the changes seem small, but will hopefully bring big change for Amy.

Amy has become much more willing to work on speech sounds at home and in the classroom. She herself has said that she is happy working on her speech stuff with her parents and sharing the activities with her classmates. She actively participates in class aloud reading activities where Danielle has embedded speech sound practice. Amy is the first to sit down for circle time each day now.

Jennifer has reported that Amy no longer throws a fit when asked to work on her speech sounds with her or her father, she enjoys it. Jennifer says that things are going much more smoothly at home and there are no more fits about practicing. Amy says that she enjoys having her parents come to speech every once and awhile, so "they can learn too." Amy likes to have a good report to bring back to Miss Amanda about what she had practiced the previous week.

Miss Amanda reports that Amy is excited to take her speech homework home to work on it with her parents, and it is making major improvements on her intelligibility and production of her sounds.

## QUESTIONS

1. Which DEC practices for the topic area of Environment did you see supported in this case study?
2. Which of the DEC practices for the topic area of Environment were not supported in this case study? How might these have been addressed?
3. What could Danielle have done differently to incorporate Amy's speech goals?
4. Do you believe Danielle handle Jennifer's concern in the appropriate manner? Why or why not?
5. If you were part of this IEP team, what would be some recommendations you would have to address this problem?
6. Did the IEP team do enough to help Amy reach her goals, and to resolve the parents concerns? Could they have done more or anything different?
7. What could have Amanda (the SLP) done differently in this situation?

# Chapter 4

# FAMILY

## OVERVIEW OF RECOMMENDED PRACTICE

The goal of early intervention and early childhood special education is to enable families to provide care for their children. And, to have the resources needed to participate in their own desired family and community activities. Families should be actively engaged in the decision-making related to their child's assessment, planning and intervention, as well as take the lead in the development of their child's IFSP or IEP. ECSE teachers should support families in achieving the goals they hold for their children.

Major tenets in family practices should include family centered practices that treat families with respect, family capacity-building practices that strengthen families' knowledge and skills and promote self-efficacy. Additionally, these practices should include collaboration between the family and professional to work on mutually agreed-upon goals.

DEC recommends the following family practices for practitioners:

- **F1.** Practitioners build trusting and respectful partnerships with the family through interactions that are sensitive and responsive to cultural, linguistic, and socio-economic diversity.
- **F2.** Practitioners provide the family with up-to-date, comprehensive and unbiased information in a way that the family can understand and use to make informed choices and decisions.
- **F3.** Practitioners are responsive to the family's concerns, priorities, and changing life circumstances.
- **F4.** Practitioners and the family work together to create outcomes or goals, develop individualized plans, and implement practices that address the family's priorities and concerns and the child's strengths and needs.

- **F5**. Practitioners support family functioning, promote family confidence and competence, and strengthen family-child relationships by acting in ways that recognize and build on family strengths and capacities.
- **F6**. Practitioners engage the family in opportunities that support and strengthen parenting knowledge and skills and parenting competence and confidence in ways that are flexible, individualized, and tailored to the family's preferences.
- **F7**. Practitioners work with the family to identify, access, and use formal and informal resources and supports to achieve family-identified outcomes or goals.
- **F8**. Practitioners provide the family of a young child who has or is at risk for developmental delay/disability, and who is a dual language learner, with information about the benefits of learning in multiple languages for the child's growth and development.
- **F9**. Practitioners help families know and understand their rights.
- **F10**. Practitioners inform families about leadership and advocacy skill-building opportunities and encourage those who are interested to participate.

(DEC, 2014, p. 10–11)

The following nine cases were designed to represent the recommended practices (RPs) for family as a whole. Each case is illustrative of a combination of the 10 RPs for family and each case does not demonstrate each of the practices. When reviewing the case studies for the RPs for family it is advised to use this chapter in the following ways. One, have individuals read each case and answer independently as a way to determine the individual's understanding of family and the corresponding practices. Two, have individuals independently read a case study and in small groups discuss what they learned regarding family and the corresponding cases. Three, have small groups read case studies and contribute to a whole group discussion as a whole. You can use any and all of these suggestions as it fits with your purposes for the teaching or review of the RPs.

## SECTION 1: CASES FOR BIRTH TO AGE 3

## Wit's End

*Unsolved*

### Background

This case study looks into the home life of Robert as well as his stay-at-home mother, Emma; three-year-old brother, James; eight-month-old twin brothers, Steve and Alan; and working father. Robert has been diagnosed with microcephaly, lissencephaly and ventriculomegaly. Robert is also considered to have epilepsy and has an absence seizure every minute that lasts for 3–7 seconds. Robert is not mobile, does not roll over and produces limited sounds. Robert recently had a feeding tube placed as requested by his mother who was concerned, he was not getting enough nutrition from a bottle of Pediasure.

Robert is considered high needs and has several service providers listed on his Individualized Family Service Plan (IFSP). He receives physical therapy, occupational therapy and speech, as well as a vision consultant who provides consultations 4 times a year. Hilda, the ECSE teacher, has limited experience as she is in her first year of home visiting.

When Hilda arrives on home visits, Robert is frequently found lying on the floor in the living room wearing only a diaper. The home is typically quite messy; food and drink are often spilled on the couch or the carpet, toys are scattered all over the floor, playdough and other messy items are smashed into the carpet and the tv is always on. Robert's older brother James is found running around the house, jumping on the couches, and frequently yelling. When the early interventionists come, James will climb on them and try wrestling and attempt to sit on their laps. Robert also has twin 8-month-old brothers who are now crawling. Robert's younger brothers, Steve and Alan will crawl on top of Robert, pull at his hair and tug at his feeding tube.

During home visits Robert's mom, Emma, is almost always preoccupied with other tasks such as cooking or cleaning or talking on the phone. Most often Emma is engaged with her phone or referencing something she previously viewed that does not directly relate to the family's needs. Emma has communicated that daily living tasks are difficult for her especially due to her husband's absence while at work. She expressed interest in moving to Colorado to access medical marijuana which she feels would treat Robert's seizures and high and low muscle tone. Emma also expressed interest in horse therapy programs and wondered if there were any available in the surrounding area.

Emma has limited understanding of Robert's limitations as she has communicated her concerns about Robert to his team, but believes God will heal him and isn't sure therapy is necessary. In response, Emma frequently cancels visits resulting in Robert only being seen two or three times a month by service providers, instead of the recommended visits twice a week. In addition to early intervention, Robert also attends an occupational therapy program in town twice a week and a physical therapy program once a week.

## Dilemma

Hilda has been Robert's home visitor for six months, and it is time for Robert's six-month review. Robert has five goals that the early intervention team is working on with the family. Hilda hasn't seen much improvement in Robert's abilities, mom's competence or confidence in working with Robert. Hilda is feeling overwhelmed with the amount of support needed by Robert's family. She is unclear of where to begin to support their needs while also building positive rapport and relationships with them. As a result, Robert has not obtained expected growth on his IFSP goals nor has the family improved on functioning in an effective manner.

Another dilemma is that Robert has limited access to home visits due to scheduling conflicts with so many providers as well as frequent cancelations by his mother, Emma. Currently, Robert gets two early intervention home visits a week due to scheduling conflicts with the early intervention teacher, physical therapist, occupational therapist, speech clinician and the family. In addition to home-based services, Robert also accesses an occupational therapy program in town twice a week and a physical therapy program once a week.

## Perspectives

Hilda called a child study meeting with Robert's early intervention service providers to talk over concerns for Robert before his 6-month review. Hilda starts, "What are we going to do with Robert? I feel overwhelmed and don't even know where to start. His home life is hectic, the house is a disaster, his siblings make everything more difficult, I don't even think his mom cares if we come or not. I am at my wit's end!"

Ginny chimes in, "I think we should consider everything that is going on in that house. Maybe we are trying to do too much at once."

I agree, said Luna the Speech Clinician. "Maybe we need to find just one or two things for us all to focus on rather than working on our own individual areas."

"How do we get mom to clean up the house so there is a place for Robert to work on some of the stretches he needs daily and how do we encourage mom to make sure they are done daily," asked Bellatrix the Occupational Therapist.

(Knock, knock, knock) Hilda knocked her knuckles on the finger smudged sliding glass door to Robert's house. She stood next to a bag of garbage that was spilling out onto the deck. On the other side of her was a shoe that had been chewed up by the family's large German shepherd. Hilda peeked in the window as Emma waived her in. As Hilda walked in, she was greeted by two smiling naked babies who crawled toward her as well as a three-year-old who was just wearing shorts and a cape.

"Hi-yah." James said as he jumped off the couch.

"Hello Davis family," Hilda said in a sing-song voice. Hilda smiled at the familiar messy house, excited kids and disheveled looking mom. Emma stood up and walked toward one of the babies and picked him up.

"These two needed diaper changes, and I decided to let their bottoms air out."

"No worries, we air out bottoms at our house too," Hilda said with a wink.

Hilda began to walk toward the living room where Robert usually is. Robert was sitting propped up in the corner of the reclining chair. That doesn't look like the safest place for Robert, Hilda thought to herself.

"Steve and Alan were bothering him so I put him up so they couldn't reach him," Lilly said. "Hello Robert," Hilda said as she picked Robert up out of the chair.

Emma scooped Steve up and began to change his diaper as well. Hilda and Ginny moved several toys out of the way to make space on the floor for Robert to lay and for themselves to sit. Same old, same old Hilda thought to herself. As Ginny positioned Robert on the floor to begin stretches, she asked Emma how daily stretches were going and how frequently it gets done. Emma looked up from her phone. "Ummm . . . it's going ok. It's been chaotic the last few weeks. We may get to them once a day." Emma looked back at her phone and began swiping away. "Have you guys seen the meme with that cute football guy? You have to see this." She turned her phone around for Hilda and Ginny to look. They both chuckled as they read the meme. James walked behind Hilda and began to climb up her back.

"James I know you want to play right now, but I have to talk to your mom first. We can play later." James continued to climb on Hilda. "James you need to stop." Hilda said with a firm tone. She was used to him trying desperately to get someone's attention during home visits.

"Get off her right now!" Emma said angrily. James then climbed off Hilda and sulked away to his room.

Ginny continued to work on stretching Robert's arms and legs and said, "I notice his range of motion is still low. When we work on his stretching and range of motion exercises daily, it can help improve his joint function and can keep them more flexible. It also helps reduce pain. Do you think you would be able to find a time during the day you can work on stretching Robert? Maybe you could find some time before bed or right when he wakes in the morning."

"Yea I probably can do that," Emma said looking up from her phone.

"Do you see how I am working his joints in his arms as I pull his arm upward and rotate it back down toward his feet," Ginny asked. At that point Steve crawled on top of Robert. Hilda picked Steve up and sat him on her lap to prevent him from crawling on top of Robert again.

"Yea, I do that," Emma said.

Ginny asked, "Will you come down here and show me what stretching you do with Robert. Maybe we can see if there are any others that we can maybe add or others that he no longer needs."

Emma came and sat on the floor and showed Ginny and Hilda what stretches she uses with Robert. "I like the way you are rotating his hips as well as his ankles," Ginny said.

Emma smiled and continued to stretch Robert. The rest of the home visit continued with Hilda holding Steve to stop him from crawling on Robert. Hilda and Ginny asked questions and visited about how the rest of the day is going with positioning Robert. James came out once more but was shooed away by Emma again. Alan quietly played in the corner with toys only looking up occasionally at the chaos that was happening five feet away.

## QUESTIONS

1. Which DEC practices in the topic area of Family did you see supported in this case study?
2. Which of the DEC practices in the topic area of Family were not supported in this case study? How might these have been addressed?
3. Should the early intervention teacher and service providers encourage Robert's mom to be more involved in his home visits? Why or why not?
4. When it comes to teaming and collaboration what could the early intervention teacher and service providers do to enhance team functioning?
5. What could the early intervention teacher and service providers do to build Robert's mother's confidence and competence for Robert's mother in the team?
6. What might the intervention providers do to provide services and eliminate disruption to the family?

# MOTHER IN DENIAL

*Solved*

## Background

Zachary is a 2-year-old boy who is cared for by his mother, Laura, in addition to his nanny, Jennifer. Laura's husband, Zachary's father, filed for divorce shortly before Laura gave birth and is not involved in raising Zachary. Laura is in her mid-thirties and Zachary is her first child. She has noticed that unlike other toddlers his age, Zachary does not make eye contact or seem interested in the world around him. Zachary's nanny first started having concerns about Zachary's development as an infant. When the nanny approached Laura with her concerns, she was fired. Taking notice of Zachary's development herself, Laura became fearful about the stigma a label like "autism" can carry for a child.

## Dilemma

Laura was confident she would be able to keep her full-time job and still be supportive and involved in Zachary's life after her husband left. Laura hired Jennifer to stay with Zachary while she worked. When Laura arrives home each day, she says Zachary doesn't seem to notice her. Laura felt guilty for working so many hours and being away from Zachary, but she was able to assure herself that a consistent nanny was the next best option.

One particular evening when Laura returned from work, the nanny seemed exhausted, on edge, and eager to get out of the house as soon as possible. Laura asked the nanny why she seemed so eager to leave. The nanny, looking scared and uneasy, began explaining to Laura, "When Zachary is not crying, he is unfocused and does not make eye contact, and doesn't interact with me. I try all day to get Zachary to notice his surroundings, but he seems to be in his own world. He cries all day without being soothed, and I worry that Zachary is not developing normally." Without hesitation, Laura asked the nanny to leave and not return. Laura took the next day off work and began searching for a new nanny. As she searched, however, she reflected on what the nanny said, and her gut told her that the nanny was not so far off.

Zachary was not sitting up at 7 months, nor babbling at 8 months. The crying continued, and little to no eye contact existed between Zachary and others. During his 10-month check-up, the doctor raised concerns about Zachary's development. The pediatrician suggested Zachary receive in-home intervention. Laura was hesitant. Laura told herself that Zachary was a "late bloomer." Laura said she would consider intervention after he turned one and has had time to "grow out of it."

As Zachary's first year went on, it was evident that he had more serious problems than Laura initially imagined. Zachary was not walking or speaking, and because of his frustrations, cried and seemed uncomfortable all the time. Laura felt hopeless and frustrated that she was not able to soothe him. At his next check-up, the pediatrician referred Zachary to a neurologist. "Throughout this neurological assessment we found Zachary to have tendencies that are most prominent for people with autism." Laura's mind became blank, trying to process if the neurologist had actually used the word "autism" and Zachary in the same sentence. She listened in a daze and decided this doctor could not be correct. "Autism, that cannot be possible," thought Laura. She grappled with the idea of people seeing her son as someone who has autism and wanted these "tendencies" to be fixed. Laura decided to begin receiving services from early interventionists in the hope that Zachary's tendencies would diminish. Reluctantly, she followed the doctor's advice and moved forward with service delivery shortly before his second birthday.

Zachary, now at 2 years and 10 months in age, is still not speaking, other than grunting and using basic sign language to communicate despite having an early intervention team working with him for an hour, two days a week. Laura thought that things would get better because Zachary had made great progress with his physical therapy and occupational therapy and was now walking. Laura didn't see signs of autism at all. He flapped his arms when he became excited, which she interpreted to be normal. Zachary is obsessed with Thomas the Train, but Laura knows that intense obsessions are a staple in all children at some time or another. Laura did, however, take notice of Zachary's lack of eye contact, and she found herself wondering if Zachary even notices and cares for her as other infants do for their caregivers.

As Laura prepared for Sharon, an Early Interventionist, and Samantha, a speech language pathologist, to visit and discuss Zachary's 3-year-old placements, she reflected on her experiences with Zachary's therapists.

## Perspectives

The team was meeting as a whole at Laura's house to discuss Zachary's placement once he turned three. Sharon, the early intervention teacher, felt nervous about sharing her recommendation that Zachary be placed in a self-contained program for children with autism. She would not be surprised if Laura refused the placement. Samantha, the speech language pathologist, was accompanying Sharon to the meeting. In the car on the ride over, Sharon shared her concerns with Samantha. "We need to emphasize that this placement has the highest likelihood of helping Zachary. In a typical 3-year-old setting, Zachary would be unable to participate in most activities, even with adult assistance. He needs to receive more support as he enters this new placement." The two agreed that they would broach the subject gently, explaining the benefits of the self-contained placement to Laura.

During the meeting, Sharon and Samantha went over the results from Zachary's re-evaluation tests with Laura. They each described the progress Zachary was making towards goals and objectives for speech and language, as well as occupational therapy. Sharon told Laura their recommendations for Zachary's pre-school placement. "From the testing results, Zachary's progress, recommendations from his pediatrician, and discussions with the early childhood staff at the Carl Strom Early Childhood Center, we think it would be best if Zachary was placed in the SPIRE program, which is for children who demonstrate indications of having autism." Samantha said, "We think Zachary will thrive and continue his progress in the SPIRE program. We would like to take you and Zachary there for a tour next week to meet the teacher and paraprofessional and see how the program works." Sharon sensed Laura was having a hard time taking everything in. Laura sat in silence, with her head down, processing this information. Tears welled up in Laura's eyes as Sharon and Samantha glanced at each other as if to determine what steps to take next. Sharon spoke to Laura: "Laura, we want you to know Zachary has made great strides. He is walking now and learning more signs each day. I know it's hard to see this progress because it is not happening overnight, but we are confident Zach will continue to progress positively in the SPIRE program." Laura said, "I know I have not been the easiest to work with. I take my career seriously and I work long hours, but I want what is best for my son. I just never envisioned this being our future. I am scared for my son and I want him to have the best life possible."

Samantha said, "We know this is hard for you. There are groups in the metropolitan area for parents with children who are demonstrating tendencies of autism, or who have a diagnosis. Within the neighborhood early childhood center, there are after school support programs for parents going through some of the same things you are." Laura said, "Thank you. I think I need to start coping and process all of this. A support group sounds like it could really help me as I want to be the best I can be for Zachary. I am not completely sold on the SPIRE program, but I am willing to take a tour and meet the teachers. If possible, can I speak to any parents who have children in the program?" "Yes, we can definitely arrange that for you," said Sharon. She and Samantha shared a look of relief with one another. They knew they were making strides with their relationship with Laura and hoped with time they would be able to earn her trust even more.

## QUESTIONS

1. Which DEC practices in the topic area of Family did you see supported in this case study?
2. Which of the DEC practices in the topic area of Family were not supported in this case study? How might these have been addressed?
3. What do you think is Laura's perception of autism? What information can Sharon and Samantha provide to support her at this time?
4. What are Laura's strengths as a caregiver? How can Sharon and Samantha promote these strengths during decision-making?
5. How might the team help Laura in making a decision that is right for her family?
6. How can the team provide Laura with support and connection?
7. What conversation might you have with Sharon in the car ride over the team meeting to help her in being mindful of Laura's concerns?

## RHETT'S CASE

*Unsolved*

### Background

Rhett is a two-year-old recently diagnosed with hearing loss and some developmental delays. His mom, Kami, had brought him to the doctor noting his lack of any verbal communication and that he did not seem to respond to his name. Rhett had several ear infections since birth. There is a family history of hearing loss as Rhett's father, Dean, suffered from hearing loss in one ear due to repeat ear infections and Kami has a maternal cousin who was born deaf. The doctor did a hearing test and determined Rhett had hearing loss in both ears. Not knowing how long Rhett had experienced hearing loss, the doctor conducted a developmental assessment. This assessment showed Rhett twelve plus months behind in several developmental areas; particularly cognitive and language.

Kami had been very diligent on taking Rhett for his regular developmental check-ups and is quite frustrated this was not caught earlier. She is feeling guilty for not noticing or acknowledging signs of problems earlier and getting Rhett in. After the diagnosis, the Heideman's were connected with in-home instructional services that consisted of a child development specialist, a speech therapist and a physical therapist. This family lives in a very rural area. To get any services outside of the home, it is usually an hour commute, one way, to a larger community. Ann, the speech therapist, has been coming into the home two times a week for the past eight weeks to work with Rhett, as well as with Kami and Dean. She has introduced a voice box device to train the family so that Rhett has some ways to communicate. Currently his main way of communicating is by pointing and grunting.

Ann is also working with both Rhett and his parents on some basic sign language that relate specifically to daily routines or behaviors such as asking for "more," "drink," "please," "thank you," "up," "eat." Rhett uses sign language with Ann very infrequently. Mom has tried to use it at home and Rhett does not use it at all with her. Dean is attempting little to no sign language with Rhett. Since Rhett is functioning developmentally at an infant level, Kami still responds to him in that way. Rhett will be getting his hearing aids in the next week. This will prove to be a real determinant on what will happen with services.

## Dilemma

In the beginning, Kami was very diligent on using sign language with Rhett. Ann had introduced a couple of words each session and had Kami demonstrate and practice at that time. As time progressed, with all the pressure of running the household alone the majority of the time, she slowly decreased her consistency of using sign language. "It is such a battle to try and get him to use it." For her, it is easier to continue to respond to Rhett's pointing and grunting. Kami did put lots of photos and items in the voice box upon receiving it. Kami figures out what Rhett wants before he can find it on the voice box or again, it was less time consuming for Rhett to point and grunt than to go get his voice box, find the picture of what he wanted and touch it to speak. By introducing the voice box and sign language, Ann has worked on creating a more inclusive environment at home, particularly as it relates to his social development.

During her sessions, Kami is very engaged and participates in activities. Ann involves Kami in the decision-making and they work together to create an action plan each week on things the family will work on. So far, Kami is the only family member that has been involved with home sessions. Ann has demonstrated several activities of the DEC practices in regards to family, such as promoting the active participation of families in decision-making related to their child and the development of a service plan. She has used family-centered practices, family capacity-building practices and family and professional collaboration.

With Rhett turning three in six months, in-home services will stop and then the school district will need to provide and fund continued services if needed. Because the family is in a rural area, many of these services will require a significant time commitment with travel. With the significant time needed to receive outside services in the future, Ann is concerned with the parents' engagement with in home services and how this will affect instruction with Rhett moving forward; especially if further changes in the home environment need to be made and additional instructional support is needed at home.

## Perspectives

Kami and Dean seem to be on a different page as far as the severity of Rhett's developmental issues. Dean believes "He is making some progress. He is fine." Kami says, "He doesn't seem to be making very fast progress. He has been getting help for two months and is only caught up on two months of development. Shouldn't he be doing better? At that rate he will never be caught up."

Ann has expressed her concerns with the child development specialist and physical therapist that there are deeper issues than just hearing loss that has affected Rhett's development. Both of the other specialists have had similar concerns. Due to his age and lack of verbal skills, the initial assessment for autism proved to be somewhat inconclusive. Ann feels the parents are holding out a lot of hope that the hearing aids will quickly remedy the developmental issues with Rhett and that he will automatically get caught up developmentally. Dean "I am not sure why we have to do all this since he will get his hearing aids and then will be able to hear us."

## QUESTIONS

1. Which DEC practices in the topic area of Family did you see supported in this case study?
2. Which of the DEC practices in the topic area of Family were not supported in this case study? How might these have been addressed?
3. What additional strategies could Ann incorporate to support the family in achieving their goals for Rhett?
4. Considering the family dynamics, how can Ann support the family functioning and build instructional services that support the family?
5. How could the team introduce Rhett's use of sign language and the voice box that is more supportive of the family?
6. What strategies could Ann employ to help the family with the transition from in-home services to outside services?
7. Should Ann be concerned with getting more of the family engaged during her home visits? Why or why not?

# FAMILY ENGAGEMENT THROUGH INTERPRETATION

*Unsolved*

## Background

Georgia is thirty-two months old and is of Latino descent. She lives in an apartment with her mother, father, and older sister who is in first grade. Georgia was originally referred to the Help Me Grow program with concerns about her motor and language development in January 2017. She received a Part C Birth to three-year-old evaluation and was found to not meet the eligibility guidelines at her age. In December of 2017, Georgia began to show an increase in activities that caused injury to herself, her siblings and parents. Georgia is throwing dishes, toys, and glasses. She is biting and kicking family members and hits herself into walls when angry. The parents expressed concern with the behavior and that Georgia was not talking. Georgia has a limited vocabulary of less that twenty-five words at thirty-two months of age when counting both English and Spanish words. In Georgia's home her eight-year-old sister speaks only English, but understands Spanish. Georgia's parents speak and understand only Spanish. Georgia's parents have friends that speak both English and Spanish and have told Georgia's parents that they do not understand the words that Georgia is saying. The family has expressed that they would like Georgia to learn both English and Spanish in order to preserve their culture. Georgia's parents are concerned they will not be able to talk to their daughter. An interpreter is needed for communication with both the family and Georgia.

## Dilemma

At the time of Georgia's referral there are currently no individuals within her direct service team that speak Spanish and can directly communicate with Georgia or her parents. The dilemma is that in working with the family how does the service team ensure relationships are built with the family when all communication is occurring through an interpreter. The delivery model is in Part C Family Guided Routine Based Intervention. All reflective goal and activity decisions and relationship building both with the family and the student is occurring through an interpreter and the usage of gestures and facial expression.

Parents have expressed through the interpreter their fear that Georgia will hurt herself again and that she might injure her sister. "She hits, but only family members." "She has never hit her cousins or other children she plays with." Georgia has hit her head on the floor and wall when angry and recently broke her tooth off. Georgia's direct service team includes an occupational therapist, who also looks at Georgia's sensory and motor needs. A speech language pathologist who is working on helping Georgia and family understand a gesture and routine for teaching Georgia how to wait. Georgia is also learning about social emotional techniques such as belly breathing, expending physical energy and calming techniques through an Early Childhood Special Education Teacher Birth-3. Georgia and her family will have ten joint home visits under the guidelines of Part C before she will turn three years of age. Georgia's third birthday is at the end of May. She is not eligible for services in the summer. She will transition to school system services in August. The family has limited access to a vehicle and can only communicate with the school system personnel using a telephone and an interpreter.

Georgia's parents have expressed that the goal they would like to focus on for the ten Part C visits with Georgia is language development within her behaviors. The family expressed concern over encouraging only English or if they could also continue to speak Spanish to Georgia. They did not want to confuse her and contribute to her inability to communicate her needs. The team encouraged the family to continue to use both English and Spanish, as they would like Georgia to be bilingual. At the reflective meeting last week where assessment and evaluation information for Georgia was shared by her parents, Georgia's mom shared that Georgia has learned if she goes to mom that her mom does not give in. Georgia has learned that if she goes behind her dad and kicks or pushes on him that he will get up and go get her what she wants. During evaluation Georgia looked at her dad and let him know that she was going to pinch him. Her dad left the couch and returned with the drink Georgia had requested. During the meeting to review results at the family's home Georgia determined that she wanted yogurt and went behind dad's back and tried to push him off of the couch.

In designing services while meeting with Georgia's parents and the multidisciplinary team it was decided that visits will only occur when the interpreter can be present. It has also been determined that for all meetings when agenda's, reports, team meeting notices, and prior written notices are required that both oral interpretation and written translation will occur to ensure the family are active participants in deciding the activities for the upcoming visits.

## Perspectives

**Family.** Georgia's family is looking for assistance from the school, family facilitator, Early Childhood professionals, with addressing Georgia's behaviors towards herself and others and helping her to be successful as she enters school. They have expressed concern that if Georgia hurts herself or her sister that parents are afraid it will become a child protection report of concern. The family wants to do whatever they can to ensure their family structure and help learn how to work with their daughters. Parents have expressed their daughter in first grade is struggling with learning reading and they were asking for help because they cannot read in English or help her read in English. They call the interpreter when they have questions on working with Georgia or questions regarding services.

**Early Childhood Special Education Teacher/Case Manager.** The time of intake with the family is often the beginning stages of developing relationships with the families. The initial contact had to occur with an interpreter. The setting of all appointments, the review of data all occurred with the interpreter. When the parents had questions about something, they would ask the interpreter. It feels like there is a distance between me and the family and they seem to trust the interpreter to get their needs met. As we begin to provide services it will be difficult to ensure a quality reciprocal relationship with the family.

Speech Language Pathologist. The speech pathologist feels she does not want to have a home visit without the interpreter present for Georgia. The Pathologist feels that through translation you may lose some connection with the family. She feels she can increase the child's outcomes but keeps directions simple so families can repeat them without her present.

## Child Behavior

Georgia lives in a home where her parents work a rotating shift. Her mom works overnight and her dad works during the day. Georgia will sometimes stay up until midnight until her dad returns home from work. Dad reports that Georgia will sometimes grab the remote if dad is watching boxing and she wants the television off and she will shut it off. Dad commented that sometimes she will choose an activity such as building with blocks and will repeat the building of a three-block tower and knock it down for several hours until dad is exhausted and they go to bed. Both parents remarked that Georgia often will throw items as a symbol that she is all done including; dishes, glasses with liquid in them and toys. During the multiple visits for evaluation and assessment Georgia never exhibited throwing or injurious behaviors. She did exhibit some refusals to complete a task.

## QUESTIONS

1. Which DEC practices in the topic area of Family did you see supported in this case study?

2. Which of the DEC practices in the topic area of Family were not supported in this case study? How might these have been addressed?
3. In what way have early education professionals ensured that family members who speak another language are active participants in the home visits?
4 If nothing changes in this situation, how might this impact Georgia?
5. How can the team ensure that Georgia's parents are active participants in goal setting during the transition from Part C to Part B services?

## SECTION 2: CASES FOR 3-TO-5-YEAR-OLDS

## Kindergarten Placement for the Fall

*Unsolved*

### Background

Bennett is a 5-year-old male who attends the Monday/Wednesday/Friday small group Early Childhood Special Education (ECSE) class. He has been diagnosed with Autism Spectrum Disorder (ASD). There are seven students who range in ages 4 to 5 years old in Bennett's class setting. In Bennett's class there are five adults who work with the students; Makalynn is Bennett's ECSE teacher, Sophie is Bennett's ECSE paraprofessional, Megan is Bennett's Occupational Therapist, Katelyn is Bennett's Speech Therapist, and Natalie is Bennett's Physical Therapist.

Bennett is aggressive in many ways such as; he breaks crayons, he hits other students, and has broken numerous toys because he does not realize his strength. Bennett is also obsessed with fans. He is very knowledgeable about different kinds of fans and how they work. This makes it difficult to divert his attention back to the classroom activity when he sees a fan. Bennett is receptive to completing tasks when allowed to be rewarded with his fan book, which is a book that the teachers made with various fans. Bennett is a very caring child to his peers and teachers. He tries to please others. For example, he shares his toys with others, he will ask others to play with him, and he will allow other students to join in the activities that he is doing.

### Dilemma

Bennett will be starting kindergarten in the fall of 2018. Makalynn believes that he will be best placed in a regular kindergarten classroom setting at the school he is currently attending. Katelyn, speech therapist, believes that Bennett will be best served by attending a level three kindergarten class-room in a different school. She believes that he needs more services than can be provided in a regular classroom setting. Bennett's parents, Kelsey and Jay, feel that Bennett would benefit from staying in the regular kindergarten classroom at his current school. They have a concern that, if he is placed in a different school setting, he may not academically and developmentally excel. They are also concerned that he will not build further social relation-ships with his peers, whom he lives by, if he is placed in a different school.

This is where family and professional collaboration, as stated in the DEC recommended family practices, is needed in order to work together and find a mutually agreed upon placement for Bennett in the fall. This situation has not been discussed with the occupational therapist or physical therapist. Bennett's family is aware of this current dilemma, however in order to have collaboration between the practitioners and the family, this situation will need to be discussed together with Bennett's family and the school IEP team.

**Perspectives**

Makalynn and Katelyn had a conversation regarding Bennett's place-ment for this coming fall. Makalynn explained to Katelyn, "Bennett is mak-ing progress in many ways this school year and should attend kindergarten in a regular classroom this fall."

Katelyn said, "We do not have all of the services and personnel that Bennett needs to be successful in a regular kindergarten classroom because he needs more one on one instruction time and he will not be able to get as many minutes in occupational therapy and physical therapy in a regular classroom without losing time with his peers in the regular class."

Makalynn responded, "Bennett is gaining more self-control this year and has made a lot of academic growth in the classroom. Last year, Bennett was not able to focus for more than 5 minutes and this year he has been able to focus for almost 10 minutes."

Katelyn replied, "He needs to be in a smaller group setting where there is a greater support system to help him better meet his needs. He will make more improvements if he is not in a large group but gets more individual support."

Makalynn said, "I disagree with this, but I believe this is something that we need to discuss with Bennett's family and the rest of the ECSE team."

Makalynn called Kelsey and Jay to set up a meeting to discuss their con-cerns and the concerns that Bennett's IEP team has about his future class-room placement.

Kelsey and Jay met with Makalynn at Bennett's school to discuss every-one's thoughts and concerns about his progress and future placement.

Makalynn asked the parents, "How are you feeling about Bennett's progress this school year?"

Kelsey responded, "I feel that Bennett has made a lot of gains this year socially and academically. At this time last year, he would not play with any other children and now it is so exciting to see how he interacts with others."

Makalynn asked, "Do you have any thoughts about Bennett's classroom placement next school year for kindergarten?"

Kelsey said, "Yes, Jay and I have talked in depth about it as we feel that Bennett will benefit most by staying at his current school and attending kindergarten in a regular classroom setting."

Makalynn explained, "There are some concerns between members of the IEP team as to whether Bennett would benefit most from attending kindergarten in a regular classroom setting or if he would be best served in a level three kindergarten classroom at another school. That is why I asked for you to meet today because we want to hear your thoughts and feelings and we want to make sure that the decision is made with everyone's input so that Bennett is successful this fall."

Jay expressed his concern by saying, "We are afraid that Bennett will not do as well in a different school setting. We are afraid he will not be able to build as many friendships or do as well in school."

Makalynn suggested, "How would you feel if we were to arrange for Bennett to visit both kindergarten classrooms so that you can see what each setting would be like? Let's set up a time that works for you to bring Bennett to each of the classrooms. I will contact the teachers in both of the classrooms about our upcoming visit and after the visit, the teachers may also be able to offer insight which may help know where Bennett will best be placed." Makalynn felt it was best for the family to have all of the information they needed in order to advocate for their child and make an informed decision.

Jay interjected, "That is a great idea and I feel that would be the best option for all of us right now. We would hopefully get a better understanding about the placement that would benefit Bennett." Kelsey agreed that this would be a wonderful idea and said she thought it would be helpful.

Makalynn responded, "I appreciate you expressing your thoughts and concerns. I will bring this information back to Bennett's IEP team. I appreciate you coming in today and want you to know that we all want the best for Bennett. I also want you to know that, as parents, you will have the right for the final say in where Bennett is placed for kindergarten. We will set up a case study to be well written and thorough. It had all of the elements of another meeting closer to the end of the school year to discuss the placement for the fall after Bennett has visited both schools."

Makalynn will take this information back to the rest of the IEP team and explain the concerns that Bennett's parents have expressed during our meeting. His progress in the next few months along with the desires and recommendations of his parents and teachers will need to be considered before any final decision is made.

## QUESTIONS

1. Which DEC practices in the topic area of Family did you see supported in this case study?
2. Which of the DEC practices in the topic area of Family were not supported in this case study? How might these have been addressed?
3 How could the team provide the family with a range of placement options?
4. What other personnel should Makalynn discuss Bennett's placement with?
5. What more could Makalynn do to help make the placement decision easier?
6. What could the team do to support the family in advocating for Bennet?

## HELP FOR HOME

*Unsolved*

### Background

Ms. Julie is a veteran teacher teaching the Pre-Kindergarten (Pre-K) class for four and five-year-olds. She is prepared to meet with incoming students and their families. She is hopeful to form many new partnerships. Ms. Julie is scheduled to meet with five families, one being Sally and her family. Ms. Julie only knows that Sally is entering her Pre-Kindergarten (Pre-K) classroom as a 4-year 10 mo. student and that she lives close to school according to the address on the class list. Ms. Julie hopes to form the beginning of a trusting and respectful partnership and plans on being respectively responsive to any of Sally's family's concerns, and/or priorities that may arise during their meeting time today. Ms. Julie is ready to take notes, write down questions or seek out any additional resources for families to help ease any worries or concerns with entering school.

## Dilemma

Sally, her Mom, Dawn, and her younger sister entered the early learning building. They had just paid the cab driver and told him to stay because they were not sure how long this visit would take. It was their first time visiting the school and their first-time meeting Sally's preschool teacher. Dawn was nervously thinking, *What will Sally act like here? Will the teacher know how to help her? I hope I am doing the right thing.* They entered the office and signed in. Sally stood close to her Mom. Sally was quiet, reserved and not wanting to be too far away from her Mom. Sally pulled on her Mom's shirt as she noticed an adult walking toward them. The teacher had arrived. "Hi, my name is Ms. Julie. I am happy to meet you." Dawn shook Ms. Julie's hand and introduced herself and the girls.

"Hi, I am Dawn and this is my daughter, Sally, she is coming to preschool here. This is her sister Sophia. Girls, please say hello to the teacher. I would like you to say, it is nice to meet you Ms. Julie." Sophia responded quickly and greeted Ms. Julie. Sally looked at the teacher, looked in her direction but did not speak. Dawn quickly spoke, "Sally, please tell your teacher it is nice to meet her!" Sally looked down at her feet, and quietly spoke the words, "nice to meet you."

The teacher guided Dawn and the girls down the hall to the classroom door. Dawn was walking with the teacher, she was anxiously thinking, *Will this be a safe place for my daughter? Will she be ok coming here?*

As they entered the preschool classroom, Sally and her sister stood and stared at all of the things in the classroom. Ms. Julie spoke, "Sally and Sophia, it is ok to play with any of the toys that are out while I talk with your mom right here at this table, we will be right here."

The girls both looked up at their Mom and waited for her to give approval to play. Dawn said, "The teacher said it is ok, you may go and play."

The girls headed for the pretend play area and began to play very quietly. Sally spoke in a whisper to her sister as they began their play. Dawn and Ms. Julie sat at a table across the room from the girls.

Ms. Julie spoke first. "This is a very informal meeting for us to meet one another, review paperwork and answer any questions you may have about school." "Let's start with questions or concerns." "What is important for us to know as Sally starts school?"

Dawn quietly spoke "I am really worried about sending her to school. I have many concerns about some of her behavior and am worried how her behavior will be here."

Ms. Julie asked, "I understand how sending her to school for the first time may make you feel worried or nervous, what is your main concern?"

Dawn answered, "There are many things happening at home, we have been through so many things, I am not sure what to start with. Sally does not talk a lot. She seems nervous a lot and she has things that she does over and over like counting with her hands while we are waiting and pounds her fists on the table when something new is happening." After a small amount of time, she continued, "oh, yeah, she bangs her head against the wall or stomps her feet a lot when she is angry, and I don't always know how to stop her. She is also afraid of loud noises; she will scream until noises stop." Dawn paused again, this time with a more worried look on her face. Ms. Julie stated, "I can tell you are worried or concerned about school and the behaviors you are talking about. I am willing to listen. Has Sally ever attended school before?"

Dawn responded, "No, this will be the first time she will ever be away from me. We have just recently moved into an apartment and this is the first time we have had a home since she was six months old. We have been living in many shelters before this. We, also, do not have a car. I am not sure about putting her on a bus." Ms. Julie said, "It sounds like you may be feeling nervous and/or anxious, but I want you to know that I can try to help you along the way."

Dawn took a deep breath and looked at the girls playing in the far part of the classroom and with a whisper; she began to share more information with Ms. Julie. Dawn spoke of siblings of Sally's that do not live with her, and how she does not get to see her Dad but maybe once a year. She spoke of many times witnessing unsafe things and that she is scared that some of the situations that she and her family have been a part of may be causing some of Sally's behavior. Ms. Julie could see the sadness and worry in Dawn's face and the possible need for help. Ms. Julie continued to acknowledge Dawn's concerns and worry and wanted to help Dawn create a plan for next steps. Ms. Julie was, also, observing Sally in her play and was not noticing any behaviors like what Dawn had mentioned. Ms. Julie knew this was a new setting and thought Sally may exhibit some mentioned behaviors, but Ms. Julie was not observing any of them today.

Ms. Julie asked if Sally had attended her developmental screening appointment and Dawn nodded her head yes. Dawn provided a copy from her bag. Ms. Julie asked if it would be ok for her to look at the screening results. Dawn handed it to Ms. Julie. Ms. Julie noticed that the only area of concern was from the Ages and Stages Questionnaire: Social Emotional-third edition (ASQ-SE: 3). A screening nurse had written that a referral was made in the social-emotional area based solely on the reports of concern from home. The screening nurse had also made comments regarding thoughts of Sally's screening appointment. The screening nurse wrote, "Sally seems happy, and shy. She shows the ability to separate, answer questions and participate. I did not observe any concerns with behavior or emotional needs during this appointment, although Mom, Dawn, spoke of concerns at home: see ASQ." Ms. Julie read some of the concerns that Dawn had reported on the ASQ: SE-3. She noticed that they were some of the same concerns she just spoke of. It was reported that Sally can be overly worried, not use words when upset, will be upset for long periods of time, uses repetitive actions, and has little to no eye contact in new situations. Ms. Julie then asked if Sally had been through any form of assessments after her screening appointment. Dawn spoke of "tests" that Sally had attended about six months prior and the people at the "testing place" told her that there were no services that Sally qualified for at that time. The only suggestion that was made was to register Sally in a preschool. Dawn was thinking, *Will this teacher be able to help Sally?*

Ms. Julie asked, "Have you or are you receiving support from anyone that comes into your home?" Dawn shook her head, "no."

Ms. Julie described what a home visit may look like and the support it can provide to and for a family. Ms. Julie did not feel that their relationship was trustworthy enough to make a suggestion of setting a home visit up at that moment, but instead waited for Dawn to add to the conversation. There was silence. Dawn looked down at her phone. Her phone beeped, reminding her that the cab was still waiting. Ms. Julie wanted more time with this family, but knew it was time for them to go. Ms. Julie said, "I would like time to get to know Sally and your family more. I would like us to prepare for the start of school and I will make observations and stay in contact with you regarding home and school. I would like us to meet again after the first two-three weeks." Dawn did not respond, only picked up her papers, asked the girls to clean up and told them that it was time to go. The girls cleaned up and followed their Mom out the classroom door. Ms. Julie was thinking, *Did I make her feel uncomfortable? Was it too much for her? How can I best reach out to help address her concerns?* Dawn was thinking how nervous she was about Sally starting school and was maybe rethinking her decision to send Sally to school. She thought, *What if this school does not know how to help?* As they were walking toward the front of the school, Dawn thanked Ms. Julie for her time and told her it was nice to meet her. Dawn had both girls say goodbye as well.

After walking Sally, Dawn and Sophia to the cab, Ms. Julie walked back to her classroom deep in thought . . . *how can I support the concerns of this family? Did it seem like Dawn wanted help? Or just to share information? Would it be helpful for a home visit? How can both Dawn and I address Sally's strengths and needs together?*

## Perspectives

School started one week later. For many following weeks, Dawn would call Ms. Julie after Sally got on the bus. She would speak of concerns, outbursts or behaviors that may have hindered getting on the bus, or anything that may have been hard as preparing for school. Ms. Julie would also call home every day after school to talk about Sally's school day. Ms. Julie was noticing that the behaviors that were most concerning to Dawn were not being observed at school, but that Dawn was still concerned about the continued behaviors of head banging, foot stomping, repetitive actions and withdrawal that were happening at home. Dawn and Ms. Julie were fostering a relationship over the phone through discussions of daily behaviors both at school and home. Ms. Julie was feeling that Dawn was comfortable with sharing information and receiving suggestions from Ms. Julie of school routines that may help at home. Ms. Julie would suggest a home visit and even at times, more forms of observations or assessments that may be helpful for answers on the differences in behavior. Each time outside or other resources were mentioned, Dawn would not respond or would state a reason why she was thinking the behaviors were happening. Ms. Julie would listen, respond and validate all of Dawn's concerns. Ms. Julie would state that she can continue to talk with her, check in with her and let her know of her options, choices and/or actions that may or could be helpful.

Dawn would ask, "Are you sure she isn't doing this at school?" "Why is it so different at home than in school?" "What am I doing wrong?" Ms. Julie continued to work on promoting Dawn's confidence and competence in that she was doing great things for and with Sally at home and offered ways to use their family strengths to assist.

Ms. Julie was not sure why Sally's behaviors were so extremely different at home than at school. She would ask herself, "How can I help Dawn when it seems like she is not willing to accept outside resources?

Ms. Julie felt like Dawn was reaching out or maybe seeking help, but it seemed like she was not willing to accept help or suggestions, except over the phone. The dilemma becomes: Dawn was noticing many concerning behaviors at home that were not being observed at school. From the ASQ: SE-3 and assessment results, it was stated that Sally would not qualify for any special education services within school. Dawn continues to share information with Ms. Julie and Ms. Julie continues to provide verbal support and suggestions but wondering how to help or if to help at home.

## QUESTIONS

1. Which DEC practices in the topic area of Family did you see supported in this case study?
2. Which of the DEC practices in the topic area of Family were not supported in this case study? How might these have been addressed?
3. Why do you think Dawn appeared to be so comfortable during the first meeting with Ms. Julie, but showed apprehension when the meeting was over?
4. Building a respectful partnership with parents is very important. How could the team build this relationship?
5. How can the parent's concerns of home behavior be supported by the team?
6. What intervention strategies could Ms. Julie have implemented to help Dawn feel more confident in implementing interventions in the home?
7. What are the next steps that can be taken to help with Dawn's behavior concerns for Sally?

## TROUBLE IN PARADISE

*Unsolved*

### Background

Tara is a 4-year-old student who attends preschool four afternoons a week at Early Childhood Family Education (ECFE). Tara meets Part B eligibility criteria in the area of Developmental Cognitive Delay. Tara also receives Occupational Therapy twice a week for 15 minutes to increase upper body strength. In an educational setting, Tara receives Special Education services for her Developmental Cognitive Delay. Interventions are currently in place to support Tara's academic and personal success at school. These include visual schedules, modifications and breaks during academic tasks, and hands on activities. A paraprofessional named Becky, has been working with Tara since she began pre-school last year.

Tara is a very kind and energetic student. She is social and actively seeks out friendships with other classmates. As stated by her general education teacher; "Socialization is a personal strength of Tara's." During free play in the classroom setting, it was observed that Tara enjoys doing the following: visiting with friends, looking at books from the classroom library, and playing math games. Tara's general education teacher stated that typical problem behaviors for Tara include, "speaking out of turn, staring off into space for several minutes, watching other students, and socializing during academic time."

Tara currently resides with her grandparents and one older biological sister. She has several other siblings but they reside elsewhere. She is not in frequent contact with her siblings other than the sister who lives with her. Tara's father lives in Minneapolis, Minnesota; however, she has very little contact with him. Her mother resides in Mankato, Minnesota but she is currently unable to support her children. For two years Tara resided in Arlington, Minnesota with her aunt and uncle. Her aunt and uncle received guardianship of both children and remained as the sole providers until the end of her second year with them. At that time, guardianship was awarded back to Tara's mother. Tara and her sibling lived in Mankato with their mother during the next year. Due to a drug relapse and subsequent failed drug test, Tara's mother was deemed unable to care for both children and custody was given to Tara's grandparents.

## Dilemma

Recently, Tara's general education teacher has reported seeing a sharp decline in her social interaction with peers and adults, as well as a significant increase in the number and severity of emotional outbursts. Tara has been observed withdrawing from adult attention or assistance during academic tasks, and has been seen hiding under classroom furniture during free play. When Tara is confronted about her behaviors, she will burst into tears and is often inconsolable. The staff members present within Tara's preschool classroom are becoming increasingly concerned about Tara's physical and emotional wellbeing, seeing as Tara is typically described as a happy, energetic, and playful child.

## Perspectives

Tara's paraprofessional, Becky, has worked with Tara in a preschool setting since the age of three. She reported feeling concerned towards Tara's recent atypical behaviors. She stated that uncharacteristic behaviors and/or emotional outbursts in the past were typically attributed to changes in Tara's home life. While it does not appear there has been a significant change in Tara's home life as before, Becky stated, "Tara's grandparents have a great relationship with me and Tara's general education and special education instructors. They are usually really good at informing us of any changes in Tara's life but we haven't heard from them recently." Becky expressed that she felt a more concrete communication forum could aid all of the staff members in limiting Tara's emotional and behavioral outbursts at school.

While Tara's grandparents did not reach out to the instructors at ECFE, Tara's aunt and uncle did. Tara's aunt apologized for lack of communication and stated "Tara's mom is in rehab once again. It can be very confusing for Tara, especially when Tara is not allowed to visit her mother." Tara's aunt also reported that Tara is exhibiting very similar emotional and behavioral outbursts at home. Tara's aunt also stated "Tara's sister and grandma have been fighting very frequently, to the point that the police were called for a noise disturbance in their apartment complex." Tara's aunt suggested that it may be embarrassing for Tara's grandparents to report on their most current life situation and suggested that an informal meeting be held to discuss future plans to assist Tara in navigating her school environment positively and successfully.

The ECSE team, along with Tara's family members, met to discuss how to limit or prevent emotional and behavioral outbursts in the school and home settings. The ECSE team suggested introducing and implementing a daily communication log which would aid in facilitating communication between the ECFE staff and Tara's grandparents. Tara's general education teacher shared, "A new daily and nightly log will be sent home with Tara every day. The daily log will describe Tara's school day; it will also provide an area for ECFE staff to write questions or concerns. In the nightly log, we ask that you describe Tara's night and any concerns or questions you have for us." The ECSE team and Tara's family members agreed upon the new communication log, and it was implemented the following week.

## QUESTIONS

1. Which DEC practices in the topic area of Family did you see supported in this case study?
2. Which of the DEC practices in the topic area of Family were not supported in this case study? How might these have been addressed?
3. What obstacles stand in the way of ensuring daily communication between Tara's family members and the ECFE staff?
4. What other modes of communication could be attempted to ensure continuing collaboration between home and school?
5. What other types of resources or strategies do you think might be helpful for this family?

# FAMILY FRUSTRATIONS

*Unsolved*

## Background

Curt is a 5-year-old student who participates in early childhood special education through the Early Childhood Family Center (ECFC) run by his local school district. Curt has a dual diagnosis of Spastic Cerebral Palsy and a mild Intellectual Developmental Disability. Curt uses a wheelchair for mobility and is non-verbal. He will point to items that he wants, as well as, shake his head yes or no. Next year, Curt will be transitioning from ECFE to the local Elementary School to begin kindergarten.

Curt's mother Lila appears to be a great deal older than the average mother with children attending the ECFC. In addition to Curt, Lila also has two adult daughters, Bonnie and Becky from a prior relationship. Bonnie is the older of the two sisters and lives at home with Lila and Curt. Becky is married and has a son around Curt's age. Lila, Bonnie, and Becky are all legal co-guardians for Curt and live in the same neighborhood. Since all three of his family members are legal guardians, they all need to attend his planning meetings and agree upon decisions that are made relating to Curt's education and health goals. This can be very challenging at times because of their differing opinions on what they believe is best for Curt, and their level of approachability and communication amongst themselves and the other members of the IEP team.

## Dilemma

What are you supposed to do when guardians can't agree on anything? Curt has 3 legal co-guardians who need to agree on what outcomes they would like him to work on so that an IEP can be created before transitioning from ECFC to kindergarten.

## Perspectives

"How are we supposed to help Curt get ready for kindergarten next year if his family can't agree on what they want him to work on," I asked my fellow teacher Maurita. Working with Curt's 3 legal guardians, who over the past few years have never seemed to agree on anything, was causing me to become increasingly frustrated. Trying to play mediator in an attempt to help them see each other's points of view and agree on the things that they would like Curt to start working on was becoming harder and harder as the year drew to a close. "I know that they all love Curt, and each other, and that they want what is best for him, but I wish that they would decide what the most important things are for Curt to learn so that I can start working with him on skills that he will need for his kindergarten IEP."

Maurita looked at me with empathy in her eyes. Having also worked with families that couldn't agree on things, she understood how frustrating this situation was for me. "What if you sit down with Lila, Bonnie, and Becky individually and talk with each of them about what they think are the most important things for Curt to work on and what they each feel Curt would like to learn? Then you can sit down as a group and see if they can agree on goals for Curt that will combine their ideas" she suggested.

"That sounds like it would be worth a shot," I said. "At this point it might be easier to get their ideas individually and then see if I can come up with a common thread between them. Maybe if I can find a common thread and then present my ideas to them, they will see that they are each getting a piece of what they feel is important and then we can focus on that goal and finally be able to move on. At this point I am willing to try anything" I said.

After talking with Maurita, I decided it would be best to set up individual meetings with Lila, Bonnie, and Becky to see what they felt were the most important things for Curt to work on. I called Lila and asked when she would be available to meet with me for an hour or so to talk with her about what she would like to see Curt work on for the remainder of his time at the ECFC and moving into Kindergarten. I sent an email to Bonnie, as that is her preferred method of communication with me. Then, I sent a text message to Becky. Each of Curt's guardians preferred a different type of communication with me, and I did my best to accommodate their preferences even though Lila and Bonnie didn't seem to appreciate anything I did. I set up meetings with each of Curt's guardians and got ready for them over the next two weeks, giving myself a pep talk that it wouldn't be so bad to meet with them this time.

The next Monday, Lila came in after class to chat with me about what she wanted Curt to work on. As Lila walked into class, she thought to herself, "This teacher is so young and always looks frazzled, I doubt that she will be open to hearing what I have to say. I really think the most important thing for Curt is for him to be able to make a good first impression with people, instead of focusing on school work. Especially when it looks like she doesn't even care about her own appearance."

As she came in, I greeted Lila and thanked her for coming to meet with me, all the while thinking that I wasn't sure I could handle her judgmental stare and condescending tone for the entire meeting. I could always tell that for some reason Lila didn't approve of me; I had yet to figure out why. I was eternally grateful that I was meeting with Lila and Bonnie separately. When they were together, they loved to team up and talk over me.

After Lila sat down across from me, with her nose in the air, I asked her to share her thoughts with me about what she felt would be the most important things for Curt to learn to help him have a smooth transition to Kindergarten next year. Looking down her nose at me she shared she felt that Curt, "stuck out," from his peers because of his wheelchair, and that if his overall appearance blended in with his peers, it would help others relate to him better and be more comfortable in his presence. "Curt is such a handsome little guy, with a smile that captures the room," Lila thought to herself, "everyone loves him once they give him a chance. I know this teacher and his sisters probably don't care what he looks like, but I just know if others take the time to get to know him, they will see what a fun little man he his. I sure hope I can convince this dumb little girl that even though she doesn't care about her appearance, it is important, especially for Curt," Lila thought.

After listening to Lila, with what I hoped was an open mind, I asked her what in particular about Curt's appearance she was most concerned with. She told me that she wanted his hands and face to be clean, his hair combed, and his clothes to be always clean. We chatted for a few more minutes about what she felt would be the best way to meet these goals for Curt and then I thanked her for coming and sharing her idea with me. I let her know that I would be in touch to set up a meeting with all of the guardians after I had spoken with Curt's siblings. She said that was fine and got up to leave. While she was walking away, I heard her say, "I'm the mom, aren't I..." under her breath as she was walking out the door.

While walking to her car Lila thought about what her decision to make Curt's sisters co-guardians really meant. She had wanted them to be able to make decisions for Curt in the event that something happened to her. *I'm no spring chicken,* Lila thought to herself, *but I didn't realize making Bonnie and Beckie co-guardians with me would mean they got to have a say in what he was learning in school while I am still alive. This is ridiculous. As the mom, I should have the most say in what he is working on. Maybe I should see if there is a way to allow them to have the power to make decisions in the event that something happens to me, but not now. I will have to look into that. This is just ridiculous!*

When Bonnie, Curt's oldest sister, arrived later that week, she was on the phone with Lila having, appearing to be having an argument about something. Seeing that she was already in such a bad mood, I asked if she would like to go have coffee in the lounge instead of meeting in the classroom. In her usual snarky voice, she replied, "That would be fine" and walked in silence next to me the whole way to the lounge.

*This is just great, we haven't even started talking and she is already in a terrible mood,* I thought to myself as we walked. *Bonnie acts like she can't stand me on a good day, I can't imagine this is going to go well. What can I do to help bring her mood around so we can have a civilized conversation? I am so not in the mood for her to bite my head off today.*

*Mom is just losing it,* Bonnie thought as she was walking down the hallway. *I can't believe that she thinks Becky and I shouldn't be co-guardians anymore. All because she is hung up about what she wants Curt to work on at school. We all want Curt to make friends at school, and everywhere else for that matter. Does she really think that people give a crap about if his shirt is spotless all the time? And to make matters worse, now I must waste my time talking with this little twit. Just great, I don't have time for this, I need to figure out how to talk mom off of the ledge.*

Bonnie was always very combative with me, so I tread carefully when I started the conversation. I decided it would help get things off on the right foot by sharing how much I loved having Curt in my class. He was a lot of fun to have around and seemed to have a knack for getting others around him to engage in conversations with him, even though he was non-verbal.

*I don't know why I have to talk with this little girl,* Bonnie thought. *She is so young and always seems so upbeat, it's really annoying. What an airhead. No wonder she gets along with Becky so well.* Surprised by the teacher's insightful comments about Curt engaging others in communication, Bonnie took the opportunity to tell her that she believes Curt needs to learn new ways of communicating with people. "Smiling and nodding are fine," Bonnie said, "but not nearly good enough. Curt needs to learn how to get his point across to people for things other than just when he wants something." Bonnie said with a humph.

I took this opportunity to talk with Bonnie about some strategies and tools I had used in the past to help students expand their communication skills. I told her that it was best to start with simple things like a picture communication board. As Bonnie glared at me unkindly, I described a picture board, how it worked, the process of creating a picture book, and eventually the possibility of looking at some assistive technology that could speak for Curt as he got older. I shared that a communication board would allow Curt to choose a symbol on the board, and that the communication board would then verbalize what Curt had chosen to say.

"I suppose something like that would be a good thing for Curt to have," Bonnie said. "When can we get him this 'talk box'?"

With patience I didn't feel, I explained to Bonnie that a speech device would be something to look at in the future, and that it would be best to start Curt off with a simple picture board. I offered to provide her with some information just as her phone rang. She looked at the screen, told me she had to go, and walked out.

After enduring the first 2 meetings for Curt I was happy to see Becky walk through the door three days later. Becky was down to earth, approachable, and didn't treat me like I was an idiot. If I needed something for Curt or had a simple question, Becky was often the person I spoke with. I knew she would listen, ask clarifying questions if needed, and then try to mediate the situation with family. I knew she got tired of being the bridge between her family and the school all the time, but she was the person on Curt's team I knew I could talk to without receiving judgmental stares and condescending comments. I was sad to see that she seemed upset when she arrived. I asked what was wrong and she shared with me that she was fighting with her mom and sister about Curt, and how they are controlling his life. With tears in her eyes Becky shared, "I'm so sorry, I was just over at my mom and Bonnie's house and we were arguing about how controlling they are with Curt. They don't really let him make any decisions for himself. I know that he is still young, but I really feel they don't give him enough opportunities to be heard. They won't even give him an option to pick out his own clothes or healthy snacks for goodness sakes. It must be so hard for him to not have control over anything in his life," she sighed.

Feeling bad for Becky, who always seemed to be the odd one out in her family, I asked, "Do you think it would help if we made sure Curt had choices at school? We could focus our attention on making choices a part of his daily routine. Do you think he would feel more in control if we did that? I can't help change what happens at home, but I can help to make sure that Curt's voice is heard while he is here at school."

"That would be a good start," Becky said as she thought, "I just can't imagine how bad it is to live with mom and Bonnie. They are always fussing over him, making his decisions, and never allowing him to pick out anything himself."

"I really think it is important for Curt to start to find his voice and have more input throughout his day," Becky shared. If he doesn't get to make some decisions soon, he is going to start getting upset. When my son doesn't get to make choices in his day, to feel like he is in control of some parts of his life, he throws some impressive temper tantrums. I don't want that for Curt."

Becky continued to calm down as the meeting wrapped up and she seemed to be in better spirits by the end of our meeting. I let her know that I would be speaking with my colleague to discuss my ideas for potential goals for Curt. I shared that once I had a few ideas I would reach out to the family to set up a meeting for all of us to gather and make a decision. Becky gave me an empathetic look and said, "Yeah, good luck with that. I know this isn't an easy situation for you either. I hope that everyone can come together with an open mind so we can make the decision that is best for Curt."

Over the next week I paid attention to Curt upon his arrival. I watched to see if his appearance was in check with what Lila said she felt was appropriate. I watched to see how he communicated with those around him, the choices he was offered throughout his day, and how he let people know what his choice was. Curt was a happy child over all, who liked to be around others, but he did seem to become frustrated, spitting and becoming rigid when those around him couldn't understand what he wanted or figure out why he was upset.

After observing Curt for a week and looking for things I thought might be important to him, I decided to meet with Maurita and discuss my conversations with his guardians, and what I thought would be good ways to incorporate what they each wanted into his IEP goals for the coming year. Together we created a goal I thought would incorporate a bit of each of the family members' concerns and then tried to set up a meeting. After playing phone tag, waiting for email responses and being ignored for a week by everyone except Becky, I finally had a meeting date set. Although I wasn't really surprised that Lila and Bonnie seemed to be blowing me off, it was still frustrating. I was just trying to do my job, and I really wanted a good outcome for Curt.

At the meeting I relayed a short summary of what each person had stated their concerns were regarding Curt. I shared that after having a discussion with my co-worker, I felt that there could be a few ways to incorporate choice making, communication, and a groomed appearance together, making one goal that would address all their concerns.

I suggested creating a simple picture communication board that Curt could use at lunch time. This would have pictures to allow him to choose between two offered lunch options and whether he would like to wash his hands or face first after eating. Using the communication board would allow him to learn a new way of making choices and would also offer a new way to communicate his wishes. At this point, the guardians began to argue about what Curt's lunch options should include, whether he should wear a clothing protector while eating, and if a picture communication board would be something Curt could use to increase his communication skills. Nothing was decided upon by the time we all had to leave and Curt's potential IEP goals were no closer to being decided on.

I don't know why I was surprised that nothing got accomplished at the meeting. I just couldn't believe that even with all that time and effort I was no closer to being able to create goals for Curt's IEP. I sat at the now empty table, closed my eyes, and thought, "Now what the hell am I going to do?"

## QUESTIONS

1. Which DEC practices in the topic area of Family did you see supported in this case study?

2. Which of the DEC practices in the topic area of Family were not supported in this case study? How might these have been addressed?
3. What other methods of communicating with Curt's family, aside from one-on-one meetings, could be used to help them brainstorm ideas for Curt's Individual Education Plan (IEP) goals?
4. List 3 potential goals or outcomes that would address the families concerns for Curt as he transitions to kindergarten?
5. Who else could be included in Curt's team to offer ideas for meeting the concerns brought up in their one-on-one meetings with the teacher?
6. What other resources and supports could the teacher use to identify and access formal and informal support to help support the family-identified outcomes or goals?
7. How could the teacher help support family functioning, promote confidence and competence, and strengthen their relationships by building on the strengths and capacities that the family already has?

# Chapter 5

# INSTRUCTION

## OVERVIEW OF RECOMMENDED PRACTICE

DEC believes that "Instructional practices are a cornerstone of early intervention and early childhood special education. Instructional practices are intentional and systematic strategies to inform what to teach, when to teach, how to evaluate the effects of teaching, and how to support and evaluate the quality of instructional practices implemented by others" (DEC, 2014, p. 12).

The major tenets of instruction are that these practices should be carried out either via the practitioner or the family / primary caregiver of the child. When a practitioner is working with a family / primary caregiver coaching and consultation strategies should be used. The focus of instruction can be on adaptive, social, cognitive, and when needed dual language development and takes place in natural and inclusive environments. The adult should use the child's strengths and interests as a guide to support the instruction while using any necessary supports or adaptations to foster participation. The instruction may include strategies, interventions, or assessment to ensure learning is occurring. It is important to be mindful of both intensity and duration of the instruction to meet goals and objectives for the child.

DEC recommends the following instructional practices for practitioners and families:

- **INS1**. Practitioners, with the family, identify each child's strengths, preferences, and interests to engage the child in active learning.
- **INS2**. Practitioners, with the family, identify skills to target for instruction that help a child become adaptive, competent, socially connected, and engaged and that promote learning in natural and inclusive environments.

- **INS3**. Practitioners gather and use data to inform decisions about individualized instruction.
- **INS4**. Practitioners plan for and provide the level of support, accommodations, and adaptations needed for the child to access, participate, and learn within and across activities and routines.
- **INS5**. Practitioners embed instruction within and across routines, activities, and environments to provide contextually relevant learning opportunities.
- **INS6**. Practitioners use systematic instructional strategies with fidelity to teach skills and to promote child engagement and learning.
- **INS7**. Practitioners use explicit feedback and consequences to increase child engagement, play, and skills.
- **INS8**. Practitioners use peer-mediated intervention to teach skills and to promote child engagement and learning.
- **INS9**. Practitioners use functional assessment and related prevention, promotion, and intervention strategies across environments to prevent and address challenging behavior.
- **INS10**. Practitioners implement the frequency, intensity, and duration of instruction needed to address the child's phase and pace of learning or the level of support needed by the family to achieve the child's outcomes or goals.
- **INS11**. Practitioners provide instructional support for young children with disabilities who are dual language learners to assist them in learning English and in continuing to develop skills through the use of their home language.
- **INS12**. Practitioners use and adapt specific instructional strategies that are effective for dual language learners when teaching English to children with disabilities.
- **INS13**. Practitioners use coaching or consultation strategies with primary caregivers or other adults to facilitate positive adult-child interactions and instruction intentionally designed to promote child learning and development.
(DEC, 2014, pgs. 12–13)

The following six cases were designed to represent the recommended practices (RPs) for instruction as a whole. Each case is illustrative of a combination of the 13 RPs for instruction and does not contain each of the practices. When reviewing the case studies for the RPs for instruction it is advised to use this chapter in the following ways. One, have individuals read each case and answer independently as a way to determine the individual's understanding of assessment and the corresponding practices. Two, have individuals independently read a case study and in small groups discuss what they learned regarding assessment and the corresponding cases. Three, have small groups read case studies and contribute to a whole group discussion as a whole. You can use any and all of these suggestions as it fits with your purposes for the teaching or review of the RPs.

## SECTION 1: CASES FOR BIRTH TO AGE 3

## Culture Shock

*Solved*

### Background

Lynn wasn't sure what to think or feel at this point. After teaching in the ECE (Early Childhood Education) program for three years, her mentor Rachel was up and leaving for another state. She felt the weight of the success of the program fall on her shoulders: so much pressure for what some might still call a "newbie." Lynn already felt challenged within her position as being a teacher at a Deaf school. It takes a lot to prove oneself as an educator of Deaf students using American Sign Language (ASL), let alone to do it well with students not from native signing families. She had never done a home visit, barely knew enough about IFSPs, and had a lot of "what ifs."

"Rachel, how about I join you on your next home visit? I think it would help me learn a bit more about what my role will be and how to conduct a visit when you leave." Lynn asked. Lynn knew the only way to become more proficient at her job was to find answers to her questions and areas of weakness. She decided joining a home visit was a great first step at learning her role: she just had to jump in and get her feet wet.

"Oh sure, that would be great. I will be going to Sulekah's home this Friday. She is a Deaf three-year-old in a predominantly Somali speaking household. I'll call her mother, Fardowsi on Thursday afternoon to confirm the visit," Rachel replied. Rachel opened her file and showed Lynn the slip of paper with Somali phrases on it. Rachel also pointed out a few apps on her iPhone for learning Somali. Lynn took a gulp and gave what she hoped was an encouraging nod. She had gone over Sulekah's file briefly and recalled bits and pieces of information Rachel had shared. The big question she had running around in her head was "how is this young Somali Deaf child going to be a successful ASL user?" She feared these thoughts sounded harsh, but it is also a tough reality for children in trilingual families to overcome the language barriers. With little experience, Lynn worried how successful she would be in this role.

Lynn had so many questions on how to prepare for a home visit. Lynn decided it would be useful to ask Rachel her questions to help her understand the home visit process. Lynn walked into the classroom as Rachel was preparing her bag for Sulekah's home visit. She asked Rachel, "how do you pick what items to bring and how are your visits structured?"

Rachel responded, "when I first started working with Sulekah, I made a list of themes and topics with the family that I thought would help us to practice using ASL and English in a useful way. Today we are going to do an 'oceans' theme, so I am packing puppets, an ocean puzzle, and a toy boat with bathtub ocean animals." Lynn nodded and felt optimistic about having all the materials ready to go. Rachel added, "We need to be encouraging Fardowsi to be using two-word phrases in ASL, so she continues to build her vocabulary. For example, "WHALE WHERE" or "FISH WHAT.""

Rachel and Lynn arrived to Sulekah's house with their big toy bag and knocked on the door. Nearly six children ran excitedly around the sparse living room and Fardowsi had yet another baby on her hip as she was finishing wiping up the counter. Lynn could see that there were no toys and wondered to herself how the children play all day and how does Fardowsi help each of her children without help for herself?

Lynn followed Rachel to the carpet with the big bag and proceeded to get out the toys, practicing the signs as they went. Fardowsi attempted to say the English words and the sign. Lynn noticed Sulekah was excited to see the toys in the bag and was also very distracted by the activity of the other children. Fardowsi attempted to get her attention by calling out her name. Rachel tapped Sulekah's shoulder, bringing the toy close and signed the word. Rachel put her hands on Sulekah's to help her sign the word and gave her lots of positive praise for copying the sign.

The hour session was soon over, and Lynn and Rachel were enjoying a cup of Somali tea as the children continued to play with the toys. Rachel gathered up the toys left from the previous visit, making a note of things that the children could not yet find.

## Dilemma

Lynn spent several weeks with Sulekah's family doing home visits. Each week she came with her bag full of items related to the theme, including a vocabulary word book. Lynn felt it would help if the family had a picture book of her signing the words with the English and the pictures. Sulekah's father, Ami, works long hours as a Somali community liaison and interpreter with the Public-School District and is not able to attend the visits. He has enjoyed the ASL books and DVDs that Lynn brings to help him learn ASL along with his family.

Lynn arrived to Sulekah's house for a visit with the family. She was greeted with warm smiles and waves. She sat down on the large carpet in the living room, all the children and Fardowsi eager to see what new toys were waiting in her bag. Lynn heard the older children call out Sulekah's name, Fardowsi speaking in Somali for her to sit down and wait patiently.

This moment sort of hit Lynn in a strange place; she carried on with her activities but made sure to observe how Sulekah responded and interacted with her family members. She noticed that Sulekah did not use any signs, but more gestures such as pointing and tugging on clothes. In the few weeks that Lynn has been seeing Sulekah, she has not even used the sign for mom.

Although this toy bag routine seemed to be what the family enjoys, Lynn couldn't shake the feeling that this didn't seem best practice. She didn't like the feeling of bringing toys for a week and then just taking them away-what is the family supposed to retain if the items to help them are only taken away a few days later? On the other hand, there do not seem to be any other toys around the house. Many articles she read talked about Routines Based Interventions and how many districts practiced this strategy for home visits. To her, this seemed like the best way to go, since it put responsibility on the family to practice skills and strategies in real day-to-day activities. Since Lynn only comes once per week for an hour, she felt it better to help Sulekah and her family learn ASL to help with these activities rather than focusing on toys.

Lynn decided to bring it up to Fardowsi and Ami. "Fardowsi, I've been reading a lot about home visits and I'm realizing that bringing toys is an old way of teaching and learning. I'd like to try something a little different by talking about your daily activities. I can help you with the language you need to help Sulekah participate and interact with your family during these routines. What do you think about trying this out?"

Fardowsi responded, "Um, yes that fine. You say no toys?" Lynn explained that she would like to help the family focus more on daily language needs rather than toys. She went on to explain that Sulekah will use these toys and participate in thematic activities when she begins school in a couple of weeks. She will be able to pick up a lot of language and experiences in the school setting and with peers. After the visit, Lynn sent Ami a follow-up email explaining the new approach to home visits. He responded saying he was thankful for providing his family with ASL and this new plan sounded wonderful.

Lynn was pleased that Sulekah's family was open to trying something new. Whew, a heavy breath escaped Lynn's lips as she went on to look up more information about Routines Based Interventions. With a strategy she'd never tried before, she had a lot to think about.

Lynn was anticipating the start of a new school year, and optimistic that the classroom environment and peers would be good for Sulekah. On the first day, Sulekah arrived in the classroom and Lynn greeted her excitedly at the door, using signs and voice to hopefully engage Sulekah. "Good morning Sulekah! School today!" Sulekah's eyes were darting everywhere, taking in all the sights of the classroom and her new peers. She had the biggest smile on her face, hugged Lynn and walked into the classroom. Lynn observed Sulekah the next few days as she explored the classroom. Lynn noticed Sulekah seemed to be unsure of what to do, where to go. Lynn had an idea; she knew Sulekah enjoyed reading books so asked her TA, Kasey, to engage her in a simple picture book in the reading center.

"Kasey, I know Sulekah enjoys reading books. Would you choose a book and attempt to show her the pictures and ASL? I'd like to see how she interacts with you." Kasey picked up a simple picture book about animals and simple, colorful pictures in it. Kasey signed BOOK and gestured to Sulekah to sit with her. Sulekah hesitated and looked around the room. Kasey showed Sulekah the picture of the puppy playing with a ball and signed DOG. Sulekah came over and grabbed the book from Kasey's hands. Kasey attempted several other words from the book and attempted to sign the words under Sulekah's in hopes she'd imitate the words. After about five minutes, Sulekah jumped up and went to the kitchen area to play.

Lynn continued to attempt to engage Sulekah with signs and voice during center time activities over the next couple of weeks. Lynn tried everything from hand-over-hand signing, using picture cues, modeling actions with the signs, providing wait time for Sulekah to sign back, using the iPad . . . all she ever observed Sulekah do is dart her eyes away and attempt to walk away. Even after modeling signs hand-over-hand numerous times, it didn't seem to stick with Sulekah. Lynn was concerned with the data she had been collecting, for it raised a lot of questions. "Kasey, I'm worried that Sulekah isn't picking up ASL. Between Rachel and I, she's had services for 8 months now and has been in school with other Deaf and Hard of Hearing signing peers for a month. I get that it's more challenging in a trilingual family, but I would have expected more intentional gesturing and body language and one-word signs by now. I just don't know if Fardowsi and Ami really understand her language needs."

Kasey responded, "You're right, she always seems to be wandering the room and when one of us approaches her she walks away." Lynn wanted to talk with the Speech Language Pathologist, Emily to see if she'd have any suggestions. Emily has been in the classroom every morning during center time and has had some interaction with Sulekah.

Lynn nodded her head in confirmation. "Do you have any other ideas of what we could try? I feel the same during home visits as well. I just switched my home visits from toy bags to using routines-based interventions in hopes that I could help the family use more daily language concepts and signs. Between my visits and Sulekah coming to school, I would have expected more words from both her and her family."

Emily looked around the room. "What if we try a simple PECS (Picture Exchange Communication System) board at home? We could take pictures of things around the house and have an 'I want' board located in an accessible place so when Sulekah wants something, she can pick the right picture/sign and put it on the board. Her family can enforce signing the word before the object is given. We can check on progress with Fardowsi and Ami, then bring it into the classroom as well."

Lynn was hopeful, "That sounds like a great idea! I'll mention it to Fardowsi on our next visit and email Ami as well."

Sulekah's parents agreed to try a PECS board and set it up in the kitchen, focusing on foods and kitchen items first. Emily and Lynn went around the house to take pictures to use for future PECS cards. Lynn felt optimistic that this would be a step in the right direction to including more routine language into Sulekah's expressive vocabulary.

## Perspectives

Sulekah was due for a six-month review meeting to go over the progress she's made. Lynn met with Fardowsi, Ami and Emily after school one day. Because Fardowsi is continuing to learn English, Ami served as the Somali translator for the meeting. Lynn started "Well, Fardowsi and Ami, thank you for taking the time to meet with Emily and I today about Sulekah. First, I'd like to hear from you both with ideas for how you think Sulekah has improved her goals and any concerns you may have."

Ami quick translated and then responded, "Thank you very much Lynn. We know Sulekah enjoys school and you are very good with her. She always smiles when getting off the bus. My family, we watch ASL DVD every night for family time. I learn a lot of ASL from my family. Sulekah and I understand each other, have a special connection and I know what she tries to tell me. That is very much improved." Lynn was glad that Ami felt well with Sulekah's supposed progress, but she couldn't help but wonder how naïve his perspective is.

"I have loved having her here and seeing her interests grow for different activities around the room. I notice her favorite areas are reading and kitchen. She loves carrying the dolls around and likes to push the pretend vacuum. I think these are activities she sees and participates in at home as well; she has a proud look on her face when she is doing these activities. I have been keeping track of her ASL-words she signs by herself and words she will sign with a model. Ami, Sulekah is showing some improvements with copying signs, but she signs very few words independently. I think we're on the right track, but we need to keep working to find strategies and activities to encourage her to use more signs."

Emily also added in her comments, "Ami, Fardowsi, I do not hear Sulekah using her voice for any intended communication. I have only heard her call out a couple of times when she's excited or if she is upset at someone. I think we really need to focus on developing her ASL as her language foundation. Having a solid language foundation will help Sulekah learn other languages, eventually."

Ami nodded, "Yes I understand. ASL is very important. Fardowsi really needs to learn English, too. Lynn, are you able teach her English, help her learn?" Lynn felt this meeting was going in several different directions.

"Ami, our main goal is for Sulekah to learn ASL. The best options for Fardowsi to learn English from me is when we converse together, use books with English words and our PECS visuals." "Ok, thank you," Ami replied. "I miss the toys you bring to my home though. I think I learn a lot watching children play with toys, it helps me learn more English words, too."

Lynn shook Ami's hand as he and Fardowsi left the meeting. She couldn't help but feel as if this meeting led nowhere and nothing was resolved, but she kept hearing positive feedback from Fardowsi and Ami. What does she do now, where does she go from here? She wasn't sure how to restructure home visits to be more successful for Sulekah and her family. They feel as if she is making great progress, she and other staff feel that Sulekah's language has not improved. Everyone is hoping for the same goals but imagine different ways of getting there and don't exactly coincide. Lynn was just . . . stuck. . . .

## QUESTIONS

1. Which DEC practices for the topic area of Instruction did you see supported in this case study?
2. Which of the DEC practices for the topic area of Instruction were not supported in this case study? How might these have been addressed?
3. What factors seem to be contributing to Lynn's concerns?
4. Lynn changes the process of home visits from toy bag play to routines-based interventions. However, Ami expresses during the meeting that he misses having toys around as he learns more English. How might Lynn work with Ami to explain the benefits of RBI?
5. Lynn described feelings of concern that her priorities and Sulekah's family priorities differ and is possible cause for Sulekah not improving her language goals. How could Lynn work collaboratively with the family to address Sulekah's language goals?

## THE NEXT STEP

*Unsolved*

### Background

Since Cayden was born, he has struggled with a seizure disorder and has lost his sight. During Cayden's most recent evaluation, the team determined his cognitive ability to be closely related to a six-month old child. Cayden's mother, Janet, has taken the brunt of caring for him. At home, Cayden is hardly required to roll over to get a toy, and is completely dependent on his mom for eating, drinking his bottle, and moving around.

Katie is embarking on her second year of teaching Early Childhood Special Education (ECSE) and working with Cayden and his family. Cayden is now four years old and is in Maggie's preschool class. While at school, Cayden also works with Ms. Kim, his paraprofessional, Betty, the speech pathologist, and Callie, the occupational therapist. Recently, Katie has had a difficult time creating a balance in instruction while understanding Cayden's comfort level and preferences during learning.

### Dilemma

On Tuesday morning, Ms. Katie was, mentally preparing for the afternoon ahead as she ran into Cayden and his mom in the hallway. "Hi Cayden, it's Katie. How are you doing today?" asks Katie with a nervous grin as she kneels down next to the wheelchair. "Oh, he has had a rough morning. He's had two little seizures, no nap, and refused to eat any of his lunch," Janet replied. "I am sorry to hear that Janet. Is there anything you need us to do here at school?" asks Katie. "Just give me a call if he has any more seizures or gets too upset. I wouldn't have sent him to school today, but I need to get groceries and get Cayden's medication from the pharmacy," Janet replied despairingly. "Of course, Janet. We will take care of him. I'll see you at 2:30, okay?" Katie replied, as she wheeled the crying child into the classroom.

Katie parked the wheelchair and gave Cayden his favorite book to hold in hopes to calm him down. "Hi Cayden, it's Kim. How are you today?" Cayden's paraprofessional asked. "He had a few seizures today, so we should probably take it easy. Can you help me get him to his adapted chair?" asked Katie. Then they began their daily routine of opening Cayden's toy bucket and handing him a variety of toys. Cayden explores by shaking and smelling the toys, putting the toys to his ears, and throwing the toys. Cayden does not signify a preference and screams if a teacher attempts to use hand over hand support with the toys.

Cayden's screams cause the other children to cover their ears and walk away in fear. The preschool teacher, Maggie, grunts in frustration at the reoccurring disruption in her class as she anxiously scrambles to calm the other children and redirect their attention to the learning activities. Maggie can't help but think, *I have a classroom full of children that need my attention, and then we add Cayden to the mix. The poor angel has an inept first year teacher that has no clue what she is doing. I don't have time to train her in and mentor her. I don't understand why the district doesn't provide more support for these newbies. I am so tired of always getting stuck with the new teachers. I don't have time for this and I am over collaborating with new people.*

As the women quickly transferred Cayden and removed him from the classroom, Ms. Katie bleakly mentions, "I just don't know what to do, I feel like I am just not even capable of helping Cayden." Maggie smiles at her and says, "Well, I'd suggest you figure something out. This cannot go on every day and it is your job as his teacher."

## Perspectives

As a newer teacher, Katie felt overwhelmed with the responsibilities of teaching a child with such high needs. Every strategy in her "bag of tricks" seemed either inappropriate or unsuccessful with Cayden. Despite her best efforts, Cayden is still not able to engage in the classroom and is not making any progress on his goals. Feeling incompetent and underqualified for the position as an ECSE teacher, Katie reaches out to her colleagues Betty and Callie for support.

Katie was puzzled, "I am worried Cayden isn't having a meaningful experience at school. What exactly should I be teaching him?" "He's a tough one, he has been since he was a baby," Callie responded doubtfully. "I think we need to change our approach and develop more realistic expectations for Cayden," explained Betty as she looked through her notes. Callie was less hopeful, "I don't know what else we could possibly do with our instruction. We just need to build his trust."

Katie agrees, it is essential to build a relationship and establish bonds with Cayden. But she also thinks Betty is on the right track here. "If Cayden isn't learning or improving, then we need to make changes," Katie exclaimed as she thought about Cayden's current goals. "Maybe we need to take a step back and focus on his ability to explore toys in a functional way? I'd like to see Cayden understand that toys and books serve a greater purpose than how he is currently using them," suggested Betty. Still frustrated,

Callie added "I suppose we can also try building his tolerance and trust in hand over hand support by developing a goal around hand desensitizing."

Katie began feeling a sense of relief as she felt that Cayden's plan was finally coming together. "These are excellent goal ideas ladies; I feel better having a purpose for my instruction with Cayden. Since he is most comfortable laying down with toys, I think I will also start providing my instruction on the ground rather than a chair," Katie proposed. Katie began looking through the Hawaii Early Learning Profile Charts (HELP) to develop a list of skills based on how a 6-month old makes developmental steps to grow in play exploration.

Despite the team's implementation of new instructional strategies, they were still not seeing the expected results after one month. Katie began planning another meeting to go over what they have done so far and what other options they can try to provide Cayden with appropriate instruction.

## QUESTIONS

1. Which DEC practices for the topic area of Instruction did you see supported in this case study?
2. Which of the DEC practices for the topic area of Instruction were not supported in this case study? How might these have been addressed?
3. How might Katie identify Cayden's preferences in order to include more engaging materials into the classroom to promote his exploration?
4. What question might Katie have asked the family prior to Cayden's enrollment both to identify preferred materials and calming strategies to help with his transition?
5. Would a change in Cayden's environment be appropriate in this situation? Why or why not?
6. What does the role of relationship play in instruction?

## GIVING IN IS SO MUCH EASIER

*Unsolved*

### Background

Cole is a three-year-old boy who was referred for global developmental delay. He lives with his mother, Laura, and is seen by his ECSE teacher for home visits.

It is three o'clock on a Tuesday. Just like every Tuesday for the past six weeks. Akira, an ECSE teacher at Cole's school, knocked on the apartment door. No answer. She waited for a few seconds then knocked again.

"Cole! Get the door!" says Cole's mom, Laura. The door opens to reveal a plump, bright-eyed three-year-old wearing only a diaper and what appears to be a chocolate milk moustache.

"Hello Cole. How are you doing today?" asks Akira. Cole smiles and laughs and holds his arms up.

"Can you say 'please?'" Asks Akira.

"Peese!" Shouts Cole enthusiastically.

Akira picks Cole up and stands in the doorway.

"Thank you. How is everything going? Has Cole's behavior improved?"

"Lord, no! If anything, it's gotten worse! It seems like he's getting more and more demanding and fussy. I don't know what to do."

"The last time I was here, we talked about encouraging Cole to use his words, especially when it involves something he really wants, like a snack, or his favorite toy. How has that been going?"

"Not so good. I try to get him to say "please" or to use words to tell me what he wants, but he gets upset and starts screaming and throws himself on the floor and starts kicking, so I just give him what he wants and then he stops. I know I'm not supposed to, but I don't want to fight with him all of the time." Laura sighs, sits on the couch and lights a cigarette. "Sheesh," Laura thought to herself. "What does this woman want from me? It's easy for her to stand there and tell me what I should be doing when she isn't with Cole all day, every day like I am. She probably thinks that I never play with him just because she doesn't see it.

"Ok. Has he had his afternoon snack yet?" Akira asks Laura this because she plans her home visit to coincide with Cole's snack time so that he can practice during a preferred activity that's part of his daily routine.

"No, but he had a late lunch, so I'm not sure if he will be hungry."

"That's ok. We can at least try." says Akira. "Would you like to help me get ready?"

"Sure," says Laura. "What do you want me to do?"

Akira puts Cole down and says "Cole, I am going to help your mom get ready for your snack now, ok?"

"Would you mind showing me what you usually do when it's Cole's snack time?" Asks Akira.

"Well, honestly, most of the time I don't make him sit at the table."

"That's fine, but could we have him sit at the table today?"

"Sure."

"Ok. Before he comes to the table, we want to make sure that we have everything ready. Which two snacks do you usually offer him?"

"I usually offer cake or cookies."

"Since he isn't always at the table, how do you offer him the choices?"

*Geez, lady,* Laura thinks. *How the heck do you think I offer them to him? Like I can't offer him choices unless he's sitting at the table?* Laura really wanted to say something but was afraid that if she did, Akira would not come as often (or at all) and that would not be good for Cole. Cole really seemed to like Akira and Akira was great with Cole. She really got results! And that made Laura happy.

"I hold out a piece of cake and a package of cookies and he takes the one he wants," she says out loud.

Akira asks Laura what she would like to offer Cole today. Laura picks out a package of snack cakes and a package of cookies. Akira asks her to open them up and separate the two cakes and four cookies into two different piles. Akira then asks Laura to ask Cole to come to the table to have a snack. Cole continues playing in the living room and does not respond immediately.

Laura asks Cole again to come to the table for his snack. Cole comes and sits down at the table.

"Cole. We have cookies and cake today" Akira says, pointing to each as she says it. "Which one would you like to have for a snack?"

Cole starts reaching for the cookie pile but it is out of his reach. Cole points and grunts/makes an "mmmmm" noise.

"Can you use your words to tell me what you want?" Prompts Akira.

Cole sits in his chair and stares at the table. After a few seconds, Akira pushes one of the cookies closer to Cole. Cole reaches out for the cookie. Akira asks him again to use his words.

"Coookie!" Cole says.

"Good job, Cole! Thank you for using your words! You can have a cookie."

Cole eats the cookie quickly then grunts and points to the pile with the three remaining cookies.

"Laura. Would you like to try this time?"

"Ok. Cole, can you tell mommy what you want?"

Cole points and says "Coookie!"

Laura pushes the rest of the cookies in front of Cole. While Cole finishes eating, Akira talks about cookies.

"You must really like cookies. I like cookies too. Cookies are really yummy."

Cole finishes his cookies then gets down from his chair and goes to the living room to play. Laura gets up, sits down on the couch and starts watching TV.

## Dilemma

Akira left Cole's house feeling frustrated and irritated. Again. She reminded herself to stay calm and not overreact. She couldn't talk to her mentor if she sounded like an irate teenager. So. What was she really upset about? Cole was an adorable, loving, three-year-old. She was so frustrated with Laura. Laura did not seem as if she was even trying. Laura just didn't seem to care. She only participated/interacted with Cole when Akira prompted her to do so. She kept trying to encourage Laura to participate and Akira tried to set the example by always talking to Cole about what she was doing and describing things to him, but Laura still never did anything unless asked to. It was like pulling teeth.

Laura always seems to have time to smoke and sit and watch TV, yet she can't manage to spend a few minutes a day with her son talking to him and encouraging him to use his words? How hard could it be?

Akira did not feel as if she was expecting too much from Laura or giving her too much responsibility. Didn't Laura want what was best for Cole? Talking with her mentor, Kaneda would help her sort things out.

Akira arrives back at her office. Kaneda isn't there so Akira continues reflection on the session, re-running everything again and again through her head so that she would be able to be as concise and specific as possible when she spoke to Kaneda.

Kaneda arrives and asks Akira how the session went.

## Perspectives

Akira states, "I guess I just get frustrated with Laura. Cole is such a bright child. He is capable of so much yet he gets little or no interaction/stimulation at home. Laura does not seem to care about that fact that Cole is three and still does not really say any words on his own. She doesn't work outside of the home. She doesn't have any other children. All she does is smoke and watch TV. I don't know any cultural norms or religious practices that would prohibit her from doing any of the things that would be helpful to Cole. I know it's wrong of me, but I can't help but feel that Laura is just lazy and doesn't care."

"I'm sure it can be frustrating when you feel like your efforts are not appreciated or are getting any results. But have you ever really tried putting yourself in Laura's position?" asks Kaneda.

"I have tried, but I still can't understand why she can't just play with him for a few minutes every day and why she can't remember to ask him to use his words once in a while. It's not like she doesn't have the time," says Akira.

"Maybe time isn't the issue," says Kaneda.

"I don't understand," says Akira.

"How much do you know about Laura? Does she have any medical conditions that may cause her to be lethargic? Does she have any psychological issues like depression?"

"I'm not sure. But even if she did, as a parent, don't you think that she would do what she had to do to take care of those issues?" asks Akira.

"Yes. But a lot of things are easier said than done. If you're depressed or overly tired, even doing the most simple, basic tasks can seem overwhelming."

"I guess. But I don't think that a few minutes a day is asking too much."

"Maybe not by your standards, but for someone else, a few minutes may seem like a very long time."

"Well, even if she does suffer from a condition that impairs her ability or motivation, that's not something I am able to treat," states Akira.

"True. But it may just help to be aware of the possibility."

"Ok. So, what do I do? Having Laura practice what I do with Cole is essential to helping Cole reach his goals. The hour that I spend with him every week is nothing compared to the time that Laura does. But if I start trying to help Laura, I feel as if I am not focusing on Cole. I have tried to encourage her by stressing how vital she/her assistance is. I can't do it without her help. Do I need to shift my focus and try a strategy that may be easier for Laura to remember? I thought about maybe taking Laura out for coffee or something and just talking with her, but then I wasn't so sure. She doesn't seem to have any friends or anyone to talk to so I'm afraid she might take it the wrong way.

"Well. You know what I always say. "You never know until you try." You're limiting yourself by worrying about all of the 'what ifs?.' You know Laura and Cole better than I do. I think it may be helpful for you to sit down and really think about why you go to Cole's house every week. Laura is an integral team member and the main focus should be meeting the family's priorities. What is your purpose? What are you trying to accomplish? Is anything keeping you from doing your best to achieve it? In some cases, you may be your own worst enemy."

"Well. What would you do?" Asks Akira.

"Like I said. You know them better than I do. I really think that this is something you need to try to problem solve on your own. Try writing down ideas or talking out loud to see if you can get to the root of the problem. How are your views on Laura impacting the ability to meet the needs and priorities of the family? If what you're doing isn't working, you need to find other options."

On the drive home, Akira started thinking about how she should approach the situation and what to do at the next session. She went through a few different scenarios in her head: Should she take a chance and ask Laura and focus on Laura to get to know her better before making any demands of her, should she just spend a few extra minutes at the end of her session with Cole talking to Laura at home, should she skip getting to know Laura better? What was her purpose? Maybe she needed to give Laura more time. Akira knew that she could be impatient sometimes. She decided that she would try to get to know Laura better during her visits and determine the priorities and concerns that she has. This would allow her, hopefully, to be more aware of Laura's situation and it would be done in a neutral location that would prevent any issues concerning boundaries. She would try asking Laura about her interests and ask her to share stories about Cole. She would work with Laura to identify what she sees as the main priorities and needs she sees for Cole. If Laura did not open up and wanted to talk, then Akira would not push her. She would have to find other ways through trial and error. The reason for her doing home visits was for the family. Laura was such a huge part of Cole's life, Akira believes that if Laura were to be more active, it would only be to Cole's benefit.

Akira relaizes now that there might be other reasons that Laura is not as active as she believes Laura should be, but it is not her place to make this judgement. Akira now understands that the only way to make progress is to determine the priorities and concerns for the family and by addressing these then she may likely get more buy in from Laura. She now believes she would be able to find a way to make everything work!

## QUESTIONS

1. Which DEC practices for the topic area of Instruction did you see supported in this case study?
2. Which of the DEC practices for the topic area of Instruction were not supported in this case study? How might these have been addressed?
3. Has Akira been focusing on Laura's goals? How might this be impacting her work with the family?
4. What suggestions do you have for initial contact with families that may lay a foundation for collaboration?
5. What other ways could Kaneda have supported Akira in her role?

## SECTION 2: CASES FOR 3-TO-5-YEAR-OLDS

## Alex's Tornado

*Solved*

### Background

Alex is a four-year old Caucasian boy. He was evaluated at 2 1/2 years old at Mayo Clinic in Rochester, MN where he was diagnosed as a child who is moderately autistic and has a communication delay. He has limited verbal communication with scripted phrases. For the last year, Alex has been attending Rochester Autism Center in Rochester, MN where he had 1:1 Applied Behavior Analysis (ABA) to help him with his aggressive physical behavior and his basic communication needs.

Starting in September 2017, Alex began attending an inclusive preschool classroom at Hoover Elementary School in Rochester. He attended the morning program for 2.5 hours. Within the first two months, Alex began demonstrating signs of anxiety and physical aggressive behaviors in the classroom. When he arrived from riding the bus, he would take a toy out of his bag and start banging the toy around the furniture, on himself, and students. It was as though he was playing scenes from movies or shows in his head, and acting them out with the toys, and in the process, hit other students with his toy. When staff redirected him to put the toy away, he would begin ripping bulletin boards down from the walls, kick at staff, and try to bite them. When asked to participate in group activities, Alex would pace around the room and knock over chairs.

One of the areas Alex enjoys in the classroom is the dramatic play area. Recently, one of the staff members changed the materials in the area, and Alex has had a hard time adjusting to new content. This frustration has led him to bumping into students intentionally, and not allowing anybody play within the area. If the students touch items in the center, Alex will start throwing items across the classroom. Several students have been hit with the items he has thrown.

Due to Alex's aggressive physical behavior, a team meeting was conducted, and Alex has now been placed into an intensive autism homeroom preschool classroom.

### Dilemma

Alex needs to follow set routines and engage in learning throughout the day using appropriate behavior of keeping feet to himself, using appropriate tone of voice, self-regulation, and being kind to his peers through instructional practices.

## Perspectives

Alex's father John says of Alex, "Alex is a great kid! Transitions are difficult, especially for him. I know in my heart, once he's settled into school, behaviors will decrease. It will just take time. I just hope it's before they kick him out of this classroom!"

Alex's mother Jessica says, "I don't know how to help Alex. Maybe Alex isn't ready for Preschool. I knew we should have kept him at the Rochester Autism Center for another year! The ABA was working to reduce his behaviors; now we are moving backwards."

Ms. Lindsey, occupational therapist, and Ms. Carolina, Alex's autism intensive teacher, discuss concerns regarding Alex. Ms. Lindsey expresses her concerns with Alex's behavior and wonders if it could be sensory based or attention based. She expresses that without warning, his behavior will switch from aggressive to calm and attentive. She wonders if there is a sensory diet that will allow or help Alex to reduce his behaviors and allow him to participate in the group.

Ms. Carolina believes that they can, but questions which strategies they should use. She mentions using visuals, such as picture cards to assist him in understanding what is happening. She also wonders if using those pictures in a First/Then format would help him understand when one activity begins and one ends. Ms. Lindsay liked the idea, but wonders if it will potentially overexcite Alex to a point where he won't be able to follow the task demands. Upon pondering their conversation, Ms. Carolina wonders if Alex may not be in the proper setting for his disability. This comes at the tail end of attempting numerous strategies and interventions into Alex's school day, but have been proven unsuccessful. She wonders what she may be missing, and begins to doubt her ability to guide him to success.

While Alex has been in the intensive classroom for three weeks, he is still arriving with his plush toy and banging them on furniture and himself. This excites him more as he paces around the classroom and knocks over things. In Morning Meeting, he will pace back and forth and not sit with his peers. When redirected, he will start kicking furniture or staff and yelling around the room. Alex is beginning to learn expectations of the preschool day by following his individual visual schedule. He will rip up his laminated individual visual picture schedule card each time small group rotations are about to occur. He enjoys center time, but he only engages in solitary play. Furniture is being knocked over two to three times a day when instruction is being presented in group activities. Alex is kicking at staff when redirected in group activities. Alex is yelling towards staff for at least 40 to 50 minutes each day when asked to complete an undesired task. Alex also paces around the room 50% of the day.

A Functional Behavior Assessment (FBA) was conducted prior to Alex moving into the intensive level 3 autism classroom. The evaluation results showed that Alex is anxious during undesired activities, and when given a task demand he will exhibit aggressive behaviors. The FBA suggested creating a break card to assist him in learning to self-regulate and reduce the aggressive behaviors. The assessment included using peer-mediated intervention to teach him how to play with others.

Considering information collected on the FBA, Ms. Carolina created a visual schedule showing where he was supposed to be in the classroom, so as to ease his anxiety and guide him in transitioning to the next activity. This helped the lesson the time he wandered around the class. Adults and staff support redirected him when needed. In addition, a break card was given to Alex. When he needed a break, Alex would hand a break card to staff and then take a sensory break (designed sensory diet activity). Staff initially used hand over hand to assist in handling the card when needing to take a break.

In addition, she used carpet squares with characters that he liked taped to them, to keep him motivated to sit down during Morning Meeting. There were visual reminders of appropriate behavior when sitting and listening. These were near the area so staff could point to expectations when reminders were needed. During the morning meeting each day, Ms. Carolina focused on one expectation, and challenged her students to try and catch each other following them.

Alex came into school overly excited with toys from home. After talking to his family, Ms. Carolina understood that Alex struggles when transitioning from the vehicle to a different destination. His toys from home keep him calm. Ms. Carolina decided to create a social story that illustrated the steps upon arriving at school, and what we do with toys brought from home. She made two laminated copies of this story. She sent one home and coached parents how to use a social story with Alex. Before attending school, Alex's parents read him the social story. Alex had visual reminders on his locker of expectations which included putting his toys and items away. Each morning after he put his toy away, Alex immediately played for 10 minutes before checking his schedule.

While in group, Alex had a duration card which showed what he was working for. This visual helped him understand when an undesired task began and ended. Ms. Carolina allowed Alex to choose a reward, or something he wanted to work for. That choice picture was attached to his duration card. As he worked and stayed on task, staff gave him tokens. After 4 tokens, he earned his choice.

Ms. Carolina also introduced the peer-mediated intervention for Alex when playing in centers. Since Alex was originally in an inclusive classroom, she was able to arrange a few peers from the class to come several times a week. These peers worked with Ms. Carolina to start socially interacting with Alex. They started with the grocery store dramatic play. There were visuals of different roles students could play, as well as grocery lists. After several months, Alex was able to pick a role and interact with these peers to play grocery store. This included putting items in a grocery cart with another peer, putting items on the counter, and having his peers check him out, as if in a real grocery store. Ms. Carolina decided that the next month she was going to add a doctor's office to the center. She kept the grocery store and made a social story for Alex explaining a new center to try. Within the social story she introduced new expectations of this center. After a few weeks of doctor's office, she put away the grocery store center.

After several months of support and instructional reteaching, Alex began to settle into school. He joined group activities 80% of the time without aggressive behaviors. The sensory diet and duration card were working since staff could be flexible of demand duration and reducing anxiety. Alex had learned to put his toy in his locker because he now understood that this was a school rule. Alex began to engage and play with peers from the inclusive and intensive classroom.

## QUESTIONS

1. Which DEC practices for the topic area of Instruction did you see supported in this case study?
2. Which of the DEC practices for the topic area of Instruction were not supported in this case study? How might these have been addressed?
3. What instruction practices were demonstrated to allow Alex to promote his engagement and learning?
4. How did the teacher use peer-mediated interventions to help Alex engage and learn to play with peers within the daily routine?
5. Educators needed to apply multiple levels of support, accommodations, and adaptations to help Alex have access and participate within multiple activities and routines. How was that demonstrated in this case study?
6. As the teacher gathered and used data for her observations and functional behavioral assessment, how did they apply the data to influence instructional practices she used?

# LET'S COUNT

*Solved*

## Background

The child, Liam, is a 3.5-year-old who attends an integrated preschool program, three days per week. Liam is new to preschool this year and was diagnosed on the autism spectrum earlier this year. His Early Childhood Special Education (ECSE) teacher in the classroom is Jennifer. Jennifer's mentor is Joyce. Joyce has been teaching ECSE 3-5-year-olds for 22 years. Jennifer has guided Liam's family through the process of early intervention and she has built a trusting relationship with Liam's mom, Gloria.

## Dilemma

Jennifer is concerned because after weeks of large group instruction Liam is still unable to count to 10 in order. Each morning in their morning meeting the class counts the days of the week on the calendar as they talk about the date. It seems that other students are grasping the counting, but Liam does not consistently count in order. Knowing that the other students are grasping the concept has been feeding into Gloria's concern that Liam is overly forgetful. She has seen him learn things and she thinks he has learned it, and then he forgets it.

## Perspectives

Knowing that the other students are grasping the concept, has been feeding into Gloria's concern that Liam is overly forgetful. At times Gloria thinks to herself that Liam is doing this on purpose, "What is he doing? playing a game with me?" This has led to Gloria getting frustrated with Liam. One day, she arrived to drop off Liam and said to Jennifer, "That's it, I have had it. Everyday Liam and I count the steps leading into school, there are 7. Today as we walked into school Liam counted, 1, 2, 7, 10, 4, 5, 9. I corrected him, and tried again, but this time he said 3,3,3,3,3,3,3." Jennifer let Gloria know that she has had similar experiences with Liam. Jennifer was feeling stumped, she told herself, "Don't over react, or jump to conclusions. It is up to you to reassure Gloria and come up with a plan." Unsure if this was due to a behavior or something else, the two agreed to not react to his miscounting, and to only offer praise when Liam counted in the correct order to reinforce his skill development.

After mom left that morning, Jennifer checked in with the 2 classroom assistants to see what their observations and thoughts were. Laura, an assistant in ECSE for 10 years has spent lots of time with Liam during snack time. "Hey Laura, I was wondering at snack what your observations are of Liam. Does he count his snack regularly when it is passed out?" This was an activity that happened daily in their classroom. Laura thought for a moment and then replied "Honestly, I don't think he has ever counted his snack with me. I'm not sure why I hadn't mentioned it earlier, but Liam just skips that part when I hand out snacks." Jennifer continued consulting with the other adults in the room.

Jennifer checked in with Susan, the general education assistant. Susan works with students during station time and when asked told Jennifer "I am always hand over hand with Liam, helping him with station activities. We do counting together, but I have never had him do it alone." This made Jennifer reflect a little more on what each adult involved was doing and knew she needed to get people on the same page, *What page is that anyways?* she asked herself.

Jennifer continued to feel confused about why this skill is not clicking for Liam. And on a particularly rough day, she thought, "It must be me! What am I doing wrong when working with Liam?" Knowing she should not go down that rabbit hole, she reached out to a mentor to see if she had any recommendations for her. Joyce, has been teaching 3-5-year-olds for 22 years. She has seen many changes to the field of early childhood special education and works hard to help new teachers coming up. After listening to Jennifer vent and explain her problem, Joyce asked her, "What have you tried?" Jennifer gave Joyce a confused look, "I have done everything the way I always do it!" Jennifer stated. Joyce was sure to keep her chuckle to herself, then continued "I have had so many instances where what I am doing to teach works for everyone in the class but one or two. I would get concerned in the past and do assessments and be observed to see what I am doing wrong. One day it clicked that the ones not getting it, or not retaining it, may need more varied experiences to practice that skill. Have you tried embedding the counting into various activities throughout the day?" It was like the light bulb went off in Jennifer's head, she felt thankful for her trusted mentor. "Everyone has times that they get too close to the situation" Joyce reassured her, "and taking a step back and getting a new perspective really helps. I am glad you reached out to me!" Jennifer felt thankful as well.

## Child Behavior

Gloria found that she wanted to say "no" when Liam made mistakes and found it difficult to remain positive. She would say to herself over and over,

"This is the only way to positively change, I must stay positive." She kept at it and kept giving Liam opportunities at home to count. Soon it became second nature to her.

In the classroom Jennifer met with her assistants and the general education teacher. Each day Jennifer had the goal of embedding 5 counting activities into Liam's day and she recruited the others in the room to help her out. Now, rather than counting the calendar the group counts the number of students. Every morning they do a counting activity where each student gets a number and they match it with another student and then repeat the number once it is matched. When passing out snacks, the teacher at the table models counting the number of children at the table, and then the students will count with her.

During choice time, Liam will commonly play with cars. One day, Jennifer put numbers on all the cars. She would work with Liam one on one to repeat the numbers and put them in order. Another time, she put numbers at various points on the car mat and would ask Liam to drive to a specific number. As part of another IEP goal Liam was encouraged to participate in 5 activities each day. For each activity he completed, he received a craft stick. Before leaving for the day, Liam would count his sticks and the teacher would track them on a chart. This was especially helpful because it worked on 2 goals at once and provided a way to track Liam's progress. It was important that they all worked together in order to be sure these interventions were working.

## Final Results

Liam seemed to respond best to active learning activities. When he needed to arrange numbers with his classmates or organize the cars in order, he would often get the numbers correct and after a few weeks started the counting process on his own without even being prompted by teachers. The real sign of success was when Gloria came in during the third week of class, just beaming. "A miracle has happened. This morning when I put out breakfast Liam counted, 1,2,3,4 and said 4 cups mama! All on his own, without any prompting, and then counted 1,2,3,4,5,6,7 up the stairs just now!!" Both Gloria and Jennifer were feeling optimistic that changing how Liam learned numbers had made the difference for him. Moving forward both mom and teacher had learned to try new and varying ways before getting stuck and frustrated. They both felt thankful that they were able to work as a team to identify what needed to change.

# QUESTIONS

1. Which DEC practices for the topic area Instruction did you see supported in this case study?
2. Which of the DEC practices for the topic area of Instruction were not supported in this case study? How might these have been addressed?
3. Embedded learning activities were provided for counting, what additional embedded learning activities could be implemented?
4. What supports could Jennifer offer to Gloria for working with Liam?
5. What could Jennifer learn from this experience and apply for her role as a teacher?

# I WANT

*Unsolved*

## Background

Taylor, a 4-year-old who is on the Autism Spectrum, is a bright and cheerful girl who loves to interact with others. She loves to smile, listen to music, and play outside. Taylor has an older brother, Jacob, who is 7 years-old and loves to play with his little sister. Her parents are Maggie and James, who both work full-time while their children go to school. Taylor's early intervention team consists of a speech-language pathologist (SLP), an occupational therapist (OT), and the early childhood special education teacher (ECSE), Mrs. Gross.

## Dilemma

Taylor's parents love Taylor and want her to succeed. They frequently communicate with teachers and specialists concerning how she is doing at school. However, Maggie and James are unwilling to spend time working on the same goals with Taylor at home. Since they both work with two kids, they tell the early intervention team to "take care of it" whenever an issue arises. They can even become frustrated with the early intervention team when they are recommended to try certain activities outside of school.

Taylor's verbal skills have just started to develop. However, she only uses words at school. Her speech-language pathologist, Mrs. Wyman, says that Taylor can express her needs in two-word phrases 50 percent of the time when she is at school. She has used these two-word phrases at school with her classmates and teachers, but at home they have only seen these skills 15 percent of the time. Taylor's parents have become frustrated with the early intervention team because they feel that they are not doing their jobs.

## Perspectives

As preschool starts on Monday morning, Taylor is prompted by a classroom paraprofessional to sit for circle time. Taylor finds her rocking chair and sits down, smiling and excited to hear songs. Mrs. Gross is sitting in the front of the classroom. She chooses class helpers and Taylor is chosen for music helper. Holding up a choice board to Taylor, Mrs. Gross says,

"I want . . ." and waits for Taylor's response.

She bounces up and down in her chair and picks The Hello Song off the board. Waiting to play the song, Mrs. Gross repeats,

"I . . . want. . . ."

Taylor squeaks out, "I . . . want" while holding up the Hello Song picture.

"Yay! You said, 'I want the hello song!'" The staff are all delighted in Taylor's use of words and give her positive reinforcement. Mrs. Gross plays the song immediately to reinforce that they are pleased with her request.

When James picks up Taylor for school, he approaches Mrs. Gross, curious about Taylor's day. Mrs. Gross excitedly approaches him, reporting,

"Taylor used her words so well today!"

James shrugs. "Well, I haven't seen it for myself. I don't know what you people are doing wrong, because she never talks at home."

Mrs. Gross was taken aback. To keep the conversation positive, she expressed, "well, I'm sorry you feel that way. I've spoken with our speech pathologist Mrs. Wyman, and she says that Taylor's use of words is developing very well during speech time. Would you like to speak with her?"

"I guess. Maybe someone will do their job around here." Without making eye contact, James picks up Taylor and walks out the door. Mrs. Gross was confused and slightly offended, since she felt that they were doing all that they could at school.

The next day at preschool, Mrs. Gross decides to try something new with Taylor. Since her verbal skills are not transferring over to home, she decides to try a task that would be required in her home context. At snack time, normally the students will get a snack and some water. As all the students sit down, she gives the students each a bowl of goldfish and a cup of water. Instead of giving Taylor her snack immediately, she puts it just out of reach so that Taylor is prompted to ask for it. Taylor sits down and looks at her snack, expectant to receive it. The rest of her classmates begin eating as Taylor sits silently. Mrs. Gross says,

"what do you want, Taylor?"

Taylor reaches for her cup and bowl across the table but cannot reach it. She sits back down, and Mrs. Gross says,

"I want snack," prompting Taylor to use her words. After approximately one minute of waiting and multiple prompts, Taylor complies and says,

"want . . . nack." Mrs. Gross and the paraprofessionals respond excitedly and provide positive reinforcement.

Over the next three weeks, Mrs. Gross attempts this strategy and others like it in hopes that Taylor's use of words will transfer over to home. They continue to see success at school, but Maggie and James still report little to no verbal skills developing at home.

On a Wednesday afternoon after school, Mrs. Gross sits at her desk with her head in her hands, frustrated and feeling at a loss. Katie, a preschool teacher in the room next door, walks into chat.

"Tough day?"

"Yeah. I just don't know what to do about some parents I'm dealing with. How do I tell them that the reason their child isn't succeeding is because of their lack of responsibility? I don't feel like that's my place. Yet, I'm getting blamed for it when I've tried everything I can."

"Well, have you told them what they can try at home?"

"They say that they don't have time for that."

Katie looks perplexed. "Have you asked more clarifying questions to see why they don't have time for it? Have you shared exactly what you are doing at school and how this could be generalized at home? What might be going on at home that you aren't aware of that could be impacting their ability to work on this with Taylor?"

Mrs. Gross looked surprised and thought to herself that Katie was out of line. Was she questioning her intentions and what she was doing? "Katie, I am losing it. I don't understand why you are judging me and how I am handling this situation. I am trying to help Taylor and I feel that you are insinuating that I don't know what I am doing. I want Taylor to be successful, can't you see that?"

## QUESTIONS

1. Which DEC practices for the topic area of Instruction did you see supported in this case study?
2. Which of the DEC practices for the topic area of Instruction were not supported in this case study? How might these have been addressed?
3. According to the information provided, how could Mrs. Gross be more effective in working with Taylor's parents?

4. If Mrs. Gross could go back in time, what might be changes she could make in working with James and Maggie?
5. The case ends with Mrs. Gross upset with Katie, what might be Katie's response?
6. What supports or trainings might be needed to assist in this situation?

# Chapter 6

# INTERACTION

## OVERVIEW OF RECOMMENDED PRACTICE

DEC asserts that, ". . . interactional practices are the foundation for promoting the development of a child's language and cognitive and emotional competence. Interactional practices are the basis for fostering all children's learning (DEC, 2014, p.14). These strategies are essential for development in the areas of social-emotional, communication, cognition, and problem-solving.

The major tenets of interaction practices are the importance of observing, interpreting, and responding to the child for development of social-emotional, communication, cognitive, and problem-solving skills. These skills are fostered, developed, and nurtured through child to child and adult to child interactions. It is imperative that children and families are supported in these areas to aid in optimal development.

DEC recommends the following interaction practices for interaction

- **INT1**. Practitioners promote the child's social-emotional development by observing, interpreting, and responding contingently to the range of the child's emotional expressions.
- **INT2**. Practitioners promote the child's social development by encouraging the child to initiate or sustain positive interactions with other children and adults during routines and activities through modeling, teaching, feedback, or other types of guided support.
- **INT3**. Practitioners promote the child's communication development by observing, interpreting, responding contingently, and providing natural consequences for the child's verbal and non-verbal communication and by using language to label and expand on the child's requests, needs, preferences, or interests.

- **INT4**. Practitioners promote the child's cognitive development by observing, interpreting, and responding intentionally to the child's exploration, play, and social activity by joining in and expanding on the child's focus, actions, and intent.
- **INT5**. Practitioners promote the child's problem-solving behavior by observing, interpreting, and scaffolding in response to the child's growing level of autonomy and self-regulation.
(DEC, 2014, p. 14)

The following five cases were designed to represent the recommended practices (RPs) for interaction as a whole. Each case is illustrative of a combination of the five RPs for interaction and does not contain each of the practices. When reviewing the case studies for the RPs for interaction it is advised to use this chapter in the following ways. One, have individuals read each case and answer independently as a way to determine the individual's understanding of interactions and the corresponding practices. Two, have individuals independently read a case study and in small groups discuss what they learned regarding interactions and the corresponding cases. Three, have small groups read case studies and contribute to a whole group discussion as a whole. You can use any and all of these suggestions as it fits with your purposes for the teaching or review of the RPs.

## SECTION 1: CASES FOR BIRTH TO AGE 3

## Patience Running Thin

*Unsolved*

## Background

Bry is a single mother who is twenty years old. She had her son Ty when she was sixteen years old. By the time Ty was two years 7 months old, he had been kicked out of two different childcare centers one of which Bry was an employee. The childcares' reasoning for dismissing Ty from their care was due to aggressive behavior. Ty would scream, hit, kick and bite when he was upset. He would throw toys and knock over furniture. Feeling helpless, Bry spoke to her pediatrician. The doctor recommended a referral to Help Me Grow to see if he would qualify for ECSE services. By Ty's third birthday, he had qualified for ECSE services under the eligibility category of developmental delay. Ty qualified under the developmental areas of communication, fine motor, cognition, social emotional and self-help showing significant delays across multiple domains.

Since Ty had been kicked out of his current childcare, his home school district assisted Bry in finding a new childcare setting for him since mom works every day from 7 am to 5 pm. Ty was placed in an in-home childcare in the hopes of with less children he would be able to be more successful. The childcare provider, Vick, has also worked with young children with delays and special needs in the past. As a part of his placement, Ty also attends an inclusive preschool classroom from 9-11:30 in his home district and then he will be bussed to his in-home childcare program until 5:00 when Bry is done working.

Ty's ECSE teacher, Lana, has had a few months to get to know Ty and Bry and has been working hard to support mom on how to best meet Ty's needs at home. Lana has conducted a Routines Based assessment and used those results to develop a plan for Ty and Bry. Ty has made many great gains in his ECSE classroom but aggressive behavior is still a problem and main concern of Lana's. Lana uses many visuals to help Ty understand what daily routines and expectations are. Ty always needs an adult with him in order to keep other children in the program safe and support his learning and exploration. There have been many team meetings with Lana, the social worker, and Bry discussing how to help Ty stay calm and how to intervene in an appropriate way when he is aggressive with students or staff. The team is consistently collaborating on how to best interact with Ty so he can continue to develop and progress. Lately, Lana feels that she has run into barriers due to how Ty is handled at home. A few weeks ago, Bry reached out to Lana saying she really needed to speak with her about Ty and his in-home childcare situation. Lana, being the case manager and Ty's teacher, has set up a meeting with Bry to discuss her concerns.

**Dilemma**

The meeting, held in Ty's home, began with Bry unloading all her worries and disappointment in Ty's new childcare provider; she shared Vick is threatening to kick Ty out.

"No one except you Lana, can tolerate Ty." "Vick wants me to take parent and child class to learn how to be a better parent!" "I do not have any time for that, I am already working Monday through Friday from 7 am to 5 and do not have time for anything else." "Vick says that he is mean to the other children, that he will try to hit the babies and bite the older children." "At home Ty does get mad but if you just keep him happy and give him what he wants he is fine." Most of the time he watches TV or plays on his tablet and is happy." "Trust me it is better to just give into him because he is going to eventually get his way." I do not have time to deal with tantrums and screaming." "I do not like getting bit, hit and scratched by him. It hurts too much and is too much to deal with." "He falls asleep in front of the TV when he is tired and just eats when he wants to." "I have told Vick over and over again this is the best way to handle him."

As Lana is listening to Bry she is very concerned that Ty does not have any consistency in his interactions with his mother and that there are no established routines or predictability in his day outside of the school's inclusive program. During the meeting and home observation, Lana had noticed Ty does a lot of stimulating behaviors and hardly speaks to Bry or goes to her when he has a problem. Lana is overwhelmed and is not exactly sure how to approach Bry's concerns.

Lana continued to listen to Bry as she expressed and unloaded her frustrations with childcare. At this time, Lana thought it would be best to listen and then try to speak to Bry about different strategies that are used at school to interact with Ty or thought maybe a natural scenario would occur where she could model how to deal with difficult interactions with Ty.

Over the course of the meeting Ty replayed the Magic School Bus song on his tablet over and over again. Anytime anyone tried to touch his tablet or take it away he would scream and hit. One time Bry tried to change his diaper but he refused even though Bry said he is soaking wet and there was a brown spot appearing. She appeared to Lana very frustrated but she said, "I will just wait for him to rip it off because that is what he normally does." Lana thought she would take this as an opportunity to show Bry how these types of situations are handled at school. Lana told Bry that often at school the staff will work to promote all children's social-emotional development by interpreting, and responding contingently to the range of the child's emotional expressions. She asked Bry if she would be willing to walk through how this would be handled at school? Lana pulled pictures from her bag to show Ty a picture of the bathroom. She stated, first diaper then more tablet. Ty screamed in Lana's face and tried to hit her. Lana then demonstrated using simple language to label Ty's emotions. "You are mad. You can be mad but time to change," all while pointing to the diaper picture promoting the child's communication development by using language to label and expand on the child's requests, needs, preferences, or interests. Ty again screamed and fell on the ground as he threw his tablet. Lana turned to pick up the tablet and said, "I will wait." Lana turned to Bry and said "this is what we see at school and now we will just wait him out and see what happens, but I think it is important to follow through with situations like this so he can learn. One strategy we use at school involves working on simple first, then phrases with pictures like these."

Bry in an understanding but frustrated tone said "but now he is mad and he almost hit you." Lana explained that it is okay. She has been hit before and there is nothing for her to worry about. Ty continued to tantrum for about 5 minutes, he ran at Lana who was holding that tablet and hit her.

Lana said, "Ouch that hurts, you are mad but no hit." Ty then sat down on the ground and then started screaming for about one minute. He then sat silently. Lana took the opportunity to show him the picture of the diaper by just pointing to it while saying nothing. Ty then got up and reached for the tablet. Lana again stated first diaper then tablet. As Lana patted the floor, Ty laid down. Bry quickly fetched a clean diaper as Lana started to sing the Magic School Bus song as she changed Ty.

Once they were done, she gave the tablet back to him. As Ty ran to his room with a fresh diaper and his tablet, Bry turned to Lana and said, "I can't stay as calm as you. It is just easier for me to wait for him to throw the diaper off. What if he does not calm down like that for me?" "When I tell him no, he bites me." Lana responded by telling Bry that parents and educators need to interact with children in a way that builds upon their development (communication, social emotional, self-help and problem-solving skills) using strategies consistently. Lana emphasized Ty is not learning anything when he is always getting his way and running on his own agenda. She further stated, "Children need structure and routines so they can predict what is going to happen." Lana then showed Bry some videos on how they play and interact with Ty at school where teachers balance interactions with Ty by directing the play and then by following his lead and how they work really hard to promote Ty's cognitive play skills through observing, interpreting, and responding intentionally to his exploration, play, and social activity by joining in and expanding on the his actions and intent.

After watching some short videos on Lana's iPad, Bry stated that Lana is the teacher and it is her job to do that and that she does not have the time or energy to work with Ty that way nor does she know how. Lana reinforced she can help her and they can work together to find a way that works well for her and Ty, as mother and son. Bry seemed hesitant, but said she would like to meet with Lana again. She mentioned that she likes the way Ty keeps himself busy with TV and his tablet, and she is too tired at night to deal with his tantrums. She voiced that she wants Lana to just "fix him." With that the meeting had to end. Bry had an appointment she had to get to. Prior to leaving, Lana asked Bry if she would sign a release stating she is able to contact and speak with Ty's day care provider Vick about some of Ty's behavior.

As Lana was leaving, she was able to hear the battle occurring between Ty and Bry as she was trying to get Ty to transition from home to the car so they could leave for an appointment.

## Perspectives

Lana left feeling frustrated and not sure what to do next. She thought that modeling how to interact with Ty would help mom see he has the ability to follow through and needs to learn how to cope, so he does not always get his way. Lana strongly feels that by using visual supports, simple language, and by following Ty's lead and expanding his play he is able to grow. She is having a hard time understanding why Bry does not want things to get better, and is having trouble understanding how she is happy with the way things are?

Bry drove the car to her appointment with Ty screaming in the back. She felt frustrated and incompetent. She kept trying to understand why Lana wants her to pick fights with Ty, why not just keep the peace? She hates having bite marks and bruises on her body that she has to try to hide from friends and family. Bry just kept thinking that it is the educator's job to fix her child and make him cooperate. Bry believes she is too busy and tired keeping Ty fed and clothed to take on more tasks. She is twenty years old and raising her child all alone, and most of the time it feels like her child does not like or want anything to do with her.

## QUESTIONS

1. Which DEC practices for the topic area of Interaction did you see supported in this case study?
2. Which of the DEC practices for the topic area of Interaction were not supported in this case study? How might these have been addressed?
3. How might including the behavior support specialist, Kay, support Lana in implementing the RPs?
4. As an ECSE teacher, how might you meet the multiple demands of hone and childcare to support the RPs?
5. What resources do you think could be provided by the social worker to support Bry?

## NEW BABIES

*Unsolved*

### Background

Aria is a two-year-old little girl who lives in a rural town in Minnesota and receives Early Childhood Intervention (ECI) services. She lives with her mother and father, and just welcomed two twin siblings, Ellie and Mikey. Aria has been very loving with the twins but does not understand that she is not the only child anymore. Currently, parents are struggling balancing their time between all three kids and life's obstacles that keep getting thrown their way. The early intervention team visits their house twice a week as Aria has been receiving early intervention services. The team consists of Denise, the physical therapist for the twins, Jenny the school social worker, Katie the early intervention teacher, and Nicole the Head Start Teacher.

## Dilemma

Katie, the early intervention teacher walks up to the home and hears Aria screaming. She knocks, with no response.

"Hello?" as Katie walks in the door.

"Hi Katie" Ashley the mom replies.

"I heard Aria screaming form outside, what's going on?"

"Aria started randomly screaming when she wants our attention, actually she just wants to scream all day, it's getting old" Ashley stated.

Aria is in early intervention services because she has difficulties using her words. The early intervention team have been coaching the parents to have Aria try and use words, rather than just giving in to her right away. She was saying more words and had more interactions prior to the twins being born 6 months ago.

"When she is screaming, what are some things that you have done to communicate with Aria?" I know we have talked about redirection, does that ever work?"

"We just keep asking what's wrong and give her suggestions on what we think she wants, but it only makes it worse. She throws her body to the ground and we get very worried when she hits her head."

## Perspectives

As the early interventionist, we have passed several ideas onto the family as to working with Aria on communication. We have talked about giving her choices, redirection, and simplifying language. With so many options and never any follow through on the part of the parents, this can be frustrating as an early intervention teacher. Often, Nicole the Head Start teacher talks about her lessons that she brings for the family, and she also voices that the follow through is minimal at home. Nicole tells the team that her focus on visits has been supporting the family during the financial crisis the family has been in after having the twins.

Katie sits on the floor playing blocks with the twins, Ellie and Mikey, and Aria sits near us watching. Aria then brings over a block to Ellie. Ellie starts clapping the blocks together.

"Aria! I love how you shared you block" Katie says to Aria with excitement.

"Mom, Dad did you see how Aria was sharing?"

"That is so nice, Aria. See how Ellie likes you sharing? She is clapping the blocks together because she is happy."

Ashley comments to Aria how she likes her sharing. Katie immediately talks through the situation with parents.

"Ashley, when you complimented Aria on sharing, her face lit up!"

"I bet that made Aria feel joyful, she will want to share again because she saw that made you proud." Katie says to parents

"It's easy when you guys are here because there are so many people paying attention to Aria and it's easier for her to get that one on one time to work on language," Dad reports.

"What are some ways that we could work on communication and give Aria that one on one attention?" Katie asks.

Ashley stated, "We've done everything, and nothing seems to work."

Katie followed up with the question, "In the last week, what were some activities that you did with Aria, with just her? I know this can be tricky with three kids and two adults, but it seems that Aria is seeking a lot of your attention and some of the acting out may be because she is not getting the attention she needs."

## QUESTIONS

1. Which DEC practices for the topic area of Interaction did you see supported in this case study?
2. Which of the DEC practices for the topic area of Interaction were not supported in this case study? How might these have been addressed?
3. What are some ways that Aria's parents can incoporate language development into their naturally occurring routine?
4. How can Katie coach the parents to address Aria's behaviors while they are happening?
5. What are some redirection techniques the parents can try?
6. What else might the early intervention team do to support the family?
7. What DEC Recommended Practices might need to be examined to assist in solving this case and why?

## PARENTING A CHILD WITH SPECIAL NEEDS
## WHILE HAVING SPECIAL NEEDS

*Unsolved*

### Background

Vicki rings the apartment buzzer and waits for the clicking sound signaling her to enter. No click. She waits a minute and buzzes again. No click. After 2 minutes pass, she digs in her bag for her cell phone and calls Katie. A crackly voice on the other line answers, "Hello?"

"Hi Katie, it's Vicki, I'm here for our visit."

Katie yells, "Oh no! I forgot!" Vicki asks if it will still work for this week or if she needs to reschedule. Michael is 2 years, 6 months and will be going to preschool in the Fall. Katie, Michael's mom, has a chromosome deletion that causes many developmental disabilities. When Michael was born, the hospital would not release mom and baby until public health, the school district and social services were in place. The school district conducted an evaluation soon after Michael's birth, qualifying him for special education services. Vicki, an Early Childhood Special Education teacher, started home visiting when Michael was 3 months old.

Vicki rubs her shoulders, hoping to release some tension as she walks down the hall to Katie's apartment. Once inside, Vicki is greeted by Michael in an overflowing diaper. Katie exclaims, "I was sleeping so I have to get dressed," and leaves the room. Michael begins grabbing at Vicki's bag and whining. His speech consists of a lot of grunts and whines with very few words.

Vicki models, "Oh Michael, I see that you are excited to play today. Let's go to the living room and wait for mom." Katie currently lives in an apartment with Michael's dad, Dale. Dale also has some developmental delays and has a hard time holding down a job. Dale is often home sleeping during home visits as he stays up late each night playing video games. This causes Katie to be "on edge" during many visits.

### Perspectives

Although Michael is typically pretty cooperative for Vicki during home visits, he does not take direction well from his mom or dad. Michael does not have a lot of functional language; he has a limited vocabulary of 20 words and most are expressed as approximations of words. Michael presently uses gestures to point to wants and needs. He will tantrum, run away, and often throw things at them. The professionals that are in the home weekly, continue to work on finding ways for Michael to effectively communicate.

The team feels that there are several factors that contribute to these behavior problems including a lack of consistency in parenting, lack of sleep due to no sleep routine, and overall frustration. Vicki continues to try to help Katie see the connection between her actions and his behaviors. Katie often blames Michael and says, "He is just a bad kid!"

## Dilemma

Vicki struggles with this visit on many levels. Aside from helping the family meet their basic needs, Vicki is attempting to help Katie make the connection between her parenting and Michael's development. She knows that using sensitive and responsive interaction is the foundation for promoting Michael's cognitive, language, and social emotional development. However, working with Katie and getting her to understand these strategies and their importance has been a challenge. Katie presents with developmental delays and has an IQ of 65, putting her well below the average intelligence range. Her inability to understand basic care and development is a challenge to all who work with the family. She inconsistently reacts to Michael and because of this, Michael always seeks her attention in negative ways.

Katie returns to the living room and starts telling Vicki about her night, "Dale was up all night playing video games so Michael did not want to stay in bed." Vicki responds, "That sounds really tough, bedtime can be one of the most difficult things about being a Mama. I remember how tough it got with my youngest, he fought it so hard. Have you been able to use the bedtime routine schedule that I brought out last time?" Katie tells her that she tried it one night but it did not work so she threw it in the kitchen drawer. Vicki gently says, "Remember Katie, we talked about needing to give it some time before he would understand it and want to follow it. Would you be willing to get the schedule so we can look at the parts he struggled with and think together about ways it might be easier for you?" Katie rolls her eyes and goes into the kitchen to find the schedule. Vicki reminds her that the goal is to get bedtime to be a positive experience and in the process a bonding interaction between Michael and herself. They discuss where the schedule got hard and Vicki gives her some feedback on how to overcome the obstacles. Vicki praises Katie saying, "I'm proud of you for giving it a try. I know parenting is very hard. Let's keep working on it and see if we can make bedtime a more enjoyable experience for everyone. By getting Michael to bed, it gives you some time to unwind and maybe spend with Dale." Katie complains, "I doubt that! He only wants to play his games and feed his lizards!"

Vicki has been especially concerned with getting Katie to interact with Michael in a positive way because she is worried that there has been little attachment and bonding between mother and child. She knows that encouraging positive interactions between children and adults during routine activities will promote positive social development. She attempts to incorporate this into Michael's daily routines and activities through modeling, descriptive feedback and direct instruction to Katie.

"I brought out some new playdough for you today Michael!" Michael runs to Vicki and starts grabbing in her bag. Vicki asks Katie's permission to use the playdough on the floor with a tablecloth that she brought. Katie hesitantly agrees but yells, "Michael you better not get any on the floor!" Vicki replies with a smile, "We will be very careful, and if someone gets on the floor, we will just pick it up won't we Michael?" Vicki reminds Michael that he needs to sit down and wait while she gets things out of her bag. Michael sits in school style and smiles. "Oh, nice job waiting Michael! Katie, do you see the great job that Michael is doing?" Katie looks up from her phone and angrily says, "He never listens to me like that!" Secretly she wonders why Vicki is so excited about him sitting down. When Michael is having a hard time opening a playdough container, Vicki suggests that he brings it to mom and says, "help" Michael does and Katie opens the container. Vicki praises Katie telling her that Michael really looks up to her and likes playing with her. She continues this kind of dialogue and invites Katie to join them on the floor.

While they interact with Michael on the floor, Vicki begins to follow Michael's lead, making several balls of playdough and placing them on top of one another. Vicki models language, "Oh we are building snowmen. Brrrrr, is your snow cold Michael?"

Michael laughs and says, "NO!!" She then asks if she can please have some of his blue playdough. Michael hands her the playdough and she said, "Thank you for sharing!" Vicki explains to Katie that talking with and playing (interacting) with Michael helps him to expand his vocabulary and focus. She goes on to explain that it helps him to practice his social skills.

Katie does not look up or acknowledge Vicki. Although in her head she is thinking, *What do you know about parenting, you just always tell me what to do?* Katie wonders if Vicki has any idea how hard it is to parent a child like Michael. She thinks of the fancy car that Vicki drives and feels a warm feeling of anger wash over her. She thinks, *How can this lady tell me what to do when she has no idea what it is like to raise a baby on your own with no money, no friends and a stupid boyfriend,* She says nothing aloud, but suddenly feels sad and does not want to talk to Vicki. She continues to look down, making "snakes" with her playdough.

Internally Vicki thinks, *If only this little boy was born to a different family. I wonder how his life would be different?* Vicki and the team that works with Katie and Michael often wonder how long Katie will be allowed to parent. Katie does not mean malice, but lacks the functional skills necessary to raise a child. The team strategically plans their visits so that a professional is in the home at least 2 times per week. Many worry about what will happen to Michael if they are not checking in on the family weekly.

Besides Early Intervention, the family receives several services due to Katie's special needs including Public Health, Early Childhood Family Education home visiting, and Nystrom's counseling. Katie has a rep payee to manage her money and guardian ad litem for when child protection has been involved. Although child protection has been involved, there has not been enough evidence to remove Michael from the home. Michael also receives outside speech and physical therapy services as well as specialty doctor visits including an allergist, a feeding specialist and an ENT.

Vicki knows that she walks a fine line with Katie because Katie could stop letting her in for visits at any time. This makes Vicki fearful that it would be one less person checking in on Michael and trying to assist the family. This stems from Katie's past history of leaving doctors and professionals when she did not like the answers or suggestions that they gave her. Vicki and the team feel at a complete loss of how to provide the services that Michael desperately needs. They wonder if they should continue to try and get Katie on board, or if they just use their time at the home giving Michael direct instruction.

## QUESTIONS

1. Which DEC practices for the topic area of Interaction did you see supported in this case study?
2. Which of the DEC practices for the topic area of Interaction were not supported in this case study? How might these have been addressed?
3. Vicki wonders if the home visits are helping Katie meet Michael's needs; how can she determine if Katie's assessment of the home visits?
4. Vicki wonders if the team is addressing the holistic needs of the family; how can she determine Katie's assessment of the team's support?
5. Vicki and Katie have identified different priorities for Michael; how should the team move forward when this occurs?
6. Some team members have concern for the well-being of Michael; what other professionals could be included on the team to assist with this concern?

## SECTION 2: CASES FOR 3-TO-5-YEAR-OLDS

# The Distant Child

*Solved*

## Background

John is a 3 1/2 year old boy who is attending his first year of preschool at his local Head Start program four days per week. He lives at home with his mother, Jackie, and two siblings, a brother in 9th grade and a 3-month old baby sister. John is exposed to two languages, but his primary language is English. In his classroom there are 15 other students, the teacher (Ms. Jamie), and one paraprofessional (Ms. Rachel). This is Ms. Jamie's first year teaching Head Start and Ms. Rachel's fifteenth year as a paraprofessional. The transition from home to a school setting has been stressful for both John and his mother. This is John's first school experience and, so far, has been a negative one.

## Dilemma

John resists separating from his mother every morning resulting in behaviors of crying, screaming, and chasing after her as she leaves. Jackie becomes frustrated with the intense crying and promises John he will get a new toy if he stops crying. Sometimes this works and he will stop crying. Sometimes it doesn't, and he will cry at the door for 15-20 minutes after his mother leaves. At school, John seems very anxious and tends to isolate himself. John does not engage in appropriate social communication, is rigid and has difficulty adjusting to routines and changes. John also demonstrates limited interest in others, primarily in a group setting. He does not initiate or respond to social interaction with his peers or adults. Since John refuses interaction, it is very difficult to give him the assistance he needs in order to move through the daily classroom routines such as dressing, eating (which he refuses to do at school), and clean up. Whenever an adult or peer approaches him, John runs and hides in the corner or turns his back away from them. John refuses to participate in classroom routines such as circle time, meal time, small group, and gym. When his teacher tries to include him in the classroom activities he will scream, cry, yell, and hide his face.

## Perspectives

John's teacher, Ms. Jamie, feels overwhelmed with the intensity and duration of John's behaviors upon separating from his mother in the morning as well as his isolating behaviors during the school day. "He's done this every day since the beginning. I have tried to build a relationship with him but it is very difficult when he always moves away from me. I don't know what to do except just give him his space at this point." Ms. Jamie has talked to Jackie about how John doesn't participate at school. "John's mother said that her older son had problems with school too and he just kind of grew out of it. I would like to be able to talk to her about the importance of John having positive early school experiences." Ms. Jamie wonders if Jackie has ever consulted with anyone outside of school to help John, such as his doctor or a therapist.

Ms. Rachel, the classroom paraprofessional, thinks that more needs to be done to help John and the teacher build a trusting relationship. "Ms. Jamie is stressed and doesn't know how to get John to interact with the class. She has tried many times to help him but he refuses. I feel bad for her and John. The only time that John isn't isolated is during free play and even then, he still takes toys to a corner and plays by himself." Ms. Rachel said she would like to build a relationship with John, and thinks she probably could if she had the time. "I work with another student in the class who has an IEP and needs full assistance with almost everything. There are not many opportunities in the day for me to try to get to know John. The few chances that I have had, when I walked towards him, he ran and hid under the Lego table."

John's mother, Jackie says that John has always been shy and he has never liked being away from home. "John just takes a while to warm up to new things and new people." Jackie is confused as to why John has started to have such intense trouble in separating from her since he started school. "At home if I go into the kitchen, he has to come with me. He refuses to sleep in his own bed and has nightmares now." Jackie wants the morning tantrums to end and then she thinks he will open up more at school.

## Final Results

Ms. Jamie consulted with the learning coordinator and they decided to propose a special education evaluation. Jackie agreed to have John assessed and observed by the school district's early childhood special education team. They came to Head Start in order to assess and observe John in his natural setting (the place he spends much of his day). After the team completed their assessment and observations, they met with Jackie to review the results of the evaluation and to let her know that John did qualify for special education services. There was a recommendation to write an individualized education plan for John.

## QUESTIONS

1. Which DEC practices for the topic area of Interaction did you see supported in this case study?
2. Which of the DEC practices for the topic area of Interaction were not supported in this case study? How might these have been addressed?
3. What changes should the teacher and paraprofessional make to the way they currently respond to John's behavior (specifically, when he separates from his mother in the morning and when he hides?
4. How will staff encourage John's participation in classroom activities, routines, and social interactions with peers?
5. How will staff support John's ability to communicate his own requests, needs, preferences and interests?
6. How can staff members support John's cognitive skills while he is engaging in solitary play? What is the next step in supporting John to expand his play to include other children?
7. What strategies and interventions can be used to support John's ability to regulate his emotions and solve problems?

## DAILY DILEMMAS OF A NEW TEACHER

*Unsolved*

### Background

Emily is a new teacher teaching in an inclusive pre-kindergarten classroom with eight general education students and eight students with Individual Education Plans (IEP). She has a co-teacher, Hannah, with almost 10 years of preschool teaching experience as well as an experienced Educational Assistant. The needs of her students seem vast and varied. One student, Taylor, is new to a school environment and has not been around children. He is expected to go to Kindergarten next year, but has not been exposed to letter or number concepts nor to his peers. Taylor's parents have expressed their concern for his social emotional development and worry that he will be too far behind to catch up. They feel he has many needs in all areas including cognitive, social emotional, and language skills.

Emily decides to set up a meeting time with Hannah in between classes to help her get to know their students. Emily makes an IEP at a glance sheet for each student. The two co-teachers sit down to discuss each individual student's needs, accommodations, modifications, and so forth.

Emily would like to use a "I Need . . ." visual strip for Taylor and other students that are not using words to communicate their needs in an appropriate way. Emily states, "I know that fostering their language can help create better interactions between the student and their peers and teachers." Emily shows Hannah a visual example of the I Need strip and explains that this is a support she will fade over time. Hannah seems to be on board with this accommodation. Emily continues to list accommodations such as facilitated play and social stories. Emily leaves the conversation feeling that they are on the same page and would both like to implement these strategies for their students.

Four months later, Taylor is doing well with some of the accommodations Emily and Hannah have put in place, but others have not been working at all. Emily feels that not enough progress has been made with Taylor and it is almost Winter Break. The good news is that Taylor's "I Need" visual strip is not used very often anymore as he has generalized using, I Need statements to verbally communicate what he needs across environments. His language skills have really come a long way since September and Emily only sees them improving more with time. However, she is most concerned about his social-emotional skills. She worries that his interactions with peers are limited and often inappropriate. Currently, Taylor is not wanting to engage with peers, and when they come to join him in play, he typically yells, throws the toys and/or hits the other child. Emily and Hannah have been trying to use facilitated play, but Taylor gets upset and runs to hide under a table instead. Emily's next thought was to try using social stories with Taylor. She made some specifically for him and added pictures she thought he would like. He was very interested in sitting down with Emily the first few times they read the story but lately he has been refusing to read any and will run and hide when Emily brings them out. She knows that she needs to find another approach but isn't sure where to go from here. She decides to talk with her instructional coach, Kelly, for some feedback and as a result decides to incorporate The Zones of Regulation social emotional curriculum suggested by Kelly. Emily and Hannah decide that Emily will teach a social emotional lesson during their station rotation time.

## Dilemma

Hannah, a general education teacher, has made remarks that she doesn't know how to teach special education students and hopefully Emily can help teach her throughout the school year. This leaves Emily to wonder if it is her responsibility to teach Hannah how to work with their students.

Another dilemma within this case is finding curriculum and resources to support social emotional needs for Taylor as well as his Pre-Kindergarten peers. The Zones of Regulation curriculum is taught at too high of a level to support his and others' cognitive needs and therefore Taylors' social emotional development is not growing as expected. With 4 months left in the school year, Emily feels that she is running out of time with Taylor and other students like him who have yet to be progressing in their positive interactions with peers and adults.

## Perspectives

Hannah is reluctant to accept the child's accommodations. Hannah thinks, *If we let Taylor have a choice board, won't we be giving in to his negative behavior and showing the other kids that we will reward them for this bad behavior, too?* Emily believes, *The choice board is being used as a preventative strategy, giving Taylor a choice between pre-selected educational and positive choices. It also gives him a sense of independence. As we keep working with him this year, this is a support we can fade. At this point, this is a way to prevent him trying to escape the room when he must do too many non-preferred tasks in a row. We also have to remember that he is new to a school setting and he may require some adjustment time with so many transitions in a day.*

## QUESTIONS

1. Which DEC practices for the topic area of Interaction did you see supported in this case study?
2. Which of the DEC practices for the topic area of Interaction were not supported in this case study? How might these have been addressed?
3. How can Emily facilitate collaboration with Hannah to eliminate the division of "her students" and "Emily's students"?
4. How can Emily support Hannah in her interactions with their students?
5. How else could Emily incorporate the students in her classroom as peer models for social emotional development?
6. How can Emily improve the interactions among her students to build social emotional skills?

## CONCERNING SOCIAL INTERACTIONS IN A SMALL TOWN

*Unsolved*

## Background

It was a chilly, yet sunny fall day the day after Labor Day in the small town of International Falls, Minnesota. Marc, the new early childhood special education (ECSE) para was eager for his first day. He had been taking classes online since the previous fall to obtain an ECSE licensure. He had previously worked in a before- and after- school program but did not have much experience working in a school setting or with preschool children. He was ecstatic to get some classroom experience before he began student teaching. He was hoping to see the evidence-based practices he was continuing to learn about from his classes in a real-life context. He got in his car and arrived at the International Falls Head Start ten minute later.

"Hello Marc, it's great to see you again! Are you excited to start the school year?" Miss Anna said, the ECSE teacher who had been with the International Falls Public Schools for the past 18 years.

"I am extremely excited," responded Marc, who had not worked the last month since returning to International Falls from Fargo, ND.

"Great! I will introduce you to the rest of the staff," Miss Anna says with a smile on her face.

"Good Morning, Beryl. This is Marc. He is the new special ed para. He will be working with George this year. Marc, this is Beryl, one of the assistant teachers in Miss Michelle's classroom.

"Nice to meet you, Marc," exclaims Beryl, a woman in her late-fifties, who looked much older due to her habit of smoking.

"Nice to meet you, Beryl, replies Marc.

Miss Anna also introduces Marc to Miss Kathy, the other assistant teacher, and Miss Michelle, the lead teacher. Miss Kathy is a tall woman in her early-fifties and Miss Michelle is a heavy-set woman in her mid-twenties. This is Miss Michelle's second year teaching and her first-year teaching preschool.

Amy introduces Marc to George, the student he will be working with for the year. George is a three-year-old boy with Down Syndrome. He knows how to say about ten words. He is a child who loves people and likes to say "hi," to everyone he meets.

Marc meets the other children as well. Some of the children are excited to be at school, barely noticing their parents tell them "goodbye," as they are already engaged in play. Other children have a hard time saying goodbye to their parents as they cry and beg their parents to stay.

Most of the children start to feel comfortable at school as they eat lunch, sing songs, play on the playground and with toys inside. George smiles and laughs throughout the day. Marc thinks that he is building a positive rapport with George and his coworkers seem nice and friendly. Marc is excited about the rest of the school year and can't wait to tell family and friends about his first day.

## Dilemma

Throughout the week, Marc notices that the assistant teachers seem to always be taking notes. The assistant teachers take notes on the children at circle time, and table time, and even Ms. Michelle often takes notes on the children at play time. Marc thinks that the teachers' constant note taking interferes with building relationships with the children. He also learned in his classes that assessing every activity a student completes can have negative consequences for children. He decides to ask Miss Amy why the teachers take constant notes on nearly everything the children do. "It seems that the teachers are taking notes on nearly everything the children do. Is there a reason they take so many notes?" Marc asks Miss Amy.

"The State requires that Head Start programs provide examples of children completing several objectives. The teachers also have to enter the notes they take into a computer program," replies Miss Anna.

"It seems a little overdone and that time could be better spent playing and interacting with the kids," responds Marc.

"I agree, and Beryl is getting burnt out from all the note taking but it is a state requirement and there is nothing we can do about it," Miss Anna says in a matter-of-fact tone.

Marc is saddened by the conversation but doesn't feel he can do much about a state requirement. As the school year continues, Marc becomes more concerned about the note taking and assessment process. Miss Beryl would often tell the students that they were being tested and that she would be taking notes on their performance. "We are testing how many letters you can name, and I will be taking notes on how well you do, so do the best you can," Miss Beryl informs her small group of students one November morning.

Marc feels uncomfortable hearing this as it doesn't seem to be in line with the evidence-based strategies he has been learning about in his classes. Should I say something?" Well, it would be inappropriate to say something in front of the children, but should I say something in private," he wonders. I don't want to step on any toes and besides I have only been working here for a few months and she has been working here for years, he concludes.

Later, the teachers decide to test the children's kicking and throwing skills. Miss Beryl rolls the ball to Emma, an athletic five-year-old girl, steps up and kicks the ball confidently. "That was high," Miss Beryl tells Miss Kathy in a voice loud enough for the entire class to hear, referring to Emma's kicking skill level. "It was," responds Miss Kathy from half across the room. "She is such an athletic girl."

Next, Miss Beryl rolls the ball to Lakeisha, a shy four-year-old girl who just joined the class a week before after other students were dropped from the program. Lakeisha nervously tries to touch the ball with her foot, but completely misses the ball. "Let's try this again, Lakeisha, Miss Beryl commands. "Okay," Lakeisha responds in a quiet voice looking down at the floor. Miss Beryl rolls the ball to Lakeisha one more time and Lakiesha just barely touches the ball with her foot. "She is very low," Miss Beryl tells Miss Kathy who is still halfway across the room. "Yes, she is. I don't think her parents do very much with her," responds Miss Kathy.

Marc is busy trying to keep George preoccupied, as the students in the class are expected to wait quietly in line until all 18 of them have finished kicking and throwing two times through the line. He is shocked by the conversation they are having in front of the children and are hoping the children are not paying attention to it. He looks at Miss Michelle for any clue on how she feels about the situation, but she is busy reprimanding two of the students for tickling each other. He is contemplating talking to Miss Beryl or Miss Kathy about their conversation but doesn't like confrontation and doesn't know what to say. He decides to talk to his mom about it when he gets home.

When Marc gets home he tells his mom, Darla, about the situation. "Mom, what do you think I should do? Should I talk to them about it?" Marc asks."It's just a temporary job. Getting involved might cause problems and they have been there longer than you, so if it came down to it, you would lose your job before them. I think you should just lay low and do your job. This is just a temporary job for a year before you student teach next year and if it came down to it and they teamed up to get you fired, it would look horrible when you try to find teaching jobs," Darla replies.

Marc thinks his mom is being a bit dramatic, but also thinks his mom has a point. I don't want to make my work environment miserable; he thinks to himself. I will just keep quiet. Marc was thoroughly enjoying the semester. He was learning a lot of new information and teaching strategies. Over halfway through the semester his professor, Dr. Funk, said something that surprised him: "Making kids apologize when they are not nice to their friends is more harmful than helpful. Often, the apology is insincere, and it teaches children that they can get away with anything if they just say sorry afterwards."

Marc had made many children apologize throughout his short time working with children, but what Dr. Funk said made sense to him. He decided that he would try to never force the children he was working with to say they're sorry again.

The next day Andrew hit Evan because Evan took the firetruck Andrew was playing with. Miss Beryl runs over to Andrew and says, with an angry tone of voice, "Andrew we do not hit our friends at school. You need to sit out for a minute. Then, after the minute is up, you need to say you're sorry before you can play again. Do you understand?"

"But he took my toy!" exclaims Andrew.

"I don't care," Miss Beryl responds. "You need to apologize. Do you understand?"

"I guess so," Andrew replies, folding his arms.

When the minute is up, Miss Beryl brings Evan over and asks Andrew, "Is there anything you would like to say to Evan?"

"No!" exclaims Andrew.

"Remember that you will not get to play until you apologize," Miss Beryl reminds him.

"Sorry," Andrew replies with an insincere tone of voice, while rolling his eyes and folding his arms.

"You can go play now," Miss Beryl replies.

## Perspectives

Marc sees the situation go down and thinks about what he learned from Dr. Funk the night before. He doesn't want to step on any toes but thinks that if he explains what he learned from his professor in a polite voice, maybe it will make a positive change in the classroom. He decides to talk to Miss Beryl privately.

Later that day, Marc finds the perfect opportunity to talk to Miss Beryl. He respectfully tells Miss Beryl what he learned from Mr. Funk. "That is the most ridiculous thing I have ever heard," Miss Beryl responds angrily. "You have only been working with children for less than two years, I have been working with children for over 30 years and have two sons. You need to mind your own business!"

It is now February and there is still a hard feeling between Miss Beryl and Marc. Miss Beryl often sits next to Allen at circle time. Allen is a bright and funny four-year-old boy, who sometimes is stubborn and has difficulty paying attention at circle. Allen has a special connection with Miss Beryl. Allen has been especially stubborn this week. He is now refusing to stand for music and every student is required to participate in all activities. Miss Beryl has had enough and says as she is walking away from him, "I cannot handle you right now Allen. I need a break from you!" Allen breaks down crying, "You don't like me anymore, Miss Beryl?" Allen asks through his sobs.

"I like you, but I don't like you right now!" Miss Beryl exclaims.

Allen continues to cry. His friend, Jaxon, rubs his back. No one says anything. After a moment of silence, Miss Michelle says, "It's time for small group."

Everyone gets up and goes to their small groups. Marc can't help thinking about the situation. That was so uncalled for, he thinks to himself. I should say something, but what and to who? Remember the last time you said something? Maybe, I shouldn't say anything. Marc is still contemplating what to do when small groups are over. It is almost time to go home for the day, and he still has no clue what he will do.

## QUESTIONS

1. Which DEC practices for the topic area of Interaction did you see supported in this case study?
2. Which of the DEC practices for the topic area of Interaction were not supported in this case study? How might these have been addressed?
3. Although socially uncomfortable, teachers have an ethical obligation to ensure that children are treated with respect. How might you handle the situation with Miss Beryl?
4. Miss Beryl decided to force Andrew to apologize to Evan after hitting him. What would have been a better way to handle the situation?
5. Marc decides to tell Miss Beryl that forcing children to apologize isn't the most helpful way to handle a young child's inappropriate behavior toward another student. Do you believe he best handled the situation? Why or why not. If not, how could he have better handled the situation differently?

## INTERACTING THROUGH THE CHALLENGING BEHAVIORS

*Unsolved*

## Background

There is a little boy, Kenny, who has severe behavior problems. He is currently in a self-contained classroom with 4 other children. The other children are afraid of Kenny because he has hit, kicked and bit most of the other children in the class. Kenny does not get much peer interaction because whenever he goes near other children they run away from him. The staff is having a hard time getting Kenny to interact with the other children because they are worried about everyone's safety. However, they think it would be good for Kenny to have a friend that is his age.

Kenny is a 4-year-old (52 months) boy with no known medical conditions. He lives with his grandma (Jean), grandpa (who is an alcoholic) and older brother in a small, rundown home. Kenny's mother is a drug addict and is in and out of the picture at unknown times. Jean is in the process of trying to get full custody of Kenny and his older brother. Kenny also had a younger brother who died when he was 1 year old from possible SIDS.

Kenny started attending ECSE classes 2 days a week when he was 3 years old. He was in an integrated classroom and was showing many challenging behaviors. He would swear, throw items, spit, kick, hit and bite the teachers and other children in the class. After 2 months in this classroom the 3-5 team met and discussed other options for Kenny. It was decided that he would be placed in a self-contained classroom with 4 other children, 1 teacher and 2 paras. Everyone thought that the smaller class would be a better fit for Kenny because it would be quieter, less stimulating and he would be able to get more of the attention he needed in this class. Kenny has now been in this self-contained classroom for 1.5 years. He has the same teacher and paras and he is still with most of the same children. Kenny has a hard time interacting with adults, let alone unpredictable children in his class.

## Perspectives

Kenny got off the bus one afternoon, hit Mary (one of the paras in his classroom) in the face and took off running toward the classroom. Mary chased after Kenny and turned to the classroom teacher Allie, and said "I think it might be a Sally kind of day." Allie went into the school's psychologist's office and said "Sally I think we need you." Sally came into the classroom and sat with Kenny in the back of the classroom. Kenny would yell out "Me hate you! You go to jail!" randomly throughout the hello circle time and spit at Sally. The other 4 children in the room would turn around and watch Kenny as he screamed at Sally. One little boy started crying and ran to sit on Mary's lap. Another boy scooted his chair closer to Allie with a frightened look on his face. Allie continued on with the hello circle and tried to distract the other children from Kenny's yelling and spitting. When circle time was over Allie said "Alright, let's get our jackets and go outside." One of the little boys turned to Kenny and said "No Kenny you stay inside today." Kenny turned to the child and started to spit at him. Allie and the paras in the room tried to get the children ready quickly and head outside to the playground.

Once the children were outside Kenny came and joined the rest of the class 5–10 minutes later, after he had calmed down a bit. When Kenny would go near other children they would run away from him. The teachers and paras would try to get other children to play with Kenny while he was calm, but all of the children seemed to be scared of him and would try to run away. Later that day, during free play, while Kenny was calm, Julie (another para in the room) brought out the bubbles. They are a class favorite and she thought it was a good opportunity for Kenny to interact with the other children. It started out smoothly and Kenny was laughing and popping bubbles. Another child, Davis, came over and started laughing and popping bubbles too. This continues for about 2 minutes until both Kenny and Davis went to pop the same bubble. Davis hit Kenny's hand on accident and Kenny started screaming "Me hate you! You bad boy! You go to jail!" hitting and spitting at Davis. Davis started crying and screaming "No! No! No! You mean!" and then other unintelligible screaming. Julie picked Davis up and Kenny kept trying to hit and kick Davis. Allie came running over to block Kenny and Julie took Davis out of the room to calm down.

This is a fairly typical day for Kenny at school. However, some days Kenny can go without having a single outburst or challenging behavior and he can interact/play perfectly fine with the other children. The team has talked and they think Kenny's day depends on how things went at home that morning. Kenny seems to do better when his mom is out of the picture. The 3–5 team think her drug addiction is intense and unpredictable and causes Kenny a great deal of stress. Kenny's mom was in jail for 2 months and those two months were when Kenny had the least amount of challenging behaviors. Kenny was able to participate in class, laugh and play with the other children. Kenny's mom is now back in the picture and the behaviors have started again and the other children seem scared to be around Kenny. Also, Kenny's grandpa's alcoholism also seems to cause a great deal of stress in the home. The team has talked to CPS (Child Protective Services), and grandma is trying to get custody of Kenny and his older brother. The team has also talked about getting Kenny a one on one para, or trying to get him into a day treatment program.

## QUESTIONS

1. Which DEC practices for the topic area of Interaction did you see supported in this case study?
2. Which of the DEC practices for the topic area of Interaction were not supported in this case study? How might these have been addressed?
3. What might Kenny be trying to say through his challenging behaviors?
4. How would different programming options impact Kenny's social interactions with his peers?
5. What other strategies could be used to help Kenny manage his challenging behaviors?
6. What other strategies could be used to help the social interactions between Kenny and his classmates?

## MICHAEL'S ROLLERCOASTER RIDE

*Solved*

### Background

Michael is a 36-month-old boy who loves everything about trains. He is the youngest child of a single mother, Suzie, and he has four older siblings who range in age from 4 to 14 years old. Michael and his siblings have been in and out of daycare for the past 18 months, due to Suzie being unable to hold a steady position with her employers. In the past, Suzie has been in and out of jail due to drug and alcohol violations and Michael's four older siblings have all been in a foster home at varying lengths of time. When Suzie became pregnant with Michael she tried to turn her life around, but is still struggling with addiction and mental illness, which makes the relationship with Suzie much like a rollercoaster. Michael's 14 year old brother, Jack, walks to his daycare center most evenings to pick Michael up, so the teachers have limited interaction with Suzie. Jack cares for his siblings most evenings until Suzie gets home from work.

### Dilemma

When Michael began at his daycare, he was meeting all of the expected developmental markers across most areas. His teachers filled out a portfolio to track Michael's development, just as they did for all the other children. He was a very social child and interacted well with his peers. In the months nearing his third birthday, his teachers noticed a change in Michael. He became withdrawn from his class, had major social anxiety, became angered easily, and was regressing in his developmental milestones. He was acting out towards his peers with anger and showed fear when other parents would enter the classroom to pick up their children. His teachers expressed their concern with Suzie and she refused to accept that there was anything "wrong" with her child. After weeks of addressing their concern, Michael's teachers finally received approval from Suzie for a referral to Early Childhood Special Education (ECSE) services.

### Perspectives

At the first team meeting to set up Michael's Individualized Family Service Plan (IFSP), Suzie arrived late with an overpowering smell of cigarette smoke on herself, as well as inappropriate attire for the cold weather outside. She seemed distracted by her cell phone, looked at the clock numerous times, and at one point less than halfway through the meeting asked, "When will we be done here? I have a date to get to." The meeting continued and Ashley, the ECSE teacher working with Michael, discussed that the results of the evaluations revealed signs of Autism. The mention of Autism didn't seem to attract Suzie's attention at all and she continued being passively disengaged.

The team agreed on providing ECSE services to Michael within his classroom at daycare three times per week for thirty minutes each session. Since Suzie does not work on Wednesdays, home visits were set up for every other Wednesday morning as well. After agreeing on the direct service minutes, Suzie stated, "I'm fine with whatever you guys want to do with Michael. There's nothing wrong with him anyways, he's just being a little boy." The team reminded Suzie of the importance of her role as a mother to be a positive role model and provide support for her son's learning and development.

Services began shortly after the IFSP meeting with Michael's team. The classroom services are mainly focused on the social-emotional development of Michael, since that has a major impact on his daily learning and developmental growth. Ashley engages Michael in a variety of activities individually, as well as within small groups to promote the positive interactions with others. Michael's behavior has typically been very good when he is receiving one-on-one attention, but when he isn't getting the direct services his behavior and mood dramatically changes. His teachers explained one situation in his portfolio log, "Michael was sitting at a center working on art, when a different center began making music with instruments. Michael immediately stood up, began shouting, covered his ears, ran to the instrument center and kicked the drum out of a classmate's hands. When we asked Michael why he did that, he refused to make eye contact or respond verbally." Based on the information from Ashley and from Michael's classroom teachers, it is clear that Michael's ability to communicate is not effective or safe. During the next session, Ashley begins working on Michael with sign language and picture cards at daycare, which seems to be helping ease Michael's frustration.

Only two home visits have been conducted since the initial IFSP meeting. Suzie has been very distant with the ECSE team and has cancelled her home visits three times. The two home visits that were completed seemed "very chaotic and distracting," according to Ashley. Two of Michael's siblings were at home during the visit causing numerous interruptions, the family dog was barking non-stop, and the home was filled with a smoky haze. Ashley spent the majority of the sessions trying to educate Suzie and her other children on the importance of positive social interactions with Michael, enhancing his communication skills through signing and picture cards, and expanding Michael's understanding of emotions through examples with puppets. Suzie seemed uninterested, but agreed to keep the resources and work on it at home with Michael. The next home visit that Ashley went to, the resources were unable to be found, and Michael's progress was minimal. "I'll be back in two weeks! And we may have to set up another team meeting to adjust Michael's services before then," stated Ashley as she walked out and waived to Michael. Suzie stood at the door and stated, "Nah, Michael will be fine," and then abruptly the door slammed.

## QUESTIONS

1. Which DEC practices for the topic area of Interaction did you see supported in this case study?
2. Which of the DEC practices for the topic area of Interaction were not supported in this case study? How might these have been addressed?
3. What should the next step be for Michael's home visits? Are there other methods of interaction and instruction that would be more effective for Michael and his family?
4. What are the pros and cons of one-on-one time versus working in small groups with the ECSE teacher? Explain what you think the best use of time would be for Michael's direct service time with Ashley.
5. How could the team engage the family in the IFSP meeting? If you were Ashley, what strategies could be used to communicate the importance of parental support?
6. What resources could be provided for Suzie to better understand or cope with Michael's disabilities? What resources could be provided for Suzie regarding her personal health issues?

## PARAS NOT UP TO PAR

*Solved*

## Background

Sophia is a happy, fun-loving five year old, who has Epilepsy and developmental delays. Sophia was diagnosed with Epilepsy at the age of three. Shortly after the diagnosis, her parents started to notice little changes in her abilities. Sophia would forget how to sing the ABC song, or couldn't recall colors. Her mother, Mary and father, Steve started to have some serious concerns about the Epilepsy affecting her growth and development. At about the same time, Sophia was scheduled to have her preschool screening at the local elementary. This was a turning point in the family's life, as Sophia's performance at the screening resulted in a referral for further testing.

After further testing, Sophia was diagnosed with developmental delays. The IEP team recommended integrating Sophia in a preschool program where she would spend mornings with her regular developing peers and afternoons in an ECSE classroom. Mary and Steve wanted what was best for their little girl, but they were also uncertain of the impact Epilepsy was going to have on her future. Sophia's parents often found themselves wondering if Sophia would always need special education services, or would her abilities improve as she got older.

Sophia has been attending preschool in an integrated classroom and an ECSE classroom for almost two years now. As the years went by, Sophia's Epilepsy worsened and she began to have Grand Mal seizures regularly when she slept. The seizures were so intense that Sophia would need several hours of rest afterwards. As a result, Sophia missed preschool often. When she did attend class, Sophia had much difficulty retaining information and needed lots of prompting to follow the classroom routine, especially during transitions. However, her behaviors were manageable and she was able to participate appropriately in the majority of activities.

Over the past six months though, not only has Sophia's Epilepsy worsened, her abilities to participate appropriately at school have decreased drastically. Sophia has several meltdowns throughout the day, refusing to do academic tasks and follow the classroom routines. Her meltdowns range anywhere from five minutes to thirty. Sophia's preschool teachers have become extremely concerned about the regression in both her social emotional and academic skills. Some days are especially daunting, as the teachers feel Sophia's behaviors are so intense that they affect the other students' learning.

## Dilemma

Sophia's preschool teachers have a strong rapport with Mary and Steve, and have communicated their concern with Sophia's behavior and regression. Sophia' teachers have said "some days Sophia does a wonderful job following directions and participating in academic activities, while other days she damages materials and kicks and screams at her teachers. Her behaviors are on such different spectrums, that it is difficult to determine if Sophia is in control of her behavior or if it is a side effect of Epilepsy." While Sophia's teachers try to exhibit patience and compassion when she is acting out, some of the paras working with her have started to become extremely frustrated. The paras feel that the meltdowns and noncompliance are strictly behavioral and that Sophia is choosing to act out. Much to the teachers' dismay, the paras sometimes tell Sophia that she is bad or naughty when she exhibits inappropriate behaviors. They even sometimes take special toys away from her that she had earned previously for good behavior, and threaten to give the rewards to the other students. This has become a big concern for Sophia's teachers, and they have tried to subtly redirect the paras' behaviors.

At home, Mary and Steve do not see the same intense behaviors as exhibited at school. They feel that this is because there is less structure and demands placed on her there. While Sophia has been struggling at school and doesn't possess the academic skills of her regularly developing peers, her communication skills are exemplary. Recently Sophia has been coming home from school and telling her mom about how the paras have been treating her. Mary and Steve were very disheartened to hear this. Mary stated "we have entrusted the emotional and academic care of our daughter in this school, and to hear that she is being called naughty and having her items taken away is simply not acceptable. She is a little girl, she wants to be good. Her brain is different from other children's. Sophia doesn't always have control over her actions."

## Perspectives

Mary and Steve immediately reached out to Sophia's teachers in regards to their concerns about the treatment of their daughter. While the teachers were aware of some of the paras' unacceptable behaviors, there were other concerns during lunch and recess where the teachers were not present. For instance, when Sophia was misbehaving the paras told Sophia she could not sit by her friends at lunch, and the other students were told not to talk to her. Sophia's teachers were saddened to hear that the paras had been acting that way, and couldn't help but feel responsible.

Mary and Steve feel their trust and rapport with Sophia's teachers and paras has been significantly damaged. However, they have built such a strong support system at the school over the years that they don't want to send Sophia elsewhere. Sophia's teachers feel terrible about the situation. They have always wanted what was best for Sophia and have shown her and her family unyielding compassion and support over the years. They know they should have done more to encourage the paras to change their words and actions when working with Sophia. Sophia's teachers have asked Mary and Steve to come in for a meeting so that they can work together to not only come up with a plan to remedy the paras actions, but also to consider some options to guide the growth and development of Sophia's social emotional and academic skills so that she may have a more meaningful learning experience at school.

## QUESTIONS

1. Which DEC practices for the topic area of Interaction did you see supported in this case study?
2. Which of the DEC practices for the topic area of Interaction were not supported in this case study? How might these have been addressed?
3. How can Sophia's teachers reassure her parents that the paras will use appropriate positive behavior intervention strategies from now on?
4. What are some appropriate de-escalation strategies that the teachers could help the paras implement when Sophia is noncompliant?
5. In any case, it is critical for the teachers and paras to have strong communication and a partnership based on trust and respect. With everything that has happened, how can Sophia's teachers make sure the paras understand how unacceptable their actions were, while working to maintain and strengthen their partnership?
6. What suggestions do you have that might increase the growth and development of Sophia's social emotional and academic skills?
7. How can Mary and Steve partner with the teachers and paras to create more meaningful learning experiences for Sophia?

## THE CONUNDRUM

*Unsolved*

### Background

Sandy is a first year teacher, and she has been assigned to teach a center-based ECSE classroom for the school year. She is nervous about teaching and spends a lot of time and care setting up the classroom to support structured routines while remaining engaging to students. When she gets her class list, she reads through each student's paperwork to get a picture of his or her abilities and begin lesson planning.

When Sandy gets to Alexi's file, she finds a behavior plan that was written in the spring. Alexi is a 55-month-old boy with Autism Spectrum Disorder. He was in a classroom across the hall the previous year, so Sandy goes to talk to his former teacher, Chloe. One of the things that stands out in the BIP are the antecedents to Alexi's behaviors; the word "no" in particular seems odd.

"So, when you say 'no', what does he do?" Sandy asks, curious.

"It depends, but it can be screaming, kicking, throwing chairs," responds Chloe, looking like she is trying to remember. "When he starts to do that, he sits on one of the blue chairs for a break."

It seems to Sandy that if he is having these behaviors, he's not likely to sit calmly on a chair. "How do you make him stay there?"

Chloe looks unconcerned. "Oh, he'll sit there just fine and cry, and once he's calm you can count and he can get up." This sounds easy enough for Sandy and she makes a note of Alexi's motivators and reinforcers and plans to find ways around saying "no" to avoid triggering behaviors.

Welcome Night is quickly approaching and Sandy has met with each of her paraprofessionals to debrief on the students and has shared the plan to use positive language, such as "hands down" instead of "no touching," in the classroom. She is a little wary of Alexi since his described behaviors are so physical.

At Welcome Night, the occupational therapist and autism resource specialist are in the room along with Sandy to welcome families and assist with a getting-to-know-the-school scavenger hunt. When Alexi walks into the room, he looks around and walks straight to the circle time carpet where some chairs are stacked. He pulls down a cube chair, points it toward the board, grabs a fidget from the fidget basket, and says "music!" His face is beaming and Sandy is amazed at this immediate comfort with the room and new surroundings. The autism resource specialist is impressed with Alexi's ability to advocate for his needs, and Sandy agrees that they will use the cube chair and fidget at large group time.

A stationary picture schedule is set up in the room for Alexi and he transitions with this independently. He uses a PECS book to initiate communication with staff and uses some echolalic spontaneous language. Music is a favorite time of day for Alexi, and he sings to every song and grins from ear to ear. This toothy smile is contagious and it always manages to make Sandy smile when she sees Alexi singing every word and doing the actions to a song. She takes advantage of his love of music by having him request songs and expanding on his language by choosing to sing loud, quiet, fast, slow, etc., using visuals.

One of Alexi's IEP goals is to follow a structured play routine, so Sandy observes Alexi's play and engages in a play session with him to establish his current skills. She also observed Alexi during free play to see which toys he chooses and how he plays with them. Alexi typically chooses toys with wheels and either lines them up in a row or spins the wheels. Sandy wants to see Alexi play more functionally with these preferred toys, so she creates sequence strips. One for the car ramp has the following: go up the elevator, drive down the ramp, get fuel.

Alexi makes progress during the play session with these visuals and he is requesting toys using his PECS book. He seems content with the routine and has infrequent behaviors, none of which are physical. Alexi is easily redirected from these behaviors with the use of First/Then visuals and reinforcers.

**Dilemma**

Throughout the fall, Sandy has been in contact with Alexi's mom every couple of weeks. Alexi is Mom's only child and she is separated from his father. After winter break, all of the students take a couple of days to get back into the classroom routine. Sandy also feels like it's difficult to get her head back in the game, so she can see how the kids need to relearn some things from before break.

However, Alexi seems different even with the break factored in. One day, he runs out of the room at full speed and is stopped by a staff member down the hall. He walks back and the day continues. Sandy praises him for using "slow feet" when they transition to the gym later and he immediately drops to the floor. There are peers behind him in line and the class stops while Alexi makes whining noises. Sandy is baffled. What set him off? He loves the gym, so why is he laying on the floor?

The paraeducator takes the rest of the class to the gym and Sandy stays with Alexi. She tries the First/Then visuals, and Alexi shakes his head and looks the other way. When Sandy tries to take Alexi's hand to help him up, he tears it away, stands up, and runs to the gym and in the door.

After school, Sandy calls Alexi's mom and discovers that he spent a week at his dad's house over the break. Mom says that Dad does not fully understand autism and is kind of hard on Alexi. Sandy thinks this helps explain the change in behavior. She wants to put some strategies in place to support Alexi when he is off like this, but can't determine the immediate antecedent to the incident. She decides to see if the behavior occurs again and compare the antecedents to see if any are the same as the first incident.

This winter is brutally cold and school is cancelled 5 times for dangerously low temperatures alone. It is now February and whether because of this or other precipitating factors, Alexi continues to run away and show refusal behaviors during transitions. Sandy has asked Amy, the autism resource specialist, to come and observe Alexi to see if she can offer any insight on the situation.

Amy has been very pleased with Alexi's progress this fall. He was a perfect case of evidence-based strategies for students with ASD working in the school setting. When she comes to observe him now, the class is in the bathroom and she can hear Alexi in one of the stalls saying, "Water! Water!" Amy finds Sandy in the stall with Alexi trying to use a visual sequence to use the bathroom, which is a change since he was previously independent in this routine. Now he is hitting the wall and repeating the word "water."

Interested in this request, Amy asks Sandy if he has said this before.

"Yeah, the past week or so he has been running to the water fountain every 10 minutes or so. Sometimes he yells 'water!' first, but other times he just bolts out of the room," Sandy supplies. "I talked to his mom and she said he hasn't been drinking any more than normal at home. Why is he doing it here?" she asks Amy, baffled.

During this exchange, Sandy has turned away from Alexi to direct her conversation at Amy, and Amy suddenly sees what Sandy cannot: Alexi has bent down, put his head into the toilet, and started to lick the water from the toilet bowl. Amy exclaims, "Stop!" which draws Sandy's attention to the situation, and Sandy pulls Alexi away from the toilet. Alexi reacts by screaming and running out of the bathroom. Sandy manages to stop him, and Amy suggests walking to the water fountain. It takes about 10 minutes to get there because they stop each time Alexi tries to run and once they arrive, Alexi drinks a good amount of water.

Amy watches Alexi drink and wonders why this behavior is only occurring at school. Alexi attends school for 21/2 hours in the afternoon 3 days a week, and he is cared for at home by his mom the rest of the time unless he is with his dad. Amy wonders aloud to Sandy if maybe he was thirsty one time and this has become a new routine for him. They decide to schedule regular drink breaks into Alexi's day to satisfy his need for water in an appropriate way and to use a transition object of Alexi's choice to walk through the school.

Regardless of the interventions the team implements, Alexi's behaviors not only continue but also intensify. The transition object he chose, a tube that makes noise when you turn it over, worked for a couple of weeks, and he continues to hold it, but the calming effect has diminished. Alexi now transitions by either running full speed or lying on the floor with no in-between. Katy, the occupational therapist, has been following Alexi's case and now she is becoming concerned that his sensory needs have increased in a short amount of time.

Alexi no longer seems to enjoy music during group time and covers his ears and closes his eyes during songs. He now drops to the floor in the classroom during activities and wiggle around on the ground. Katy finds it curious that he doesn't seem upset if left alone like this, but if anyone approaches by trying to talk to or touch him, Alexi will start to scream "No! No! NOOO!" and thrash around on the floor or try to run away. Sandy now has to keep the door closed when Alexi is in the room, and he still attempts to open the door.

Seeing that he is covering his ears, Katy brings Alexi a pair of noise-reducing headphones and prompts him to wear them right away at arrival before behaviors have started. This seems to calm him as far as people speaking to him, but he still screams and yells "No!" when staff approach get within a couple of feet from him. Katy wonders if Alexi may be experiencing some mental health issues since his reactions and behaviors are so intense and repetitive.

**Perspectives**

Sandy is overwhelmed by the flurry of service providers in and out of the room and trying to implement strategies suggested by different sources as well as herself. She has called a team meeting, and would like to problem-solve as a group and look again at Alexi's behavior plan. His behaviors are very different from those described on the plan and it is time to update it and brainstorm strategies for preventing and defusing behaviors. The plan is to bring everyone's perspectives together and see how Alexi's needs can best be met.

## QUESTIONS

1. Which DEC practices for the topic area of Interaction did you see supported in this case study?
2. Which of the DEC practices for the topic area of Interaction were not supported in this case study? How might these have been addressed?
3. What factors may have contributed to the increase in behaviors that Alexi is exhibiting?
4. What do you think about the way Sandy handled Alexi's behaviors from the beginning of the year to present? What would you have done differently?
5. The end of the case study does not describe who is invited to the team meeting. Who do you think should be in attendance and why? How would you involve Alexi's mom in the team meeting and follow-up?
6. Imagine you are sitting in on this team meeting. Considering that Alexi will be transitioning to kindergarten in a few months, what would be your first priority to problem-solve? Why?
7. Given the information you know, what interventions would you suggest at the team meeting? Do you think multiple interventions should be tried at once, or should they be introduced one at a time and why?
8. Assume the team decided to investigate the possibility of mental health issues. How should they proceed, and how should this be discussed with Alexi's mom?

# Chapter 7

# TEAMING AND COLLABORATION

## OVERVIEW OF RECOMMENDED PRACTICE

Educational programs and services for young children who have or are at risk for developmental delays and disabilities, by their nature, always involve more than one adult. The quality of the relationships and interactions among these adults affects the success of these programs. Teaming and collaboration practices are those that promote and sustain collaborative adult partnerships, relationships, and ongoing interactions to ensure that programs and services achieve desired child and family outcomes and goals.

The family is an essential member of the team, which should include practitioners from multiple disciplines, as needed. Communication among team members should be respectful and supportive, to promote interaction and sharing of expertise to enhance capacity of the team. All interactions should be culturally sensitive.

DEC recommends the following practices to support teaming and collaboration:

- **TC1**. Practitioners representing multiple disciplines and families work together as a team to plan and implement supports and services to meet the unique needs of each child and family.
- **TC2**. Practitioners and families work together as a team to systematically and regularly exchange expertise, knowledge, and information to build team capacity and jointly solve problems, plan, and implement interventions.
- **TC3**. Practitioners use communication and group facilitation strategies to enhance team functioning and interpersonal relationships with and among team members.

177

- **TC4**. Team members assist each other to discover and access community-based services and other informal and formal resources to meet family-identified child or family needs.
- **TC5**. Practitioners and families may collaborate with each other to identify one practitioner from the team who serves as the primary liaison between the family and other team members based on child and family priorities and needs.
(DEC, 2014, p. 15)

The following 11 cases were designed to represent the recommended practices (RPs) for teaming and collaboration as a whole. Each case is illustrative of a combination of the 5 RPs for teaming and collaboration and does not contain each of the practices. When reviewing the case studies for the RPs for teaming and collaboration it is advised to use this chapter in the following ways. One, have individuals read each case and answer independently as a way to determine the individual's understanding of teaming and collaboration and the corresponding practices. Two, have individuals independently read a case study and in small groups discuss what they learned regarding teaming and collaboration and the corresponding cases. Three, have small groups read case studies and contribute to a whole group discussion as a whole. You can use any and all of these suggestions as it fits with your purposes for the teaching or review of the RPs.

## SECTION 1: CASES FOR BIRTH TO AGE 3

## A Child in Need

*Unsolved*

### Background

Eli is a 3-year-old who has experienced trauma. Eli lives with his mom, Amy. Eli has observed his mother being beaten by his father, Henry and at his young age tried to intervene to help her. Eli has trouble on the bus and is unbuckling himself from his harness. Eli is attending a childcare facility called Kinder Pals where he is waiting in the infant room for the bus to come in the morning before school. Natasha, Eli's teacher at Kinder Pals, would like Eli to be removed from their program because of his behaviors. At his preschool program he is having challenging behaviors and is physical towards other children and staff are worried about his safety and the safety of the other children and staff members. Miss Kelsey, Eli's preschool teacher, works with Trina, the school social worker to come up with a plan to support Eli and his mom.

## Dilemma

The Dilemma of this case study is complicated in that everyone is working with Eli, including his mother Amy who needs help. Miss Kelsey, the preschool teacher, used her professional learning community (PLC) to try to help Eli. Kelsey gained some great ideas and resources to help Amy and Eli. One of them is to start a behavior chart as Eli does respond well to a three-point scale. It also serves to communicate how the day went with home. Kelsey also learned about Trina and the Blossbrook Family Center focuses on using innovative strategies to build relationships and transform lives. They have a day program called Little Blossom for children. Little Blossom runs Monday-Wednesday for 3 hours per day. They provide services to children who have experienced trauma, show challenging behaviors, and or have a caregiver with mental health. Ms. Kelsey called Amy to present the benefits of social work and Little Blossom to her. Ms. Kelsey hopes that Amy is as excited as she is about the idea. Amy was excited to hear about the option and the next step was for Trina to contact mom.

"It's so nice to meet you, Amy! I'm Trina, the school's social worker. I have been coming in to see Eli and it's been fun getting to know him."

Looking nervous, Amy asked, "Are there any services I can receive too? I want to learn how to talk with Eli and handle issues when they arise at home."

Trina felt strongly about the dedication Amy was presenting, and she stated, "Blossbrook can also provide services where a professional can come into your home to teach you skills to use in your day to day life."

"I don't know how to communicate with Kinder Pals," Amy said nervously as she tapped the table with her red fingernails. "His teacher, Natasha, called me Wednesday and told me they don't want Eli to come anymore. Is it possible the three of us could sit down with her?"

As Amy listened, she kept thinking how much she needed Kelsey and Trina. *There is no way I can do this alone. Please ladies, help make this happen,* Amy thought to herself.

The next day, all four members sat down around a conference table.

"I'm sorry, but Eli cannot keep coming to Kinder Pals! We are having too many issues and our staff is not able to control him! He will leave the classroom, and nobody can find him. I don't believe it's the right environment for him. He is taking up too much time and the other kids are not getting the service they deserve," Natasha said firmly. "What if you approach him in a different perspective? Trina said with a calm demeanor. When he is angry, acknowledge his feelings. Eli, I see you are feeling mad. What can I do to help you feel happy?"

"That won't work! Exclaimed Natasha. He won't listen to anyone at the center. The second a staff member comes up to him, he will hide, run out the building, or throw whatever is near him."

"Wait, I have an idea Trina said! "What if we have an ECSE teacher come to Kinder Pals 3x a week for 20 minutes to provide services to Eli? We can work as a team to provide the proper interventions." Ms. Kelsey felt excited about the idea. Natasha stated that she didn't think that having an ECSE teacher there for 20 minutes is going to make a difference in Eli's behavior. "After the ECSE teacher leaves, what are we supposed to do when his behavior begins to escalate?"

## Perspectives

There are many different perspectives in this case study. Amy the mother just wants the best for her son Eli and helps for them at home for him to be successful. Ms. Kelsey is trying hard to reach out to help Eli and his family to be successful. Trina, the social worker, brought in to be the bridge between home and the childcare is trying to give the childcare center options to help them be successful with Eli at daycare. Natasha, the teacher at the daycare, is really struggling and they are at the end of their rope dealing with Eli. They do not see the options as being helpful. This is a really difficult situation and one that probably happens more than we know.

## QUESTIONS

1. Which DEC practices for the topic area of Teaming and Collaboration did you see supported in this case study?
2. Which of the DEC practices for the topic area of Teaming and Collaboration were not supported in this case study? How might these have been addressed?
3. Developing relationships with all team members is crucial in a child's development. Kelsey was aware of the difficulties Kinder Pals was having with Eli. She was given information from Eli's mother, Amy as well as the bus driver. What could Kelsey have done to form a relationship with Kinder Pals (Natasha)? Do you think by forming a relationship and communicating they would have been more willing to help solve Eli's behavior? Why or why not?
4. Amy is struggling at home with Eli and has been for a while. Do you think if Amy would have contacted Kelsey earlier and explained the

struggles with their home life, they could have provided the right support for Eli in and outside of the classroom sooner? Why or why not?

5. Natasha is firm about Eli not coming back to Kinder Pals. Why do you believe this is or not the right decision? Do you feel it was Kelsey's duty as case manager in this situation?

6. Eli's father, Henry was not a present in the discussion of Eli's behavior. Do you believe Miss Kelsey should have invited him to attend their meetings? Why or why not?

7. How would talking with the school's social worker and hearing about the community-based services help Henry become awre of his son's struggles int he school environment?

## MEDICAL MYSTERY

*Unsolved*

## Background

Joey is a 23-month-old boy who was referred in November, for speech and language concerns by his pediatric physician Dr. Jason. An intake questionnaire was completed by Tom, an Early Childhood Special Education Teacher (ECSE). The questionnaire that asks for parent concerns, strengths of the child, and medical history. After completing the questionnaire, it was determined to go through with an evaluation to determine Joey's eligibility for intervention services. During the evaluation Kristen an Occupational Therapist (OT) noted that he had some physical characteristics such as, large head and low muscle tone. It was determined that Joey qualifies for early intervention services in the area of cognitive development and communication. It was determined that Joey will be receiving services from both the hospital and school district once a week beginning December. Joey will receive services from a Speech Language Pathologist (SLP) and ECSE. In January Joey qualified for Occupational therapy two times a month, Joey was also diagnosed having an extra "y" chromosome or "Jacob's Syndrome." Some characteristics of this syndrome include; a large head, low muscle tone, speech delays and low sperm count in adult males.

While completing weekly visits it was determined that we need to set up a form of communication between Teresa the SLP representing the school district, Amanda the SLP representing the hospital, and Tom the ECSE teacher, Joey's parents Erin and Brian to best serve Joey. Erin stated, "It sometimes gets confusing with what we should focus on between Amanda and Teresa, and Tom." In the DEC Teaming and Collaboration 2 it is recommended that practitioners and families work together as a team to systematically and regularly exchange expertise, knowledge, and information to build capacity and jointly solve problems, plan, and implement interventions. Joey's case manager began an email chain that can be updated after each visit between the three service providers. During a visit Joey's mom said, "I really worry about the size of Joey's head and want to see if that is something we need to have checked." Tom stated, "This is something that you can request the next time you are at the hospital for a speech visit, or I can mention it to Amanda if you'd like." It was determined that his ECSE teacher would update Amanda and Teresa about Erin's concerns. At this time, Tom also consulted with Kristen about possible avenues to pursue for Joey's head shape. Kristen stated, "Erin can request an MRI at her next visit with Joey." A request was made to Dr. Jason for a referral to a neurologist and blood work for genetic testing from the team.

### Perspectives

In January, all testing was completed by Dr. Chad and results were shared. During the ECSE teachers first visit after testing, Erin stated, Joey's mom stated, "I don't really understand what the doctor told me when he read the results." Tom replied, "I can request the medical records for review if you sign a release of medical information." Erin said "I would like that because you can help me understand what this all means." Upon reviewing the medical records next, the team collaborated to discuss the next steps would best serve Joey's needs. The team decided to keep the visits similar between the hospital and school district. OT services were added to the IFSP for two times a month.

### Dilemma

In February Erin stated, "my mom thinks we should just do all of our doctoring for Joey in one place." "She thinks that he is being seen by too many people." Joey's ECSE teacher assured his parents he's here to facilitate whatever they feel as a need for the family and would serve as a primary liaison between the family and other team members. The dilemma is that the school district and current hospital are seeing nice gains in Joey's development and by teaming together they feel they are effectively supporting Joey and his family. Joey's grandma's opinion is that she thinks he should, "just go to the doctor." The intervention team feels that the current plan is working and by switching to another clinic would add travel to Erin's schedule.

As a team we are at a crossroads for service delivery. From the team's perspective in the time working with Joey have seen nice improvements and would like to continue with their model. We feel this is appropriate because the diagnosis does not change any of the services we are providing. The doctors feel that the service delivery model we are currently using would be just as effective as going to just the hospital. With this being said, it is ultimately up to Erin and Brian.

## QUESTIONS

1. Which DEC practices for the topic area of Teaming and Collaboration did you see supported in this case study?
2. Which of the DEC practices for the topic area of Teaming and Collaboration were not supported in this case study? How might these have been addressed?
3. What other ways can the team communicate between visits to enhance that communication between team members?
4. Who should serve as the main liaison for the team? Provide two pieces of evidence to support your choice.
5. Do you think the team included members who were best to provide services? Why or why not?
6. What would the next steps be when meeting with the parents and grandmother?
7. How could the team facilitate collaboration when there is a difference of opinion among team members?

## SURROGATE MOM

*Solved*

### Background

As Janet, a general education teacher was preparing for the beginning of a new school year, another teacher, Renee, informed Janet that she had had one of her students last year and his name is Tyler. Renee told Janet that Tyler struggled with separating from his mother, lacked communication and speech skills and could be physically aggressive at times. Janet asked Renee, "Has he completed a preschool screening?" Renee replied, "Yes. When he turned 3 this past spring, he was referred to Special Education for an assessment after the screening. However, his mom did not want to move forward with an evaluation just yet. She wanted to give Tyler some more time in a school setting, in the hopes that he will succeed if given more time." This new found information left Janet with a lot of questions. She wondered what the screening had shown, and what strategies Renee used with Tyler that may have been successful in the classroom. She decided to contact the office where the student records were kept, and take a look at the results of the screening. She hoped that by doing so she would get a picture of Tyler, and possibly incorporate some intervention strategies that may help him as he starts the new school year.

Last year Tyler was in a mixed aged 2-5 year old Early Childhood Family Education (ECFE) 1 day per week. Parents come with their child and start out in the child's classroom, and then they separate to go to parenting classes. They then come back together at the end of the class in the child's classroom. This year, Tyler will be in a 2-day-a-week ECFE class. Tuesday is the parent day and Thursday is the drop off day when the parent does not stay. Tyler who is 3 years old will come to school with his mom, Kim.

On the first day of school, Janet met Tyler and his mom, Kim. Tyler was very shy and stayed close to his mom. Kim told Janet that Tyler had been having a hard time separating from her, and that he also still wore a diaper, and that he brought his blanket because it comforted him. Kim then mentioned that separating was going to be tough for Tyler, and warned that he may scream, cry and possibly hit. Janet thanked Kim for the information and made a mental note to have her Educational Assistant (EA) Chris sit by Tyler and help him with the separation.

The first two months of school went well for Tyler. It took him some time to adjust to separating from his mom, but after the 3rd week of school he was able to leave mom and come to circle time with his blanket, crying for only a few minutes. During this time, Janet and Chris noted several things about Tyler that were concerning, and planned to talk to mom about them at conferences in October.

Chris asked Janet one day after class in September, "Do you notice that Tyler doesn't talk and when he does it doesn't make sense with regard to what is going on around him? I also noticed that he walks on his toes most of the time." "Yes," Janet replied, "I did notice those things and I am very concerned about how he seems to have trouble processing information. For example, he is unable to follow a 2-step direction even with verbal prompts and hand over hand support. When we use the sink to wash hands, Tyler will only put his hands under the water and is not able to complete handwashing without hand over hand help." This conversation prompted Janet to continue to take notes on Tyler, and how he was doing throughout the school day so she could express these concerns to Kim, Tyler's mom. *Janet wondered how Kim would react when she talked about Tyler's behavior in class. She hoped that Kim might become more open to the idea of going forward with a Special Education Evaluation.*

## Dilemma

When conference time came around, Janet had the following conversation with Kim, Tyler's mom. "Kim, Tyler has been doing well adjusting to school, however, I have noticed some things that I am concerned about and I wanted to discuss my observations and concerns with you. Tyler isn't consistently processing information when asked to do something in the classroom. In addition, he is not speaking very often in class. When he does speak, he will say something that is not related to what we are doing. For example, at snack time, we asked him if he wanted some water, and he replied with, "baseball, dad." Do you notice any of these things at home?" Kim replied, "I do, but I think that Tyler is just stubborn and doesn't want to do things when I ask him." Janet said, "Kim, it could be that he is being stubborn, yes. However, based on what I have seen and some of the struggles he is having we need to try something different. I understand your apprehension with completing an evaluation, and it is ultimately your decision whether or not we evaluate Tyler. We just want to make sure we are doing everything we can for him so that he can be successful in school." Kim replied, "I want to wait. You have stated that he has made progress which I think is a good thing." *Kim left that conference feeling confused and began to doubt her decision to wait on an evaluation. She thought Tyler was making progress. But then she wondered if she had made the right decision when she declined the evaluation. She began to doubt her decision. As Janet got ready for her next conference, she couldn't help but wonder what she could do going forward to help Tyler succeed. She knew that Tyler's mom wanted what was best for Tyler just as she did, but understood that it can be difficult for a parent to admit that their child may need more help.*

## Perspectives

As the month of November arrived, Janet and Chris saw a change in Tyler's behavior. He began to become physically aggressive when he didn't want to do something or didn't like something. They noted that these behaviors occurred mainly during circle/group time and transition/clean-up time. The behavior began with uncontrollable crying, screaming and swatting at Chris and moved from swatting to full on hitting and kicking. Janet brought this behavior to Tyler's mom's attention. Kim was very apologetic and explained that the behavior meant that he was getting very comfortable in school. She explained that what Janet saw, was behavior she also experienced with Tyler at home. Janet proceeded to ask Kim if there were any strategies she used at home with Tyler that would ward off or deescalate the behaviors. Kim said that she just had to sit back and wait until he calmed down on his own. Janet thanked Kim for the new-found information and began thinking about how to help Tyler stop his physical behavior in the classroom.

In Tyler's school, when a student displays physical aggression or behaviors, the teacher must fill out a Behavior Incident Report (BIR). Janet asked Chris to start filling out a report every time Tyler had uncontrollable crying, screaming or was physically aggressive toward someone. On the report, a teacher can ask for help from the BIR team after several reports. Janet and Chris decided to ask for help with a checkmark on the intended box on the form. In the meantime, while Janet waited for help from the BIR team, she tried fidgets with Tyler during circle time when he had trouble sitting, and this seemed to help. Chris also sat next to Tyler with picture cards illustrating the rules of the class for sitting in a group. Tyler continued to be physically aggressive towards Chris and Janet. During transitions, Janet would give Tyler a job to do to help, like putting a toy away. This worked, but only temporarily. Tyler began following Chris around during clean up time, and during learning center/time, and when something changed like a new person came into the classroom.

While waiting for help from the BIR team, Janet reached out to Special Education Teachers to see if there was anything they knew of that might help ease Tyler's mom's apprehensions regarding an evaluation. April, one of the special education teachers, offered to reach out to Tyler's mom to update her on the behaviors in the classroom. This would not be a surprise to Kim because they had previously agreed at the screening, to have April give an update on Tyler 6 months into the school year.

When classes began again in January, April and her team were able to contact Kim and set up a meeting to discuss Tyler's behaviors and difficulties in the classroom. Janet learned from that meeting that things had gotten worse at home over break and that Kim now sees that maybe Tyler does need some extra support. Together with Tyler's mom, Kim decided to go ahead with the evaluation.

Jen, the school social worker who is part of the Special Education Evaluation team, and the BIR team, set up a meeting to devise a BIR plan for Tyler. Janet began the meeting with proper introductions and stated the reason for the meeting. She mentioned that she had spoken with Kim, who expressed concerns about how aggressive Tyler had been at school, and that it had escalated as of late. From her observations, Jen thought that Tyler might be using Chris as a "surrogate mother" when he needed comforting and felt threatened. The BIR data suggests that Tyler struggles with circle/large group time, transitions and clean up times. She asked the team if they agreed with her assessment, and they agreed. Janet added different possible reasons for Tyler's aggression. She thought that his struggle with language could be frustrating for him leading to aggression. She also expressed concerns with his inability to process directions, and that these too may be leading to frustration, anxiousness and it comes out in aggression. Janet agreed, and then gave her suggestions. She said, "I would agree and here are two things I would like to try with Tyler to help him. One, I think we should use a first/then card with Tyler to help him learn the routine better and what to expect next. Also, I think you can use it in learning center time to help with Tyler's wandering and not actually playing with anything or anyone. The second thing I think we should do is have Chris only engage with him during positive interactions. Meaning, once Tyler starts to become aggressive, Chris will say "STOP" using American Sign Language and walk away. If Tyler does not stop, Janet will step in and do the same thing, and then assist him to a quiet corner to calm down. When he is calm, he can join the class again." Janet and Chris agreed to this plan and were excited to start putting it into action.

At the beginning of February, Tyler's Special Education team completed Tyler's evaluation and scheduled a meeting to discuss the test results. Janet, Jen, Kim, April, Bobbie (speech pathologist), Becca (Case Manager), and Carrie (district representative) were at the meeting. At the meeting, Kim learned that Tyler does qualify for special education services under the categories of developmental delay and speech/communication delay. This meeting allowed practitioners and Kim to come together as a team to talk about Tyler and plan for his future.

Currently everyone is waiting for the IEP to be written and signed by Kim. Once this is done, the services will begin. The BIP has begun, however, more time is needed in order to measure its success.

## QUESTIONS

1. Which DEC practices for the topic area of Teaming and Collaboration did you see supported in this case study?
2. Which of the DEC practices for the topic area of Teaming and Collaboration were not supported in this case study? How might these have been addressed?
3. What other resources or strategies do you think Janet could have used in her classroom to help Tyler?
4. How can the team collaborate regarding the special education evaluation?
5. How can the team collaborate regarding Tyler's physical aggression at home?
6. What are your thoughts on the Behavior Incident Report (BIR) plan and why?

7. What could have been done differently to help this family sooner?
8. Suppose Kim never agrees to an evaluation for Tyler. Is there anything more Janet could do to help support Tyler and Kim?

## TWO TRAINS PASSING IN THE NIGHT

*Unsolved*

### Background

"Today was another rough day for Samantha." Kara said to Mary, the Parent Educator and other half of her ECFE team. "I think it is time to suggest an evaluation to mom." "I think your right, Kara. I know that it will be hard for mom to hear but it is important to get the ball rolling so that when, I mean if, she qualifies she can start to receive services right away." "I'm sure that it will be difficult to hear, but we both see how much mom is struggling with Samantha's behavior now. Anytime she tries to engage Samantha in an activity she screams and throws herself on the ground. Her lack of language really stands out against the other children who are able to communicate their wants and needs. Samantha won't even turn to her name being called." said Kara. "And let's be honest, circle time is stressful for all of us!" "Oh, I know Kara." Mary sighed. "We really need to think about what we can do to help her during circle time. One minute she is dancing in the middle, the next minute she is screaming in mom's lap. It seemed to help for a little while when I stood up and held her so she could watch from above but then she started kicking and screaming again. Poor little girls don't know what she wants. Let's set a time to meet tomorrow to write down our concerns and then over the next month we can collect some data so that when I meet with mom we will have something to back up our concerns." Mary suggested. "That sounds like a good plan Mary." said Kara.

### Dilemma

Susan was the first parent to arrive for class on Monday. This wasn't unusual. Susan and Samantha, her 2 year old daughter, seem to arrive early every week. It seemed like Susan had a hard time being home with Samantha and looked for any opportunity to get out. If Mary remembered correctly, Susan had different activities scheduled every day for Samantha. After one of the first classes, Susan asked if they could stay and play in the children's classroom for a while longer, when we explained that we had another class coming she asked the teacher next door.

Today, Samantha was tearing through the room like a tornado and leaving a trail behind her. After greeting Susan and Samantha and chatting a bit about their weekend, Mary took a deep breath and gathered her thoughts. She knew this would be a touchy conversation but wanted to take advantage of having the room to themselves. "Susan, I wanted to follow up with you on a conversation that we were having last week in class. We were discussing language development and you mentioned that Samantha has a few words that you and your husband are able to understand but that other family members and friends have a hard time understanding her, is that correct?" "Yes, that's right. Usually she communicates by screaming when she is frustrated." Susan said. "I noticed that during parent and child interaction time as well." said Mary, "I talked to Kara, the children's teacher, after last week's class and she also mentioned that she has a hard time understanding Samantha. We have also noticed that Samantha struggles with transitions during class time. Have you noticed that at home?" "Oh, yeah! Everything is a fight with her at home. She gets mad when it's time to stop playing so we can have dinner, then she gets mad when it's time to clean up after dinner. She hates bath time and getting ready for bed is nearly impossible. By the end of the night we are both exhausted." said Susan. "That must be really hard on you Susan. Would you be open to talking with our early childhood special education team? They are a great resource and may be able to offer you some support and provide suggestions on how to best help Samantha in her development." said Mary. "Oh, I have met with them. My pediatrician suggested I contact them at Samantha's last well-check because he was concerned that she wasn't talking. They came out and did an evaluation. They said that she has some developmental delays and Missy comes out to work with her once a week. In fact, Missy was the one who suggested that I sign up for an ECFE class." replied Susan. "Oh, I wasn't aware of that." said Mary "That's great news. I am glad that you are getting some support."

## Perspectives

Everybody was slowly wandering into the cramped meeting room and finding their place at the table. Around the room, waiting for the meeting to start, some people were having side conversations while others were finishing their prep work for the week and some were clinging to their morning coffee still trying to wake up. Our Monday morning staff meeting is supposed to start at 7:30 but it never actually starts until 7:40 and even then it seems that it is the same conversations that we have been having all year; bussing, implementing the new curriculum, assessments, finding time to do assessments. Finally it is open to any questions or issues we need to talk about. Kara raises her hand, reviewing in her mind what she was going to say and how she was going to say it. "I have something I would like to talk about. I was wondering what the protocol is for notifying teachers when there is a child enrolled in their classroom that is receiving special education services?" asked Kara, trying to keep the tone in her voice light. "The teachers are notified during the initial registration process." answered their supervisor, Barb. "They would receive the child's IEP and meet with the special education teacher working with that child to discuss the services that will be provided. But you shouldn't have to worry about that because that is in preschool and we don't have any children receiving special education services in ECFE." Barb has been the supervisor for the early learning program for the last three years and oversees preschool, ECFE and ECSE. Although Kara has never had any problems with her, several of her co-workers have expressed frustration with Barb's lack of support and understanding of the ECFE and preschool programs and feel that special education is her top priority.

"Actually, we found out last week that we have a little girl who has been receiving services for the last few months. Don't get me wrong, I am not complaining that she is in my class. I agree that both she and mom will benefit from the program. I just wish we had been informed about it ahead of time instead of finding out about it the way we did." Kara waited for a reply and when there was none she continued on. "It was actually rather embarrassing the way we found out. Mary and I had been discussing our concerns about Samantha's development and decided that it was time to talk to mom. Mary sat down with mom and talked to her about our concerns and suggested an evaluation from the ECSE team. Then mom tells us that she has already done all of that and is receiving services. Mom told us that it was her birth-3 teacher that suggested that she enroll in an ECFE class. We felt pretty foolish." Kara finished her story and waited for a response. "Well," began Barb, "legally we cannot disclose any of that information and it is up to the parents to tell you if they want to. We are not providing any services to the family during your class, are we?" "No." answered Kara. "Then it is really two different programs and it is not our place to provide you with that information." said Barb. "I guess I got the impression from mom that she assumed we already knew. I also feel like we wasted a lot of time during the first few weeks struggling with the challenging behaviors, seeing the red flags, documenting it, collecting data and then meeting with mom to tell her something she already knew. If we would have been in the know from day one we could have been working together with the special education team and the family to better help this little girl. We could have been part of the solution instead I feel like we only held her back by not understanding the whole picture. I understand that it is mom's decision to inform us, but I wonder if the ECSE staff could encourage the families to do so. We all have the same goal which is to help this child to be successful. Wouldn't it make more sense if we worked together?" "Like I said," Barb sighed. "It is up to the parents to decide if they want to share that information. If they don't tell you our hands are tied."

## QUESTIONS

1. Which DEC practices for the topic area of Teaming and Collaboration did you see supported in this case study?
2. Which of the DEC practices for the topic area of Teaming and Collaboration were not supported in this case study? How might these have been addressed?
3. Kara and Mary were frustrated that they were not informed that Samantha was receiving special education services. Since ultimately it is the parents' decision whether or not to tell the ECFE teachers, is it worth bringing it up at the staff meeting? Why or why not?
4. What are some possible reasons why Samantha's mom did not share this information with the teachers?
5. ECFE is a program that recognizes and supports families in being their child's first, and most important teacher. Since neither Kara nor Mary are special education teachers, nor are they working in a special education role, is it necessary for them to know the details of Samantha's special education needs? Why or why not?
6. How could the team coordinate services for Samantha across agencies?
7. Do you agree with Kara's encouraging the parents to tell their children's teachers if their child is receiving special education services? Why or why not? Would you still agree that they should tlel their child's teachers if they attended a community child care?

## THE TIMES, THEY ARE A-CHANGIN'

*Unsolved*

## Background

Keith and Terry are first-time parents, aged 44 and 41, respectively. Terry has taught kindergarten for a number of years, but has taken a 2 or 3 year leave-of-absence from her teaching position to spend the last two months of her pregnancy on bed-rest and then to give birth to her premature son and stay at home for the first year or two of his life. She is overjoyed to be a mother and often remarks, "I am the oldest mother of the youngest child in our neighborhood. But I don't care. I waited a long time to be a mom and I have no regrets." She also describes her feelings about her baby, "I just wish I didn't have to worry so much about him and how he is developing." Her husband, Keith is very supportive of Terry's wish to stay home with Jake and sometimes feels that he is not helpful enough, or available very much, to help care for their baby. He travels frequently for his job and worries for his wife and baby. The Birth-to-Three teacher, Anna, has heard him offer some words of regret such as, "I just feel like I am never there when she needs me. But it can't be helped, I guess. It's my job." There are a very few extended family members available for support and respite for the family.

The multidisciplinary team members are mainly located in the Early Childhood Center in the community in which Keith and Terry reside. The members consist of the Birth-to-Three teacher/Interventionist, an Occupational Therapist, a Physical Therapist, and a social worker.

## Dilemma

During the course of the school year, the consistency of the program has become a problem for the teaching staff and team to navigate. Does this affect the whole program or specific age group? The OT resigned and moved to another state because of her husband's new employment. While the position was advertised and candidates were interviewed, the caseload was put "in a holding pattern," with the social worker making attempts to visit the families involved. A new OT was hired and began to work with the families; but then, the OT had emergency surgery, and they were, again, without an OT. Anna, the teacher, has had many emails and phone calls to the new OT and the social worker regarding her concerns about Jake and his family and the transition that they are facing. Many of the phone calls and emails have not been returned. Sometimes Anna stops by the offices of the OT and the social worker to see if she can speak to them face-to-face, but she isn't able to connect with either of them. Anna talked with her supervisor one morning and conveyed her frustration, "I am getting so desperate for some communication from them. I realize that the social worker has a lot of responsibility right now, but I just need to talk with her about this family that will be moving to Part B." Maybe add that they are supposed to be collaborating on some assessment work. Anna's supervisor asked her to forward the emails to her so that she could see the actual times and dates of the numerous emails. Her supervisor remarked, "It's not that I don't believe you, Anna, I just need to see how long and often you have been trying to communicate with either the new OT or the social worker so that I can explain and justify your/our concerns." Anna and her supervisor discuss the fact that the people that are covering those positions are perhaps feeling frustration about their workload as well. Can you add in one perspective that of the social worker or new OT? Anna also has some transition ideas that she would like to try with the family and she needs to be able to share those ideas with the other professionals involved with the family before she presents the ideas to Keith and Terry.

**Perspectives**

Anna had a recent home visit with the family and she listened to their concerns about changing teachers, unfamiliar surroundings, new/different people in their home are just some of the concerns that they express. Terry states, "We are just so comfortable with you and our old OT. You know Jake so well and how can someone new ever know him as well as you do?" She continued, "And we never know from one week to the next who will be contacting us-the social worker, the old OT, the new OT." Anna listens as Terry continues, "I just don't know if I really want to send Jake to preschool. Maybe it would be better if I just kept him home with me."

## QUESTIONS

1. Which DEC practices for the topic area of Teaming and Collaboration did you see supported in this case study?
2. Which of the DEC practices for the topic area of Teaming and Collaboration were not supported in this case study? How might these have been addressed?
3. Is it important that Anna's supervisor is aware of the problems Anna is facing? Why or why not?
4. What systems could be put into place to guard against the problems this study describes regarding staffing issues?
5. What supports could Anna offer the family regarding the transition?

## SECTION 2: CASES FOR 3-TO-5-YEAR-OLDS

## Mathew's Team

*Unsolved*

### Background

Jessica was an Early Childhood Special Education Teacher at North Point Elementary School. This was her second-year teaching. She taught a 3-5-year-old co-taught class with Karen, Monday through Friday from 1:15-3:45 P.M. Karen had been teaching Early Childhood for the past seven years. Jessica and Karen had eight general education students and five students with special needs in their class ranging in disabilities. One of their students was named Matthew. Mathew was a 4-year-old boy who had a developmental delay. He received speech services and occupational therapy.

Jessica was concerned with the amount of days Mathew was missing school. Over the few weeks he showed up for the entire five days, he made improvements with using the interventions she had put in place. He was beginning to be able to regulate his emotions better, identify when he was becoming frustrated, and make an appropriate choice to calm down. When he missed many days of school in a row, Jessica felt like he was starting over from the beginning of the school year where he was hitting and kicking the other students an average of three times a day.

Karen enjoyed co-teaching with Jessica, but thought Mathew needed to be in a self-contained classroom. She wanted Jessica to pull Mathew out of the class and work with him one on one when he became frustrated. Karen thought Jessica had put great interventions in place for Mathew, but Karen nor Jessica did not always have the time or enough support to follow through with the interventions when they had several students in their class who needed significant support.

Mathew's mother, Cindy was a single mother of four going through a divorce. She worked a full-time job and did not get home until late. Mathew's sister would watch him and his siblings after school. Cindy was concerned by Mathew's aggressive behavior towards his siblings and outbursts at home and in public. Mathew had not been allowed back to his previous day care centers due to his behavior. Cindy felt sending Mathew to preschool was her last chance to get Mathew help.

## Child Behavior

Mathew enjoys going to preschool. He likes to play outside on the playground and play with toy trains. He has a difficult time-sharing toys and space with his peers. Mathew was absent from school an average of three days a week. He struggles with making friends and will hit and kick his peers and classroom staff when he becomes frustrated.

## Dilemma

Jessica and Karen were getting their materials ready for their afternoon class. Jessica stated, "Karen, don't forget we have an IEP Meeting for Mathew after class today." Karen looked at Jessica and said, "yes, I remember. I'll be there. It will be nice to talk to Mathew's mother since she hardly returns our phone calls." Karen felt there was continual IEP meetings scheduled every week and she was always having to stay late at school. "I wish we had more time to discuss Mathew and some changes I would like to make," said Jessica. Karen nodded her head in agreement and stated, "We meet once a month to plan but that never seems like enough time." Both Karen and Jessica are feeling inadequate due to the lack of time they have to collaborate together.

Cindy came into school for Mathew's IEP meeting right after school was out. She was feeling helpless with Mathew's behaviors at home but she was seeing he was making gains in academic areas. As she was walking down the school hallway to Mathew's IEP meeting, she felt apprehensive about what his teachers were going to say. Jessica greeted Cindy when she entered the classroom. She passed out a meeting agenda and the team went around the table and started introductions. The team consisted of Jessica, Karen, Cindy, Mary, the occupational therapist, and Molly, the speech therapist and district representative. Jessica, Karen, and Cindy were all feeling anxious about this IEP meeting for different reasons as stated above.

Jessica started with Mathew's progress towards his goals and objectives. Karen jumped into the conversation, "Mathew has been making some great progress, but we are still concerned with him hitting the other children in the classroom when he becomes frustrated. We have seen an increase in the number of times he has hit his peers this past month. I think it would be best if Jessica took him out of the classroom when he becomes aggressive to calm down." Jessica was stunned Karen was saying this without discussing it with her before the meeting. Jessica then stated, "We have a calming area in our classroom that we have been practicing using with Mathew to make an appropriate choice to calm down when he becomes upset or needs to be alone." Jessica wanted to discuss this with Karen later, but did not feel it would be appropriate to discuss in Mathew's IEP meeting. Karen wanted Mathew to be removed from the room when he became aggressive because she did not want the other children to get hurt. When he escalated in the past, he was a distraction to the rest of the class and would take a long time before he became regulated again. Karen felt like her voice was not heard nor valued by Jessica. This was a huge issue that needed to be resolved immediately.

"I cannot stay for the whole meeting because I have another meeting, I need to attend but I would like to talk about Mathew's progress in occupational therapy," said Mary. "He is doing really well, here are a few samples of his work and the progress he has made. I would like to decrease the amount of time I see him." Jessica and Karen exchanged glances because they did not agree. They felt he had been making progress but still needed the same amount of time and support. Jessica wished Mary would have mentioned this prior to the meeting so they could have discussed this. Mathew's mom, Cindy, was happy to hear he was making progress and agreed to decreasing the amount of time he had occupational therapy. Mary had been meaning to mention this to Jessica and Karen before the meeting, but with as many students as she had on her caseload, she just did not have time. She felt a pang of guilt when she noticed they exchanged glances after she mentioned decreasing Mathew's service time. She also was frustrated at the quantity of students she was expected to service. She felt that there is not enough time in one day to get to everything accomplished. Cindy stated, "I am so grateful for all of you helping Mathew. He loves coming to school. I have seen Mathew make progress these past couple of months, but I am worried about him hurting his siblings at home and yelling when he does not get his way." Jessica told Cindy about the interventions they were doing at school with Mathew and gave her ideas to try at home. Cindy was thinking that these were all great ideas. I hope I am able to use the interventions in our daily schedule she was thinking to herself. I don't want to ask Jessica how to put these interventions in place because she may find out I am never home due to my crazy work schedule. Her suggestions are helpful but I don't know the steps to use them with my son. I don't want people to think I'm a bad mother.

By this time, the meeting had lasted over an hour. Molly jumped in the conversation stating, "I would like to increase the amount of time I see Mathew for speech and pull him out of the classroom to work with him in a less distracting environment one on one." Jessica wanted Mathew to stay in the least restrictive environment and did not agree with this recommendation. Before Jessica could say anything, Cindy said, "I like that idea." Molly felt relieved. It would be easier for her to work with Mathew one on one. This meeting was not going how Jessica planned. The team was not on the same page and the meeting was going in many different directions. They still hadn't had time to discuss Mathew's attendance before Mathew's mom stood up and said how grateful she was for all of them, but she had to go pick up Mathew's sister from basketball practice. The team thanked Cindy for coming in and she quickly rushed out the door.

## Perspectives

Jessica felt like the meeting did not go as she had planned. She was upset Karen brought up having her remove Mathew from the classroom when it was supposed to be a team-taught class. She wished Karen would have discussed this with her first. Jessica did not understand why Mary wanted to decrease Mathew's direct service time. Both her and Karen thought he needed this time. Jessica had been waiting to discuss her concerns regarding Mathew's attendance with Cindy, but was not able to address her concerns because of the time limitation.

Cindy was feeling happy Mathew was making progress. She was eager to try the new ideas discussed which would help her at home with Mathew's behavior of hitting his siblings but felt overwhelmed with all the information from the meeting and was concerned about being able to put Jessica's ideas in place. She wasn't able to spend as much time with Mathew and his siblings as she wanted because of her hectic work schedule. She felt guilty not being able to bring him to school every day because of her job and not always having enough gas money to make it there.

Karen was discouraged with the meeting. She felt like nothing was accomplished. She wanted Jessica to start taking Mathew out of the classroom more before he seriously injured one of the other students. She knows Jessica has many good interventions in place, but feels like it is Jessica's responsibility to follow through with the interventions.

## QUESTIONS

1. Which DEC practices for the topic area of Teaming and Collaboration did you see supported in this case study?
2. Which of the DEC practices for the topic area of Teaming and Collaboration were not supported in this case study? How might these have been addressed?
3. How could the team have addressed the mother's frustrations and concerns?
4 How should Jessica approach Karen about her concerns with taking Mathew out of the classroom when he becomes frustrated?
5. What would have helped the team be in agreement prior to Mathew's

IEP meeting?

6. Describe how you think the lack of team communication will affect Mathew?

7. How could the team have addressed the mother's frustrations and concerns?

8. How could Jessica and the team work on building a better relationship with Cindy so that she does not feel apprehensive to ask for help?

## IT'S HARD TO LET GO

*Solved*

### Background

Jenna and Stan are the parents of three-year-old Braxton, who was diagnosed with Cerebral Palsy when he was eighteen months old. Jenna has been a stay at home mom since Braxton was born, and spends her days caring for his unique needs. Stan works in the IT Department at a local hospital and has a demanding schedule. He hasn't let his work schedule get in the way of being there for his family though. Jenna stated, "Stan is a hard worker and is dedicated to his job, but he always puts his family first." Though their role as Braxton's parents hasn't been an easy one, Jenna and Stan are their son's biggest advocates.

Since his diagnosis, Braxton has been receiving services under Part C of IDEA. He recently turned three, and is now receiving services under Part B. Due to having Cerebral Palsy, Braxton uses a wheelchair and has a difficult time communicating orally. Despite all that he has been through, Braxton is an easy-going, happy young boy who enjoys being around others.

### Dilemma

Braxton will be beginning preschool in an ECSE classroom in a few weeks and his mother, Jenna is concerned about Braxton transitioning to the preschool program. She is concerned that Braxton will not have his needs met as much at school in a setting with other students. She is also concerned about the amount of time in the preschool setting and that in the amount of time he will be at preschool, he will not have an adequate amount of time to receive his additional services at school. Braxton sees an occupational therapist, and physical therapist and a speech pathologist. This is a major concern for Braxton's parents, who feel that Braxton needs to see all the specialists on a routine schedule to be successful. They want him to make noticeable progress and maintain academic levels close to his peers.

Another concern Braxton's mother has is about the care he will receive at school. She feels he has a large number of significant needs and that caring for him is time consuming. She worries that the school is unable to do an adequate job of meeting these needs and that there is a possibility Braxton could be neglected.

## Perspectives

Braxton's IEP team sees a great deal of potential in him. They are excited for him to begin preschool and feel that he will benefit greatly from this new experience. The team agreed that Braxton's mom has his best interest at heart, but that she can sometimes be overbearing and unapproachable. The OT, PT, and SLP recommended Braxton's new teachers work to develop a strong rapport with Jenna by addressing her concerns, no matter how small, and assuring her that parent input is valued.

## QUESTIONS

1. Which DEC practices for the topic area of Teaming and Collaboration did you see supported in this case study?
2. Which of the DEC practices for the topic area of Teaming and Collaboration were not supported in this case study? How might these have been addressed?
3. How can the ECSE staff in the preschool make Jenna more comfortable with Braxton at school?
4. What advice would you give to Jenna and Stan?
5. How can the tea support Jenna and Stan in preparing for the transition for Braxton?
6. What advice would you give to Jenna and Stan?

## KINDERGARTEN AHEAD

*Unsolved*

## Background

Kevin is a four-year-old boy in a preschool learning center. He has been diagnosed as Developmentally Delayed after developmental screening and developmental evaluation. For the last two years he has worked with his learning center as well as his community's early learning intervention program and shown some progress. He is currently working on making gains in speech and fine motor skills in order to be at a kindergarten level for the upcoming fall school year. He has interactions with several adults to work on his skills, most notably is his occupational therapist, a speech and language pathologist, his general education preschool teacher and a special education specialist, Katie, who sees him three days a week in his preschool.

## Dilemma

"Now before we begin our meeting, I want to go over your parental rights. You are the most important member of the team," Katie began as she did every IFSP meeting. The office she had her meetings in was almost as familiar as her classroom at this time of the year. "The reason we are meeting today is to discuss Kevin's transition into kindergarten and what we will be doing for the rest of the year to ensure he is ready," Katie continued already seeing a glazed over look in the eyes of Kevin's mom. As she pulled out her carefully prepared files she could not help but feel a little frustrated. It seemed every meeting she had with Jamie the young mother checked out as soon as Katie mentioned LRE or the kindergarten standards.

Despite the tired look on Jamie's face Katie continued to go over all the progress Kevin had made so far. She showed the graphs she had made to track his development in interacting with other children, his language skills, letter recognition and fine-motor skills. After each goal area Katie would pause to give Jamie a chance to ask questions but Jamie just nodded. When Katie asked, "do you understand?" another head nod was all she received. Katie turned over the meeting to the other specialist teachers who went over all the skills Kevin was working on and needed to continue to work on.

At the end of the meeting Katie told Jamie some simple ways to continue the work Kevin was doing at school at home. "Kevin loves playing with our alphabet letter app on the iPad. You could try working with something similar at home to continue to work on letter recognition. Or when you are walking to the park with him try counting the number of cars you see on the way. Just remember to keep it fun!" Jamie said what seemed to be her first words of the conversation, "okay, I'll see what I can do. Is it okay if I stop in to see Kevin before I go?" Although Katie knew it would disrupt Kevin's work, she knew the only answer she could give was "sure."

Once again Katie left the meeting feeling frustrated. She put so much time into making the graphs, tracking progress, filling out paperwork and working with Kevin to get him to the best place possible but it seemed like her work went unnoticed by Jamie. 'I know she is a good mother, but would it kill her to pay more attention to his goals?' was her final thought as she walked away from the meeting.

## Perspectives

As Jamie got off of the city bus and walked toward Kevin's school, she was full of apprehension. She always felt uncomfortable in the school not only because of the office's stiff chairs and her own memories of being in a principal's office but also because she felt out of place with all the teachers. When Jamie finally checked in and made it to the office, she was happy to sink into the uncomfortable chairs after just getting off an overnight work shift and the long-standing bus ride. Soon after Kevin's teacher Katie walked in holding her morning coffee. Katie always looked so put together with a sleek hairstyle and matching outfits and jewelry. Jamie gave her own hair a self-conscious pat down and briefly wished she would have had a chance to grab coffee.

"You are the most important member of the team," Katie's announcement caught her attention and she thought 'if I am the most important member then why do I never feel like I have control?' As Katie pushed more and more paperwork at her Jamie just wanted to ask "how is my son doing? Stop telling me about percentiles and tell me if he will be able to be in a normal all-day kindergarten class." Jamie hated how Katie constantly asked her "do you understand?" Of course, she understood how Kevin held his crayons wrong, skipped numbers while counting to ten and had trouble controlling the volume of his voice. But other kids had trouble with their indoor voices too! It was so frustrating to hear everything Kevin still needed to work on and Jamie had a sense of hopelessness as Katie started going over what to do at home.

*Don't they understand that all my free time already goes to working with Kevin? I try to work with him at home, but he doesn't always want to work after spending all day working at school. I only get a few hours with him before his bedtime and I'm back off to work.* Jamie heard Katie talking about taking Kevin to the park in the background of her thoughts and gave a silent laugh at the suggestion. *Kevin might be doing well with kids at school but at the park the older kids make fun of the way he talks.* The iPad suggestion wasn't even worth a thought since there was no way Jamie could afford to spend money on such an expensive toy.

At this point all Jamie wanted was for the meeting to be over so she could see her baby, go home to sleep and have some time with him before work. 'Kevin's teacher doesn't understand how frustrating it is to work so hard with him during our short amount of time together only to hear so few positive things in these meetings' was Jamie's final thought as she hurried out of the office and towards the classroom.

# QUESTIONS

1. Which DEC practices for the topic area of Teaming and Collaboration did you see supported in this case study?
2. Which of the DEC practices for the topic area of Teaming and Collaboration were not supported in this case study? How might these have been addressed?
3. What could Katie do to help support Jamie's involvement in the meetings?
4. Whata changes could be made to the structure of the meetings to ensure both parties leave satisfied?
5. Did this IFSP meeting demonstrate that family members are an essential part of the team? Why or why not?
6. Do you think these communication issues are common in IEP/IFSP meetings? Why or why not?
7. Did this IFSP meeting live out the idea that family members are an essential part of the team? Why or why not?

## TEAMING AND COLLABORATION GONE WRONG!

*Solved*

### Background

It was the start of a new year with a seasoned teacher in a new school. The new Early Childhood Special Education (ECSE) teacher, Beth, moved to a new location and was paired with an existing team of teaching assistants (TA's), Lorie and Linda, who had worked together at that location the year before. They had all chosen the place they wanted to be and the TA's had chosen to be with Beth.

### Dilemma

The week before school started they all met at a local restaurant with the new speech therapist and student teacher. They talked about the space and asked about each other, how they came to be where they are, a bit about how the room was put together, and Beth's high expectations. Lorie and Linda talked to each other later and both were very excited to be with the new teacher and start the year off together.

## Perspectives

**Beth's Story.** Beth was changing schools after being at the same school for a long time. She had researched the different locations and chose the one that had the best accommodations for ECSE children, running water, a bathroom, great light and storage. She was paired with two TA's who had worked at the school together the year before. They had a great introduction and everyone seemed excited to start the year together. There were troubles from the start, Lorie kept trying to tell her how to run the class like last year, and Linda seemed angry all the time. Making matters worse, neither of them seemed to know any of the interventions Beth used. It was like they had never been trained. She tried to email them about the interventions and her expectations but they still did not let the kids do their own work. They took so long doing their email and billing she began to wonder what they were doing and kept track of the time they were gone.

By the end of three weeks she had enough and sent e-mails to the TA's copying the principal and ECSE supervisor. Beth felt that she had done everything she could and was at the end of her rope. She felt unwelcome and felt the TA's were not trained and stated that in the email after school on Friday.

**Lorie's Story.** Lorie began the first day very excited and eager to see some of the children from the year before and meet the new children. The first days were a bit chaotic as they always are, learning new routines and finding materials in the class were hard especially since she had spent the last few years in and out of this room and knew where things had been kept. She found herself looking for things in the places they had been before. Lorie talked to Beth about the children that were returning and what they were doing last year. She talked about the setup of the motor room and her frustration at the dwindling space and portable walls since she thought they were not safe. When Lorie spoke of the past she began to feel like her comments were not welcome and Beth did not seem to care.

She began to feel frustration over practices that she thought were not helpful or even harmful to children. These were the very late breakfast time and a "no fussing, be happy" policy. Some of the practices and interventions that Beth was using were not familiar to Lorie and Beth had stated "I should just treat you like you are new." Beth sent e-mails detailing and intervention and assigned TA's to certain children. Lorie was trying to implement the new interventions as best she could and began to feel like there was nothing she could do right and Beth did not prepare her for small groups to let her know what was happening or what she wanted to see from the children, like her past teachers did. Conversation between adults was minimal and little said between any adults because Beth didn't allow it. Lorie started to shut down and not ask any questions or say anything to anyone unless they directed a comment or question to her.

Then came the e-mail. Lorie thought it was unprofessional to send that out on a Friday after work knowing that she checked email on nights and weekends. Lorie felt like Beth said she was not capable of doing her job and that she was untrained. Lorie thought Beth should have come to her instead of making it an issue for supervisors to deal with.

**Linda's Story.** Linda was happy to start the year and was grateful to be with Lorie since she had transferred from another program the year before. She was also grateful to be in a decent room all day because last year she was in an office turned into a classroom half the day. Linda thought the team would work well and loved the fact that Beth stated she had high expectations of the children. Right away it seemed they were at odds with each other. Beth told her she had an attitude and though she was angry all the time. Linda also thought that the breakfast time was too late, being almost two hours after school started, creating behavior from the children who were hungry.

Linda was used to having a very collaborative classroom and talked about things with Lorie and Beth. It became clear in the first week that this was not going to be that kind of classroom. Linda brought her concerns about breakfast to Beth after the first week saying "they are hungry when they get here." Beth replied to her that she thought the parents fed their children before school and "they will get used to it." Linda felt that she had not been heard and thought that Beth had a need to control everything. She also thought that Beth was not willing to listen or accept input from anyone. When Linda got the e-mail Friday night she was angry. She thought that it could have been done in a different way. She also saw in the email that Beth took no ownership in anything she did to make it worse.

Beth and the TA have a meeting with the principal the next week. Lorie and Linda stated they no longer wanted to work with Beth due to the e-mail and being asked to "renew their commitment or ask for another position" in the email. Linda was transferred to the upper grades while Lorie stayed until a replacement could be found 6 weeks later.

## QUESTIONS

1. Which DEC practices for the topic area of Teaming and Collaboration did you see supported in this case study?
2. Which of the DEC practices for the topic area of Teaming and Collaboration were not supported in this case study? How might these have been addressed?

3. How could Beth have handled this situation differently? What else could she have tried?
4. How could other team members have contributed to this situation?
5. What improvements could be made for the functioning of this team?
6. Was the outcome the best for everyone? Why or why not? What might have helped to make the outcome more desirable for all involved?

# Chapter 8

# TRANSITION

## OVERVIEW OF RECOMMENDED PRACTICE

The Division for Early Childhood has stated that Transition "refers to the events, activities, and processes associated with key changes between environments or programs during the early childhood years and the practices that support the adjustment of the child and family to the new setting (DEC, 2014, p.16). In the field of early childhood, transitions would be from both the type of setting and/or federal funding source. A child and family may transition from hospital to home services if the child had a medical issue at birth (Part C funding). Another transition may be from home services (Part C funding) to early childhood community or school services and then to kindergarten / school-age services (Part B funding).

There are two major tenets for transition. The first would be the importance of the practitioners to share information regarding the child and family from the sending to receiving program and this would occur before, during, and after the transition. The second would be the practitioners working together with the family to ensure a successful transition before, during, and after the whole process.

DEC recommends the following transition practices for transition:

- **TR1**. Practitioners in sending and receiving programs exchange information before, during, and after transition about practices most likely to support the child's successful adjustment and positive outcomes.
- **TR2**. Practitioners use a variety of planned and timely strategies with the child and family before, during, and after the transition to support successful adjustment and positive outcomes for both the child and family.

(DEC, 2014, p. 16)

The following seven cases were designed to represent the recommended practices (RPs) for transition as a whole. Each case is illustrative of a combination of the seven RPs for transition and does not contain each of the practices. When reviewing the case studies for the RPs for transition, it is advised to use this chapter in the following ways. One, have individuals read each case and answer independently as a way to determine the individual's understanding of assessment and the corresponding practices. Two, have individuals independently read a case study and in small groups discuss what they learned regarding assessment and the corresponding cases. Three, have small groups read case studies and contribute to a whole group discussion as a whole. You can use any and all of these suggestions as it fits with your purposes for the teaching or review of the RPs.

## SECTION 1: CASES FOR BIRTH TO AGE 3

### Daycare to Preschool

*Unsolved*

### Background

Mae is 34 months old and lives at home with her mom, Jamie, and dad, Lee. Mae is their first child. Mae was born with a rare chromosome deficiency called 6p deletion. At her first well child her doctor noticed that there was an abnormal amount of flexibility in her foot and referred her to a specialist, where her condition was found. Mae's condition is so rare, her developmental delays are unpredictable.

Mae qualifies for services under part C in the category of developmental delay. She receives physical therapy 2 times a month for 20 minutes, speech therapy 3 times a week for 20 minutes, and occupational therapy 2 times a month, all within the daycare setting.

She has been in a center-based daycare since she was 8 months old and now transitioning into the preschool setting. Her teacher, Angie has reported enjoying working with her and being pleased with her progress.

### Dilemma

Jamie has concerns about Mae transitioning to the preschool, and wonders *how far will she be behind the other kids, how will Mae react to the new environment, and how will the new service providers work with Mae.*

## Perspectives

Angie is the lead teacher in the infant room at the Little People Daycare. She has worked with Mae for 16 months. Reflecting on her time with Mae, Angie reports,

"When Mae first started at our daycare Jamie was nervous about every little thing, just like most first times are. It took her a long time to trust our staff, and she had a lot of questions when anything changed for Mae. Once she was comfortable with our staff you could see her relax and Mae seemed a lot happier with us in the mornings after drop off too."

"Mae has made great progress; we have seen her through all of her developmental stages. She seems to be behind the other kids by 3-6 months. We did allow her to stay in the baby room longer than usual because she wasn't crawling or walking. Jamie was very worried that she would get trampled over in the toddler room since she wasn't moving as much as the other kids. We slowly transitioned her into the toddler room, and it seemed like she started crawling immediately after she saw other kids moving. This took quite a while for Jamie to be ok with, but she was relaxed after she saw the progress Mae made shortly after being in there.

Jamie is a great mom! She makes sure Mae has everything she needs, and advocates for her needs. At times she can be overwhelming but if you listen to her concerns, give her time and give your opinion in a couple days she comes around. We will all miss having Mae with us all day long."

Jamie reported the following information when Angie was talking to her in conversation, nothing formal. "I am so worried for Mae and the next stage in her life, going to preschool. It took me a long time to be ok with her at daycare. She has a lot of people that work with her on a regular basis and she has made great gains because of those people. Going to preschool she will have all new service providers, speech, physical therapy, classroom teacher and assistants. What if she doesn't make as many gains or even worse yet, loses some of her skills? I have met the 2 different teachers, and the preschool special education teacher but no one else, and we don't know for sure which teacher she will have yet."

## QUESTIONS

1. Which DEC practices for the topic area of Transition did you see supported in this case study?
2. Which of the DEC practices for the topic area of Transition were not supported in this case study? How might these have been addressed?
3. What strategies can the preschool staff use to begin to form a rela-

tionship with Jamie"

4. What strategies can both the daycare teachers and the preschool teachers use to work together to create a smooth transition for Mae?

5. How can the family be more involved in the transition process?

## A LONG WAY FROM HOME

*Unsolved*

### Background

Sloan is a two-year old boy who lives with his mother, Maggie and father, Tom. When Sloan was 15 months old, Mom reported she started having concerns about Sloan's development. Sloan was assessed and qualified for Part C services in the category of developmental delay in the areas of communication, cognitive, and social-emotional development. Most recently, Sloan was diagnosed through a local private Autism Program as having autism. He has therapy in home with an early childhood special education teacher one hour a week, speech pathologist four times a year, occupational therapist three times a year, social communication playgroup four days a week for four hours and private therapy. Sloan was born full-term following an uncomplicated pregnancy. During delivery, it was discovered that Sloan's umbilical cord had wrapped around his neck; however, there were no other complications during delivery.

Sloan was going to daycare at a family day care, and they decided it would benefit Sloan to have his dad stay home to take him to school and therapy appointments. During the routines-based interview, his mom expressed she would like to take Sloan to Target to get groceries. Mom Maggie works during the day and is not always available to join his dad, and the early intervention teacher. The early intervention teacher added the routine of grocery shopping at Target on their list of priorities to work on. Being able to run errands is an important skill to learn and is developmentally appropriate. Sloan is working on improving his language skills, routines at home and unexpected events. Creating a routine of going to the grocery store will work on improving his language skills by asking for groceries of his choice, create social situations with other children and adults, and help his parents be able to get necessary food items for the family.

## Dilemma

When Sloan becomes upset, he will yell, cry, and occasionally push things out of the way. When he is unable to communicate, he engages in whining. In situations where he does not know what is going on, he runs out of the room or throws himself into items such as the couch, his parent's leg, and/or on the floor. Sloan enjoys opening and closing doors. At the store he runs out of the store and will not respond to the demand of "stop." He will not sit down in the shopping cart. When asked to put groceries into the shopping cart, he throws them on the floor and stomps on them. He engages in self-injurious behaviors in the form of pulling his hair or hitting his head. Both parents want Sloan to be part of the shopping experience. It is important to them to bring them with them to the store. They want him to be included and don't want to leave him behind with one of them as the other shops.

## Perspectives

**Dad.** Tom has the routine of grabbing some essential groceries at Target Wednesday mornings, the early intervention teacher meets him at Target around 8:45 a.m. The early intervention teacher and Tom get Sloan out of the car, he locks the door of the car once he is out. Sloan does not like to sit in the shopping cart, so Dad pushes the shopping cart with Sloan underneath him to "help" push the cart. Sloan pushes for a few steps and then runs off in the parking lot of Target. The teacher and/or dad run after him and help remind him to "push" the shopping cart. This cycle continues, it takes 5 minutes to get to the entrance of the store. Once at the entrance of Target, Sloan becomes fascinated with the doors opening and closing. Sloan is stuck at the entrance for 5 minutes with watching the doors open and close. When Dad says it is time to get groceries, Sloan falls to the floor, screaming, trying to break free from his dad and run. Dad lifts up Sloan to put him in the shopping cart and Sloan kicks his legs to avoid sitting in the cart. After a minute or two, Sloan is carried away from the door and prompted to "push" the shopping cart and told they need to get some milk. In the refrigerated section, Sloan opens the door and closes the door of the milk refrigerator. Sloan wants to stay at the refrigerator door and continue to open and close the door. As the teacher redirects Sloan to get "juice," Sloan runs down the aisle. Dad and the teacher run after him. As they work towards the juice, Sloan takes the juice and throws it on the floor, tries to step on them and crush them. This continues for 20 minutes until they go to check out. At the check-out dad places Sloan in the back of the shopping cart to have him help place the items on the belt to check out. Sloan leaves Target content and sits in the shopping cart. Dad loads the car with the bags of groceries and Sloan is happy to hold the keys of the car and unlock the car doors. Sloan gets into his car seat willingly. Dad and Sloan drive off back to the house where the early intervention teacher will meet them.

At the house, dad pulls his car into the garage and lets Sloan sit in the front seat of the car where he enjoys pushing the buttons on the dash and pretends to drive. Dad brings the groceries into the house and the early intervention teacher is in the garage waiting for dad to come back and get Sloan. Once dad is back to get Sloan out of the car, Sloan is screaming and crying. Dad picks him up and he kicks his dad and wiggles free from him to run back to the car and play inside the car. Dad says that Sloan can play up to an hour in the car. He loves to push the buttons and open and close the door. It takes 5–8 minutes of trying to get Sloan back into the house. In the house, the teacher is there and wants to talk to Sloan and his dad about the grocery run and a few other goals of Sloan's. Sloan is still upset and keeps running to the door. The teacher has about 5 minutes to converse before she has to leave. Dad needs to get Sloan ready to go to his therapy appointment. It is difficult to get Sloan ready and back into the car without wanting to play with opening and closing the car door.

**Mom.** The grocery run takes place at the same time and day of the week as dad. Mom drives her own car to the store to meet Dad and Sloan at the parking lot. On this particular day, Mom is able to come to work on the routine with dad, Sloan, and teacher. Mom usually works when this routine is scheduled. After grocery shopping mom will go to work.

Mom walks over to the shopping cart from her car and Sloan wants mom to hold him into the store. The same behavior takes place with Sloan's mom as does with his dad. Mom does hold Sloan in the parking lot and does not ask him to push the cart. In the entrance, the automatic doors are appealing to Sloan. Mom says, "last time I was here, I got Sloan some popcorn and he did great." The teacher runs to get some popcorn and works with Sloan to first sit in the cart then eat popcorn. Sloan was not interested in popcorn and wanted to run back to the automatic doors. The teacher then asked Sloan to "push" the cart and everyone made their way to the groceries. As mom makes her way around the store, she comments "I just shop on the weekend and leave Sloan home with his dad." Mom walks next to the shopping cart throwing groceries into the cart while dad and the teacher run after Sloan. Sloan is running and grabbing items off of the shelves and throwing them onto the floor. Mom gives Sloan a sucker at one point. Sloan takes the sucker for a few minutes and throws it on the floor. There are 20-30 items in the shopping cart. Sloan helps put the items on the belt to check out and is content standing in the back of the cart doing this activity.

**Early Intervention Teacher.** In order to get moving dad picks Sloan up in the parking lot and carries him to avoid having him run and be unsafe.

Dad does not have a list of groceries with him and just picks things up as they go and occasionally will wander off without Sloan and the teacher to grab something he remembered he needed in a different aisle. The grocery run is important to mom although she is at work and dad is at home with Sloan. I see a two year old who doesn't understand why he is there and has no concept of how long he is going to be there.

Target is a big and bright store. For children with Autism, a big space like Target can cause sensory overload. The automatic doors are distracting for Sloan and he is fascinated with the movement. Just the doors opening and closing make him uninterested in anything else. Sloan is not sure why he is going into the store; he doesn't know how long he will have to be in the store and why he is there. There isn't anything interesting for him to do while he is at the store. There isn't anything to keep him engaged and an active participant.

## QUESTIONS

1. Which DEC practices for the topic area of Transition did you see supported in this case study?
2. Which of the DEC practices for the topic area of Transition were not supported in this case study? How might these have been addressed?
3. As the family began early intervention services, they identified grocery shopping as a priority What strategies can the early intervention team provide to help the family navigate the transition to community environments for Sloan?
4. How can the tean support Sloan in anticipating the routine of *running errands?*
5. How can the team incorporate Sloan's developmental objectives into the grocery store routine?
6. What other suggestions might be provided by the teacher to the family?

## TRANSITIONING TO PRESCHOOL

*Solved*

### Background

Mayrin is a 34-month-old girl who has recently qualified for early Childhood Special Education Services. Mayrin receives services twice a week for 45 minutes in the home and will transition to school once she turns three. During this time, Mayrin works with an ECSE teacher and a speech and language pathologist. Mayrin spends her days at home with her mother, Vanessa. Since Mayrin is turning three in two months, the team has been discussing her transition to preschool. Vanessa is very nervous for her transition since Mayrin has had little exposure to other children her age. Mayrin is the youngest of four siblings and everything is done for her in the home. Vanessa has told the ECSE teacher that she is sad Mayrin is growing up so fast and not ready for her to leave home. Vanessa is worried that Mayrin will be scared at preschool and not ready for it. Mayrin is not potty trained and mom is very nervous about the process. Vanessa is very worried and anxious about the transition to preschool and is not sure she wants to send Mayrin.

## Dilemma

During Mayrin's home visits, the teachers noticed that Mayrin is missing important play and social skills that are going to be needed in preschool. Melissa, the ECSE teacher, also noticed that Mayrin does not like to do things for herself such as feeding herself and dressing herself. The ECSE teacher asked Vanessa if she would be interested in taking Mayrin to an ECFE class. During this class Mayrin will have an opportunity to play with other children her age and her mom will have a chance to be around other parents who have children the same age as Mayrin. Another part of ECSE is a parent education that may be beneficial for the family. The class is offered once a week during the day for two hours. The ECSE teacher also talked with Vanessa about giving Mayrin more independence through her daily routine. She suggested giving Mayrin options when picking out her clothing and encouraging her to dress herself. She also suggested visuals to help Mayrin through the process and a lot of positive encouragement.

Before Mayrin transitions into preschool, the ECSE teacher will set up visits for both Vanessa and Mayrin to come into the school and be comfortable with the surroundings. A social story is also made for Mayrin that mom can read with her leading up to her first day of school.

The ECSE teacher talked with mom about potty training Mayrin and the process that it would take to teach her. Making potty training a fun event will help Mayrin to want to use the potty. She also showed mom how to use positive reinforcement when potty training, such as a sticker chart and gave mom some songs to sing and stories to read. With a clear schedule of frequent bathroom breaks, a reward system and positive reinforcements, mom said she was ready to try potty training with Mayrin.

After the visit the ECSE teacher set up the ECFE class for Mayrin and Vanessa to attend, since it was during the day, she planned to come to the first couple of classes to help transition Mayrin.

Four weeks after the initial visit the ECSE checked in with Vanessa to see how things were going with Mayrin. Vanessa stated that Mayrin is doing well in ECFE classes and loves going to school. The first day she was very shy and didn't want to play with the other kids or leave her mom's side. The next time they went to school Mayrin was able to leave mom's side shortly after she started playing and warmed up to the teacher. Vanessa stated that she was happy watching Mayrin play with the other kids. Mom is feeling less anxious about Mayrin going to school now that she knows she will be fine.

Vanessa has started the potty-training process with Mayrin and stated that it was going good, Mayrin had gone potty on the potty for the first time yesterday. Vanessa has been giving Mayrin a sticker every time she sits on the potty and they sing a song. Vanessa indicated that Mayrin really seems to like it. Vanessa is going to try putting Mayrin in underwear next week and see how she handles it. Vanessa is pleased with the progress that Mayrin has made.

Vanessa also told the ECSE teacher that Mayrin is becoming more independent at home with dressing and eating. When it is time for Mayrin to get dressed, Vanessa will help her pick out her clothes then she will leave the room so that Mayrin can get dressed. Vanessa said that Mayrin is excited to show Vanessa that she got dressed all by herself.

The ECSE teacher reminded Vanessa that her and Mayrin have a school visit in a few weeks to meet with the team so that they can become familiar with the Mayrin's new classroom. Vanessa thanked the ECSE teacher for all she has done and told her that she is ready for Mayrin to come to school.

## QUESTIONS

1. Which DEC practices for the topic area of Transition did you see supported in this case study?
2. Which of the DEC practices for the topic area of Transition were not supported in this case study? How might these have been addressed?
3. What activities did the teachers provide to the family to assist with a successful transition?
4. Vanessa was concerned with ayrin's self-help skills, what supports might you provide to a family who has this same concern?
5. The ECSE teacher created a social story for Mayrin to prepare her for school, what might this have included?
6. At the end of the story the transition was successful, what additional strataegies or supports may have been provided by the teachers to assist with the transition?

## SECTION 2: CASES FOR 3-TO-5-YEAR-OLDS

## Time for Kindergarten

*Solved*

### Background

How can George's team facilitate a successful transition to kindergarten this fall? George is a five-year-old boy that enjoys interacting with the physical world around him. He has been diagnosed with developmental delays in the motor domain (affecting both gross and fine motor skills), speech and language impairments, and Attention Deficit/Hyperactivity Disorder (ADHD). George is an identical twin. He was born second and had a significantly lower birth weight than his brother. The boys' mother realized that George was not developing at the same rate as his brother. George's motor skills were not developing as quickly, he was having more problems eating and self-soothing, he developed severe skin issues, and he seemed to be significantly behind in his physical and cognitive development. When George was 18 months old, (she expressed her concerns to his family doctor who referred him to early childhood intervention through the Help Me Grow program. This began the process of assessment, which led to a diagnosis of having developmental delays. George immediately began receiving educational services through the local school district and therapy from an occupational therapist.

George attends preschool in an inclusion program. He goes to school Monday through Thursday, for three hours a day. He has attended this program for just about three complete school years. He will be attending kindergarten this upcoming year, and it is time to start planning his transition. The team wants to make it as smooth as possible for George. His preschool teacher has provided his special education services and he has received consistent services from a speech and language pathologist and the occupational therapist. While in his preschool program, George was diagnosed with ADHD and began taking medication. His teacher and his one-to-one paraprofessional both agree that the medication helps George focus, but also makes him tired. George shows significant growth in the area of social-emotional development since he began attending preschool. His preschool teacher said, "When George began attending my program, he seemed withdrawn and distracted. He had trouble focusing on any task for any amount of time. Now, he is able to spend about two minutes on a task and is able to focus and put forth a willing effort."

## Dilemma

George's family agrees with all of his diagnoses. They state that they support the services he receives and the education he has been getting at school. Although his parents state that they are supportive, staff members have not seen fond, affectionate interaction between George and his family. They describe the family relationship as "business-like," which they described as mom and dad addressing George's needs without any emotion and affection being provided. George's parents return signed paperwork only after repeated reminders which frustrate staff. Scheduling meetings with them has also proved challenging. Meetings are typically postponed several times until they absolutely must be held in order to meet deadlines required by law. Even after repeatedly rescheduling meetings to accommodate the availability of George's parents, their attendance rate is 50 percent. The school staff attempts to make up for the attention and affection that they feel George does not get at home by lavishing him with positive attention at school.

Mom plans to stop medication for ADHD over the summer and stop all educational activities, other services, and therapies over the summer. She said, "He needs a break." This is concerning to the staff because they know the value of a consistent schedule. George's parents do not provide many opinions about George's situation; his parents allow the staff at school to plan interventions and therapies as they see fit. Staff and therapists send home daily updates and work to provide consistent communication, even if it is not reciprocated.

## Perspectives

Knowing George's delays, backgrounds, and situation, the team makes a plan to support George as he begins kindergarten. The school district that George attends is small, and the Speech and Language Pathologist and the Occupational Therapist have developed strong and positive relationships with George. Both will continue to provide services to George in kindergarten and are worried about him making connections with the other adults, since they don't believe he is getting enough emotional connection from his parents. George's preschool teacher will remain his case manager, monitoring his progress and providing one-to-one services a few times throughout the week. The one-to-one paraprofessional that George has worked with for the past three years will not be able to accompany him in the same capacity when he goes to kindergarten and the current staff are concerned about this connection being gone. The preschool/Early Childhood Special Education (ECSE) teacher states that, "George has outstanding rapport with his para. It is a shame not to keep that relationship strong and consistent for him. She should stay with him for as many years as she is able."

Since many of the team members are remaining, this will provide easy exchange of information between the sending and receiving program. His parents do not want George and his twin brother in the same kindergarten classroom in order for both boys to be able to succeed and to avoid their skills being compared. George's parents also believe the current teachers dote on George too much and believe this will cause issues for his twin brother. They are worried that his twin brother will be ignored. George will have the same designated areas in the building for sensory breaks. Staff will work to maintain as much of his current routine as possible. After the first month of school, George's team will meet to assess how things are working and what can be adjusted. His kindergarten teacher and the preschool/ECSE teacher will work collaboratively and stay in good communication to provide George with the best educational opportunities possible. All of these plans align with the DEC transition practice that recommends various strategies for before, during, and after transitions.

## QUESTIONS

1. Which DEC practices for the topic area of Transition did you see supported in this case study?
2. Which of the DEC practices for the topic area of Transition were not supported in this case study? How might these have been addressed?
3. What additional educational interventions should be documented and planned for prior to his transition to kindergarten?
4. How might the staff and educational team support the parents as members of the team in making decisions for George?
5. Regarding the family's plan for the summer (no medication or services), how might the therapists address the family's concerns and develop a mutually agreed upon plan?
6. It is the family's preference to separate the twins; what are the implications of separating George and his twin brother?
7. What additional areas should be addressed prior to George's transition to kindergarten?

## SAM AND SUE

*Unsolved*

### Background

Sam and Sue are 4 1/2 year old twins attending preschool for the first time. They entered Pre-K midyear. They have had to transition to several different environments in a short amount of time. Mom passed away last year from a drug overdose, and Dad was incarcerated and recently released from prison. Grandma Linda and Grandpa Bruce have temporary custody and are fighting dad for permanent custody of the children. They want what is best for the kids, even though their lives have been drastically changed as playing the role of parents for the second time, later in their lives.

Karen, the special education teacher (SPED), has arrived at the preschool classroom, that she visits two times a week. Cindy, the general education teacher, is reading a book at group time. Andrea, the classroom special education paraprofessional, is next to Sam and looks exasperated. Sue is attending at circle time, while Sam is walking around the room avoiding the activity.

"I dressed up as the Stay Puff Marshmallow Man last night!" says Sam.

"That is your favorite costume, isn't it?" replies Karen. "What is Ms. Cindy reading?"

Sam walks away and looks around the dramatic play area.

Karen turns to Andrea, the special education para, "How is the day going?"

"He doesn't want to sit at group time and has gotten frustrated at centers and knocked down blocks because they wouldn't stand up right." Andrea sighed.

Cindy, the general education teacher, finished circle time and the students headed to snack. "I am worried about Sam going to kindergarten in the fall. He has a hard time following direction and self-regulating. I don't even know if he knows his numbers and letters, since he won't sit down and work with me."

"Have you been using the visual schedule and the calm down book?" asked Karen.

"I'm not sure what Andrea's been able to do." replied Cindy.

### Dilemma

Sam and Sue have summer birthdays, turning 5 in July. Sue is doing well academically yet has emotional trauma from their family history. Sam has significant behavior issues but doesn't know how to deal with his feelings, especially considering what he has experienced at such a young age. Both qualify for services under the developmental disability category. They are registered to start kindergarten in the fall but Cindy and Grandma are not on the same page for next school year.

## Perspectives

They are registered to start kindergarten in the fall. Cindy thinks Sam is not ready for kindergarten and doesn't want the kindergarten teacher to think that she hasn't prepared him. Grandma is concerned if they hold Sam back, should they have Sue also repeat pre-K. The SPED teacher feels they could both transition to kindergarten with the proper strategies and supports in place. In meeting with kindergarten teachers and parents, Cindy is sending and receiving information, specifically, before a transition may occur.

Grandma wants to keep the twins together and is looking for support and guidance in kindergarten. Cindy does not think Sam is ready. Karen suggests talking to the kindergarten teacher on the expectations of the class. The elementary school has an open house coming up and Grandma Linda is planning to go with the twins.

Karen has implemented a zone book to help Sam identify his emotions and what he needs to calm himself. After looking at his behavior data she sees that he avoids activities that are difficult for him. Sam enjoys slime and other sensory play, and it provides positive stimulation at the beginning of his day. He has responded well with a rewards chart and made some positive gains in behavior management. He can ask for and take a break on his own. He still avoids difficult or non-preferred activities but has some strategies in place to help him.

At spring conferences, Cindy focused on the academic needs. Karen gave a progress report on Sam's gains in behavior management. The school psychologist gave the family a counseling resource. The twins are adjusting to their new preschool environment. The ECSE teachers help transition children on an IEP to kindergarten the first week of school in the fall. Sue is ready to progress, but questions still arise about Sam.

## QUESTIONS

1. Which DEC practices for the topic area of Transition did you see supported in this case study?
2. Which of the DEC practices for the topic area of Transition were not supported in this case study? How might these have been addressed?

3. It is the family's preference to keep the twins together; what are the implications of keeping Sam and Sue together?
4. How can the team solicit input from the school physhologist or a counselor on the implications of separating the children?
5. It does not appear that the school team has information on Sam's behavior in the home; what benefits might this conversation generate?
6. What suggestions might you have on summer programming on helping Sam with both his behavior academic skills?

## WILL IT WORK OUT?

*Unsolved*

## Background

Brooks is a 4-year-old boy and big brother to his sibling, Josie, a 1-year-old girl. Brooks' parents, Heather (30) and Matt (32), met in high school and right out of college got married. A year later, Brooks was born 6 weeks early. Because of his early delivery, Brooks spent the first 2 weeks in the hospital; his lungs were underdeveloped and doctors wanted to keep a close eye on him. Two weeks went by and Brooks was ready to go home; Heather and Matt couldn't wait!

Time passed, Josie was born, and all was great, except for Heather and Matt's growing concern about Brooks' development; his play stills were underdeveloped, he always needed to have his toy care wherever he went, he did a lot of arm flapping when excited, and change or transitions appeared to be extremely difficult for him. They began noticing more and more underdeveloped play skills specifically, difficulties taking turns and sharing, trouble expressing and regulating emotions, and a preference to play alone. They noticed everywhere they went, Brooks always needed his favorite toy car and when he got excited about something, flapped his arms. Hardest of all, Heather and Matt continuously found themselves fighting with Brooks when a change occurred at home or they needed to transition to something or somewhere else. Concerned knowing Brooks was 4 and only a year away from Kindergarten, they decided to seek advice from Brooks' pediatrician who then referred them to a specialist in mental health. Meeting with the specialist a few days later, it was decided an early screening test would be beneficial in pinpointing any deficit areas Brooks may have. Getting in right away, Brooks was screened and after receiving the results—also keeping in mind Heather and Matt's concerns—Brooks definitely showed signs of Autism. Choosing to be proactive, Heather and Matt continued with a comprehensive diagnostic evaluation after which they accepted an Autism diagnosis for Brooks.

Letting it all soak in, Heather and Matt sought Early Childhood programs for students with Autism and/or disabilities alike. Finding a program in their school district, Heather and Matt scheduled to have Brooks evaluated to receive special education services. Accepted, the next step was for Heather, Matt, and Brooks to meet with their case manager and education team.

## Dilemma and Perspectives

"Welcome!" Miss Carley reaches out her hand greeting both Heather and Matt. "My name is Miss Carley and I will be Brooks' new teacher. I also have with me Miss Claire, our school behavior specialist, Miss Theresa, who will be Brooks' Speech Clinician, and Miss Rachel, our school's lead teacher." Miss Claire, Miss Theresa, and Miss Rachel reach out their hand one at a time to greet both parents.

"Hi, it's nice to meet all of you." Heather reaches out her hand. "I'm Heather and this is my husband, Matt." Matt reaches out his hand. "We also have Brooks here with us—say Hi Brooks." Brooks was being shy—he cuddled up between his mom and dad hiding his face.

"It's nice to meet you Brooks," said Miss Carley. "We can't wait to have you in our class! Brooks looks up and smirks, still trying to hide his face.

"We are meeting today to not only welcome you to our Early Childhood Special Education program, but also, personally meet with you before Brooks starts Preschool in a few weeks. We want to hear your concerns and altogether, go about creating some goal areas we can include in an IEP for Brooks." Miss Carley takes out a sheet of paper describing what an IEP is and hands it to Heather. "I will let you read more but in short, an IEP is an Individualized Education Plan that we develop as a team, you included, that summarizes a student's disability, states educational goals and objectives, and includes supports and services the student will receive while at school."

"Oh perfect. This will help us a lot," responded Heather.

"Great! Let's hear a little more about Brooks!" said Miss Carley smiling.

Heather grabs Brooks between herself and Matt and places him on her lap. "Absolutely," said Heather. "Around the age of 2, we began noticing different/unusual things in Brooks; he flapped his arms when something excited him; he would have a really hard time playing, as well as sharing when we would play with him; any change or transition taken place at home, he freaked out. *Sigh*. Of all these things, we think the transition part is the hardest; we have Josie who is 2 now and it makes it hard when he's on the floor throwing a tantrum because we need to go somewhere or he needs to clean up his toys."

Miss Carley grabs her notepad and pen. "Alright—don't mind me, I'm just jotting down some notes as you speak." Heather smiles. At this time, Matt is at another table nearby playing trains with Brooks. "Recapping what you shared, you guys seem to struggle most with change or transitions at home. Just so you are aware, these are normal behaviors we notice in children with Autism or disabilities alike; don't think it's just Brooks!" Heather laughs; Matt looks over and smiles. "I think what we can really tackle and work on here at school is helping Brooks get used to a routine schedule that will help during those tougher transitions. Our hope will then be he will get used to dealing with change and/or transitions and your home situations will become easier."

"Oh, that would be wonderful!" said Heather, smiling. Matt is listening, still occupying Brooks. "I am going to give you an online resource you can look into at home related to Autism. It's a great resource to learn more about Autism itself and what to expect in children with it. It provides great evidence based strategies for interacting with children with Autism as well as suggestions to try to make those changes and transitions a little easier. In school, we use a combination of duration maps and a visual timer for our students who struggle with transitioning. I will provide you a duration map you can start using at home. The duration map is a simple tool of showing Brooks how much time he has left in whatever activity he is doing. There are 4 removable dots; you will simply remove one at a time as the transition gets closer—when all 4 dots are removed, it will be time to transition. The best thing about this tool is you can decide how fast or slow the dots are removed. We suggest if the duration map isn't working, to use a visual timer—something that will make a sound when time is up. When we use either of these tools at school, we also provide students with a verbal 2-minute warning; it may be helpful to provide one at home too! All in all, we suggest being consistent; the first few times may be a struggle but as Brooks becomes used to this new routine, he should adjust just fine. How are you guys feeling?"

"Alright," said Heather. "I think we have some good resources to start with" Matt rejoins at the table; Brooks continues to play with the trains at the table. Matt reviews the resources provided as the conversation moves on. "What do you suggest if Brooks isn't responding," asks Heather. "Great question," responds Miss Carley. "Miss Claire, would you mind answering that?" Miss Claire smiles. "Absolutely. Follow through with whatever you are asking of Brooks. One of the biggest things when teaching students transitions or anything else for that matter, is following through. If you are asking him to do something and he doesn't want to do it, my best advice is to wait him out until he completes what you are asking of him."

"What if we don't have time to wait for him out? I mean we have Josie too and sometimes she isn't very patient," says Matt.

"I understand there isn't always time to wait children out—our schedules are busy—but still follow through. If he isn't responding, you can do hand-over-hand to help him finish what you are asking of him," replied Miss Claire.

"Ok, so following through is the biggest thing," states Heather.

Nodding her head, Miss Claire continues, "Yes, and once Brooks starts school, we will continue using the same transition warnings you are using at home as we teach and get him used to our schedule. I understand you may not always have the same daily schedule when you're at home; you may find it useful to use a first, then approach with him. The first, then approach is simply stating what you want him to do first followed by what he can do next; for example, *first* clean-up your toys, *then* you can have a snack.

Following the meeting, Brooks' parents take the information given to them and start using it at home. In the meantime, an IEP is written for Brooks based on the meeting information and decisions. One week later, Miss Carley mails out the IEP for Brooks' parents to read through and sign; at the same time, she calls parents to let them know to watch for the IEP in the mail as well as ask how things were going at home post meeting. Sighing on the phone, Heather shares that Brooks didn't respond well to the first, then at first, but with persistence, he is starting to get the hang of it. Brooks is slowly getting used to the new routine; she adds that some situations are harder than others, but they keep persisting. Happy to hear he is improving; Miss Carley reminds them how the transition to school—something new to Brooks—may be a struggle. She tells Heather and Matt that she will be mailing them a "Time for School" story for them to read to Brooks before his first day of Preschool. Ending the conversation, parents are reminded to read through the IEP, sign if they agree to it, and return it to school with Brooks on his first day.

Heather and Matt read the story Miss Carley sent to Brooks the morning of his first day of school. Surprisingly to both, Brooks got ready and on the bus with only the use of a visual timer; the visual timer was used to show Brooks how many minutes he had before he needed to start getting ready.

At school, Brooks appeared very shy at first however, as the day went on and Brooks became more comfortable, Miss Carley began noticing the behaviors seen at home during activity transitions; refusal and crying. She gave it the first week of school before putting any plan into action; until then, she had Brooks pick out a transition toy to carry during each transition.

The next week, a routine schedule and plan for Brooks before and during the transitions was put in place. Brooks started using an individual schedule of the day's activities—something he checked after each activity. He appeared interested in the schedule however, still needed a lot of transition warning. Miss Carley noticed that Brooks transitioned pretty well from a preferred activity to another preferred activity, but not from a preferred to a non-preferred activity. She continues to work with him in the classroom as well as communicate with parents.

By the end of the school year, Brooks had improved quite a bit transition wise; he still struggled taking turns with peers and playing alongside them with the same set of toys. His parents were impressed with his progress at home as well; he was showing more and more interest in playing with them and little sister Josie, as well as transitioning when necessary without the battle. Heather and Matt met with Miss Carley, Miss Claire, Miss Theresa, Miss Rachel, and the new Kindergarten team planned to work with Brooks. At the meeting, parents were informed that Brooks would be placed in an inclusive classroom; a classroom where children with disabilities and without, learned together. Miss Carley shared with the team that Brooks uses a schedule during transitions and oftentimes, needs some sort of transition warning before a change. They shared his challenge of playing with others as well as sharing. With this information, the meeting ended; the Kindergarten team seemed confident.

Summer came and went. Brooks continued to show progress, even through summer school. On the first day of Kindergarten, Brooks transitioned really well. He seemed excited for his new class and the new friends he would meet. The school year started off strong as teachers made sure to teach Brooks the routine schedule right away and provide transition warnings when necessary.

A month into the new school year, teachers were happy with the way Brooks continued to transition and follow the routine; sometimes, he didn't even check his schedule. They decided to slowly fade giving transition warnings to Brooks in hopes he would follow his peers'. Brooks responded really well at first, however, it didn't take long for him to fall apart again; only this time, it appeared more extreme. He struggled when he didn't get the things he wanted, began dropping to the floor when things didn't go his way, threw tantrums when he needed to transition to something new, and gave very little effort to a new activity after he transitioned—especially if it was a non-preferred activity. These behaviors started following him home; Heather and Matt are unsure of what to do next.

## QUESTIONS

1. Which DEC practices for the topic area of Transition did you see supported in this case study?

2. Which of the DEC practices for the topic area of Transition were not supported in this case study? How might these have been addressed?
3. How did the social story support Brooks' transition to kindergarten?
4. Brooks experienced difficulty when the transition warnings were faded, how might the team respond?
5. What additional information is missing between the school and home that may have assisted with Brooks' transition?

## YOUR OPINION IS IMPORTANT

*Unsolved*

### Background

Martha and Bill are the maternal aunt and uncle of Jane and her biological brother Clayton. Jane is 2.11 years old and Clayton is 4.1 years old. Martha and Bill do not have any biological children. They adopted both Clayton and Jane immediately following birth, as they were removed from their mother due to substance abuse issues. Martha is a stay-at-home mom, and Bill works seasonally in construction work, so Jane does not attend daycare. Clayton was enrolled in Part C preschool services and now attends Part B preschool. Jane is enrolled in Part C services. This case study will focus on Jane. Jane has no medical concerns and qualifies for Part C services through the school district for developmental delay due to low speech, cognitive, and social emotional assessment scores. Since beginning Part C services, early childhood special education teacher, Ryan, and school speech and language pathologist have visited Jane in her home every two weeks for one hour each visit. Jane's home was the environment identified by her parents as most natural and comfortable for her learning.

Recently, Jane's parents and Ryan have seen an increase in Jane's resistance to separate from her mom and decrease in her ability to transition between tasks without exhibiting negative behaviors. According to the Hawaii Early Learning Profile (HELP) 0–3 assessment, Jane did score below her age level in Strand 5–1 Attachment/Separation/Autonomy, so this has been an area Ryan and her parents have been working on during her home visits. It was initially suspected Martha's presence was affecting Jane's ability to transition, so Ryan and Martha tried some transition strategies during visits, such as having mom suggest transitions, having mom be present for transitions, and having mom exit for transitions. However, it does not appear Martha's presence affects Jane's negative reaction to transitions.

When transitioning between activities, Jane will begin to scream, yell, and throw herself on the floor. On occasion, Jane will throw toys at her teacher or parents and/or runaway when asked to transition between tasks. She has also started throwing her food on the floor when asked to finish her meal and prepare for the bath. It takes an average of 15–25 minutes to get Jane to calm down and transition between tasks. Transitions between tasks can include change in play activities, washing hands to sitting at the table to eat, preparing to go outside, playing outside to playing inside, and more. Jane's negative behaviors are appearing to increase in intensity and length.

## Dilemma

As Ryan has worked with Jane for 18 months, he understands she is very timid around males. Ryan works hard to develop a trusting relationship with Jane by speaking softly, allowing her to play near him on her own terms, and always sitting at her level. During this home visit, Ryan and Jane are playing make believe at the kitchen set when he states it is time to clean the kitchen area up and get ready to have a snack. Ryan observes that Jane initially ignores his request and continues to play. After repeating his request and stating that they can work together to clean up and then walk to the snack table together, Jane throws herself on the floor and begins to kick and scream that she wants to play and is not hungry. Ryan begins thinking about strategies that might help with Jane's transition process, such as utilizing a song, visual cards, or egg timer to signal a transition. He also watches how the parents react to Jane's behavior and thinks they appear anxious and stressed about her distress. Ryan thinks Martha is struggling to not intervene and allow Jane to continue playing. Martha tells Ryan, "It's just so hard to see her so upset! How can you remain so calm?! I just usually give in." Ryan calmly reminds Jane they need to work together to clean the kitchen area, but he will wait until she is ready to help so they can have a snack. Ryan observes it takes Jane 10 minutes to quiet herself down and quit kicking the floor, and six minutes to begin helping him clean and get ready for snack. Ryan thinks Jane will benefit from simple transition strategies if he can work with the parents to have them used consistently. Martha wonders if part of the reason Jane responds so poorly to the transition is because Jane is timid around males.

Before he leaves the visit, Martha tells Ryan she has been struggling with Jane during public outings, as she throws tantrums when transitioning between the car and the store, between departments in the store, and going from the store back to the car. Martha says, "I am becoming frustrated! I have started leaving Jane at home with Bill during outings to avoid her tantrums." Bill says, "I am so tired of fighting with her over the simplest things—like stopping coloring to take a bath!" Martha says, "I just don't understand because oftentimes we are asking her to do things she seems to enjoy!" Both Martha and Bill tell Ryan they have started letting Jane dictate her own schedule to avoid her tantrums. Ryan tells them he has some ideas on strategies to help Jane with transitions, and he will bring them to the next visit. Bill says, "Well, remember that we aren't teachers, so I am not sure if we will be able to help like you can." Ryan reassures Bill and Martha there are simple strategies that can be used to help Jane and asks if they would like to visit them this visit. Bill and Martha say they have plans and would have to visit more next time.

For his next visit, Ryan brings activity cards with one word and a visual of the activity to present to Jane, preparing her for the transition. Ryan presents the card to Jane and says, "We are going to play blocks for ten minutes. After that, we will read stories. I am going to set this timer so it signals when we should put away our blocks and read stories." Ryan shows Jane the story card and sets the timer for ten minutes. Ryan thinks Jane appears to understand the schedule of activities, and they begin to play. Jane checks the timer twice out of curiosity. When the timer goes off, Ryan has Jane help him shut off the timer, holds up the story card, and asks Jane if she would help him clean up for story time. Jane whimpers and throws herself on the floor. Ryan again holds up the activity cards and says, "Jane, remember that we were going to play blocks for 10 minutes (held up block card) and then read stories (held up story card) when the timer went off (pointed at the timer)? Please help me clean up (held up a clean-up card), so we can read our stories now (held up the story card). I will wait quietly for you by the kitchen until you are ready." Ryan asks Jane to put away the cups and begins singing the clean-up song. Jane begins to help and is ready for stories. Ryan thinks this was a good response to the strategy, as Jane's tantrum to the transition decreased to 10 minutes. Ryan gives Jane a sticker chart he brought to reward her for transitioning. Jane is very excited about the stickers because Ryan brought stickers with her favorite characters from Frozen. Ryan knows her room is decorated in Frozen and this is her favorite movie. Ryan thinks Bill and Martha appear encouraged by the result of the strategy. Ryan reinforces this strategy throughout the visit, and Jane appears to respond well, never exceeding a 10-minute resistance to transitioning.

**Perspectives**

At the next visit, Ryan explains transition strategies are most successful when both the educator and family form a collaborative plan and work together. Ryan speaks to Bill and Martha about establishing consistent transition strategies between home and his Part B classroom. Not only will it help Jane transition better in her daily routines, but she will also be entering the classroom environment in four weeks and this might make the transition more comfortable and familiar to her. Ryan says he is concerned Jane will not comfortably adjust to the transition between the home environment and the school environment if she does not begin to practice established transition strategies. Ryan asks if the strategies he demonstrated at today's visit would work well for Bill and Martha as an individual family. Martha says, "The strategies you used were easy enough. I think we could do things like that at home." Bill agrees. Ryan says they can work together to determine what cards they would like him to make to correlate to their family's routines and tells them he will leave the stickers and sticker chart to reinforce her positive transition behavior. Ryan asks Bill and Martha to provide him with more information about Jane's reaction to transitions in other situations, such as church nursery, bedtime routines, going to a friend's or grandma's house, visiting her brother at school, or others. Martha and Bill write down different transition situations that they both think are important to helping Jane. While they are working, Ryan asks Jane to color pictures of her home and family to hang up in her classroom so she can feel more comfortable in her new environment.

Ryan asks if they can work together to create a transition referral packet to share with other staff, so all of Jane's teachers and therapists can get to know Jane as an individual and understand what strategies work best for her prior to her entering their program/room. Martha and Bill think this is a great idea! Ryan works with Martha and Bill to fill out a get-to-know-me form for Jane, and Martha gives Ryan a picture of Jane. Ryan explains the file will continue to grow with tips and strategies as her team gets to know her better. Ryan discusses the importance of Jane being familiar with and feeling comfortable in the school environment prior to her first day of Part B preschool. He asks Martha and Bill if they would like to bring Jane to the school for a special tour and hold her last two Part C visits in her soon-to-be classroom. Martha and Bill both agree it is a good idea to introduce Jane to the transition of working with Ryan in the classroom environment instead of the home environment.

Ryan explains to Martha and Bill that transitions can be difficult for some children, but it is beneficial to implement strategies that can help make Jane feel safe and comfortable while she adjusts. Ryan reassures Bill and Martha they are a valuable part of Jane's team. He states everyone involved is there to support them and Jane in this process. Ryan encourages them to continue offering feedback and suggestions to help make Jane's transition more successful. Ryan asks how often Martha and Bill would like to meet with him to discuss Jane's progress during this process. Bill and Martha are relieved they will not feel alone after Jane transitions out of Part C services and ask to meet every two weeks until they feel confident Jane is making progress, and they have a "handle" on using the strategies at home.

## QUESTIONS

1. Which DEC practices for the topic area of Transition did you see supported in this case study?
2. Which of the DEC practices for the topic area of Transition were not supported in this case study? How might these have been addressed?
3. The family identified that Jane was timid around males; what strategies did Ryan use to both increase Jane's trust whle also addressing her compliance?
4. How did the ECSE team help support Martha and Bill in implementing transition strategies at home? What remains to be addressed?
5. The school transition process can be challenging for parents and students alike. What strategies can the school district employ to help families transitioning students?

# Appendix

# RESOURCES

## *Research on CMI*

Harman, T., Bertrand, B., Greer, A., Pettus, A., Jennings, J., Wall-Bassett, E., & Babatunde, O. T. (2015). Case-based learning facilitates critical thinking in undergraduate nutrition education: students describe the big picture. *Journal of the Academy of Nutrition and Dietetics, 115*(3), 378–388.

The vision of dietetics professions is based on interdependent education, credentialing, and practice. Case-based learning is a method of problem-based learning that is designed to heighten higher-order thinking. Case-based learning can assist students to connect education and specialized practice while developing professional skills for entry-level practice in nutrition and dietetics. This study examined student perspectives of their learning after immersion into case-based learning in nutrition courses.

Mostert, M. P. (2007). Challenges of case-based teaching. *The Behavior Analyst Today, 8*(4), 434.

Over the past 20 years, teacher educators have increasingly turned to case-based instruction with Pre-service, novice, and even experienced teachers. However, advocates of case-based teaching rarely point out the many challenges that might detract from effective case-based instruction. I briefly outline some of the more obvious challenges facing case instructors as they attempt to use the method for improved teacher education

Popil, I. (2011). Promotion of critical thinking by using case studies as teaching method. *Nurse education today, 31*(2), 204–207.

This paper examines the use of case studies as teaching strategies to promote critical thinking. Critical thinking and case studies are defined as teaching method. The benefits and limitations of case studies are also discussed. The literature review investigates research studies that have indicated how case studies facilitate and promote active learning, help clinical problem solving, and encourage the development of critical thinking skills.

Sanders-Smith, S. C., Smith-Bonahue, T. M., & Soutullo, O. R. (2016). Practicing teachers' responses to case method of instruction in an online graduate course. *Teaching and Teacher Education, 54,* 1–11.

This is a study of two cohorts of practicing teachers enrolled in an online graduate course using Case Method of Instruction (a pedagogical technique based on realistic case studies) to facilitate students' learning.

## *CMI Online Resources*

*Case-Based Learning: Poorvu Center for Teaching and Learning.* Case-Based Learning Poorvu Center for Teaching and Learning. (2020). https://poorvucenter.yale .edu/faculty-resources/strategies-teaching/case-based-learning.

Case-based learning (CBL) is an established approach used across disciplines where students apply their knowledge to real-world scenarios, promoting higher levels of cognition (see *Bloom's Taxonomy*). In CBL classrooms, students typically work in groups on case studies, stories involving one or more characters and/or scenarios. The cases present a disciplinary problem or problems for which students devise solutions under the guidance of the instructor.

*The Case Method.* CITL. (2020). https://citl.illinois.edu/citl-101/teaching-learning /resources/teaching-strategies/the-case-method.

Cases are narratives, situations, select data samplings, or statements that present unresolved and provocative issues, situations, or questions (Indiana University Teaching Handbook, 2005). The case method is a participatory, discussion-based way of learning where students gain skills in critical thinking, communication, and group dynamics. It is a type of problem-based learning.

*Case Method Teaching.* Undergrad Main Site. (2020). https://teachingcommons.stanford .edu/resources/learning/learning-activities/case-method-teaching.

In Case Method Teaching, students review a real-world situation (a case) that poses a thought-provoking problem or dilemma. Students are placed in the role of decision maker and asked how they would resolve the problem.

*The Case Study Teaching Method.* Harvard Law School The Case Studies. (2020). https: //casestudies.law.harvard.edu/the-case-study-teaching-method/.

It is easy to get confused between the case study method and the case method, particularly as it applies to legal education. The case method in legal education was invented by Christopher Columbus Langdell, Dean of Harvard Law School from

1870 to 1895. Langdell conceived of a way to systematize and simplify legal education by focusing on previous case law that furthered principles or doctrines. To that end, Langdell wrote the first casebook, entitled A Selection of Cases on the Law of Contracts, a collection of settled cases that would illuminate the current state of contract law. Students read the cases and came prepared to analyze them during Socratic question-and-answer sessions in class.

*Christensen Center for Teaching & Learning.* Teaching by the Case Method—Christensen Center for Teaching and Learning—Harvard Business School. (2003). https://www.hbs.edu/teaching/case-method/Pages/default.aspx.

Chris Christensen described case method teaching as "the art of managing uncertainty"—a process in which the instructor serves as "planner, host, moderator, devil's advocate, fellow-student, and judge," all in search of solutions to real-world problems and challenges. Unlike lectures, case method classes unfold without a detailed script. Successful instructors simultaneously manage content and process, and they must prepare rigorously for both. Case method teachers learn to balance planning and spontaneity. In practice, they pursue opportunities and "teachable moments" that emerge throughout the discussion, and deftly guide students toward discovery and learning on multiple levels.

The Clearinghouse for Special Ed. Teaching Cases. (2001). http://cases.coedu.usf.edu/.

This project is designed to develop, evaluate (field test), and nationally disseminate teaching cases that will aide in the attainment of knowledge (by preservice and inservice teachers) around the knowledge areas/competencies that the Council for Exceptional Children (CEC) has identified as necessary for teachers who work with children and youth with disabilities and their families.

University of Buffalo Libraries. (2020). *National Center for case study teaching in science.* About the Collection—National Center for Case Study Teaching in Science (NCCSTS). https://sciencecases.lib.buffalo.edu/collection/about.html.

One of the primary goals of the National Center for Case Study Teaching in Science is to develop and maintain a nationally accessible refereed collection of exemplary STEM case studies for use at the undergraduate, graduate, and high school level. We have been working toward this goal for over 25 years and our collection of more than 830 peer-reviewed cases has become the centerpiece of our website.

Velenchik, A. (2018, May 7). *Teaching With Case Method.* Teaching with the Case Method. https://serc.carleton.edu/sp/library/cases/index.html.

The case method combines two elements: the case itself and the discussion of that case. A teaching case is a rich narrative in which individuals or groups must make a decision or solve a problem. A teaching case is not a "case study" of the type used in academic research.

*What is the Case Study Method?–Executive Education–Harvard Business School.* HBS
    Executive Education. (2020). https://www.exed.hbs.edu/hbs-experience/learning
    -experience/case-study-method.

Simply put, the case method is a discussion of real-life situations that business executives have faced. On average, you'll attend three to four different classes a day, for a total of about six hours of class time (schedules vary). To prepare, you'll work through problems with your peers.

## Recommended Practices Modules

*Early Childhood Recommended Practice Modules. RP Modules.* (2020). https://rpm.fpg.unc
    .edu/welcome.

Early Childhood Recommended Practice Modules (RPMs) are free modules developed for early care and education, early intervention, and early childhood special education faculty and professional development providers. The modules support the implementation of the Division for Early Childhood (DEC) Recommended Practices.

## Practice Improvement Tools

*Practice Improvement Tools: Using the DEC Recommended Practices.* ECTA Center. (2019).
    https://ectacenter.org/decrp/.

The Practice Improvement Tools help practitioners implement evidence-based practices. They are based on the *Division for Early Childhood (DEC) Recommended Practices.* These tools and resources guide practitioners and families in supporting young children who have, or are at-risk for, developmental delays or disabilities across a variety of early childhood settings.

## Performance Checklists

*Practice Improvement Tools: Performance Checklists.* ECTA Center. (2012). https://ecta
    center.org/decrp/type-checklists.asp

These Performance Checklists are intended for practitioners (and leaders where noted) to increase their understanding and use of the DEC Recommended Practices and for self-evaluation of one's use of the practices.

## *Practice Improvement Quizzes*

Practice Improvement Tools: aRPy Pop Quiz! ECTA Center. (2012). https://ecta center.org/decrp/arpy.asp

These quizzes are based upon the knowledge in our *Performance Checklists* and *Practice Guides for Practitioners and Families.* Review the checklist and practice guide linked in the quiz, then watch a short video clip, and answer the question using what you've learned!

## *DEC Recommended Practices with Examples*

The Division for Early Childhood of the Council for Exceptional Children. (2016). DEC Recommended Practices with Examples. https://fpg.unc.edu/sites/fpg .unc.edu/files/resources/presentations-and-webinars/Recommended%20 Practices%20with%20Examples.pdf.

The DEC Recommended Practices were developed to provide guidance to practitioners and families about the most effective ways to improve the learning outcomes and promote the development of young children, birth through five years of age, who have or are at-risk for developmental delays or disabilities.

## *CMI Books*

Storey, K. (2018). *Case Studies in Transition and Employment for Students and Adults with Disabilities.* Charles C Thomas Publisher.

This book is intended to give support providers the understanding, knowledge, and skills for providing transition and employment services in school, employment, community, and residential settings and thereby improve the quality of life for the individuals that they support.

Storey, K., & Haymes, L. (2016). *Case Studies in Applied Behavior Analysis for Students and Adults with Disabilities.* Charles C Thomas Publisher.

This book responds to a critical need for highly qualified personnel who will become exemplary professionals because of their advanced knowledge, skills, and experiences in working with students and adults that have varying disabilities, including Autism Spectrum Disorders (ASD). Since Board Certification for behavior analysts was introduced, there has been an expansion of training programs in Applied Behavior Analysis to meet the demands from school districts, health insurers, and families.

Torres, T., & Barber, C. R. (2017). *Case Studies in Special Education: A Social Justice Perspective.* Charles C Thomas Publisher.

Special education law and practice have undergone profound transformation over the past 50 years. Students with disabilities are now more likely to receive a free and appropriate education in the least restrictive environment possible; however, the ideals of the law have not always been manifested in effective practice. Although special education services are vastly better today than they were in the early years of public education, current policies and practices continue to result in the under-education of many children with disabilities.

# REFERENCES

Bailey Jr, D. B., McWilliam, P. J., & Winton, P. J. (1992). Building family-centered practices in early intervention: A team-based model for change. *Infants & Young Children, 5*(1), 73–82.

Bailey Jr, D. B., McWilliam, R. A., Buysse, V., & Wesley, P. W. (1998). Inclusion in the context of competing values in early childhood education. *Early Childhood Research Quarterly, 13*(1), 27–47.

Banbury, M. M., Janz, J. R., & McDermott, L. M. (2003). Essential elements of 4 teaching methods: Linking rubrics to teaching. *The College Quarterly, 6*(1).

Barnett, D. (1991). Building a case-based curriculum to enhance the pedagogical content knowledge of mathematics teachers. *Journal of Teacher Education, 42*(4), 263–272.

Boavida, T., Aguiar, C, & McWilliam, R. A. (2014). A training program to improve the IFSP/IEP goals and objectives through the routines-based interview. *Topics in Early Childhood Special Education, 33*(4), 200–211.

Boehrer, J., & Linksy, M. (1990). Teaching with cases: Learning to question. *New Directions for Teaching and Learning, 42*, 41–57. https://doe.org/10.1002/tl .37219904206

Carter, I. (1999). *A measure of freedom.* Oxford, UK: Oxford University Press on Demand.

Cicchetti, D., & Barnett, D. (1991). Attachment organization in maltreated preschoolers. *Development and Psychopathology, 3*(4), 397–411.

Council for Exceptional Children & CEEDAR Center (2017). *High-Leverage Practices in Special Education.* Baltimore, MD: Council for Exceptional Children.

Division for Early Childhood. (2014). *DEC recommended practices in early intervention/ early childhood special education 2014.* Retrieved from http://www.dec-sped.org /recommendedpractices

Division for Early Childhood. (2018). *DEC Recommended Practices: A quick overview.* Retrieved from http://www.dec-sped.org/dec-recommended-practices

Dolmans, D. H. J. M., & Snellen-Balendong, H., Wolfhagen, & van der Vleuten. (1997). Seven principles of effective case design for a problem-based curriculum. *Medical Teacher, 19*(3), 185–189.

Erskine, J. A., Leenders, M. R., & Mauffette-Leenders, L. A. (2003). *Teaching with cases.* London, Ontario: Ivey Publishing.

Erskine, J., Leenders, M., & Maufette-Leenders, L. (1998). *Teaching with cases.* London. Ontario: Richard Ivy School of Business, University of Western Ontario.

Ertmer, P. A., & Russell, J. D. (1995). Using case studies to enhance instructional design education. *Educational Technology,* 23–31.

Gideonse, H.D. (1999). What is a case? What distinguishes case instruction? In M. R. Sudzina (Ed.), *Case study applications for teacher education: Cases in teaching and learning in the content areas* (pp. 1–7). Boston, MA: Allyn and Bacon.

Hendricks, S., & Bailey, S. (Eds.). (2016). *Preparing educators for online learning: A careful look at the components and how to assess their value.* Lanham, MD: Rowman & Littlefield Publishers, Inc.

Johnson, S. M., & Marietta, G. (2009). Taking human resources seriously in Minneapolis. *Public Education Leadership Project at Harvard University, PEL,* (055).

Kerns, G. M., & Watkins, C. R. A. (2007). *Using case studies to enhance the understanding of learning differences.* International Association of Special Education. Available from https://www.iase.org/Publications/2007.HongKong.pdf#page=112

Kim, S., Phillips, W. R., Pinsky, L., Brock, D., Phillips, K., & Keary, J. (2006). A conceptual framework for developing teaching cases: a review and synthesis of the literature across disciplines. *Medical Education, 40*(9), 867–876.

Kim, O., Utke, B. J., & Hupp, S. C. (2005). Comparing the use of case studies and application questions in preparing special education professionals. *Teacher Education and Special Education, 28*(2), 104–113.

McWilliam, P. J. (1992). The case method of instruction: Teaching application and problem-solving skills to early interventionists. *Journal of Early Intervention, 16,* 360–373.

McWilliam, R. A., & Bailey Jr, D. B. (1995). Effects of classroom social structure and disability on engagement. *Topics in Early Childhood Special Education, 15*(2), 123–147.

McWilliam, P. J., & Kersgard, M. (Eds.). (2002). *Lives in progress: Case stories in early intervention.* Baltimore, MD: Paul H. Brooks.

McWilliam, P. J., & Killoran, I. (2002). Lives in progress: Case stories in early intervention. *The Canadian Journal of Infancy and Early Childhood, 9*(1).

McWilliam, P. J., & Snyder, P. (1993). Teaching through the case method. In *International Conference on Children with Special Needs.* San Diego, CA.

Naumes, W., & Naumes, M. J. (2000). Case writing: A tool for teaching and research. *Journal of SMET Education, 1*(1), 24–32.

Pindiprolu, S. S., Peck/Peterson, S. M., Rule, S., & Lignugaris/Kraft, B. (2003). Using webmediated case-based instruction to teach functional behavioral assessment skills. *Teacher Education and Special Education, 26,* 1–16

Porges, S. W., & Bohrer, R. E. (1990). The analysis of periodic processes in psychophysiological research. In J. T. Cacioppo & L. G. Tassinary (Eds.), *Principles of psychophysiology: physical, social and inferential elements* (pp. 708–753). New York, NY: Cambridge University Press.

Schmidt, H., Norman, G., & Boshuizen, H. (1990). A cognitive perspective on medical expertise: theory and implications. *Academic Medicine, 65*(10), 611–621.

Shulman, J. (Ed.). (1992). *Case methods in teacher education.* New York, NY: Teachers College Press.

Silverman, R, Welty, W., & Lyon, S. (1992). *Case studies for teacher problem solving.* New York, NY: McGraw-Hill.

Snyder, P., & McWilliam, P. J. (1999). Evaluating the efficacy of case method instruction: Findings from preservice training in family-centered care. *Journal of Early Intervention, 22,* 114–125.

Snyder, P., & McWilliam, P. J. (2003). Using case method of instruction effectively in early intervention personnel preparation. *Infants and Young Children, 16*(4), 284–295.

Sudzina, M. R. (1999). Guidelines for teaching with cases. In M. R. Sudzina (Ed.), *Case study applications for teacher education: Cases in teaching and learning in the content areas* (pp. 9–19). Boston, MA: Allyn and Bacon.

Sutyak, J. M., Lebeau, R. B., Spotnitz, A. J., O'Donnell, A. M., & Mehne, P. R. (1996). Role of case structure and prior experience in a case-based surgical clerkship. *American Journal of Surgery, 172*(3), 286–290. doi:10.1016/S0002-9610(96)00108-0

Svinicki, M. D., & McKeachie, W. J. (2013). *McKeachie's teaching tips: Strategies, research, and theory for college and university teachers* (14th ed). Belmont, CA: Wadsworth, Cengage Learning.

Watson, S., & Sutton, J. M. (2013). An examination of the effectiveness of case method teaching online: Does the technology matter. *Journal of Management Education, 36*(6), 802–821.

Whitehouse, C. (2012). Case studies in summative assessment: An investigation. *Centre for Education Research and Policy.* Available from https://research.aqa.org.uk/sites/default/files/pdf_upload/CERP-RP-CW-10112009.pdf